There were times throughout my life I felt certain I'd travelled a million miles to get to where I am right now, and that I must surely be 100 years old, at the very least, that's how old I feel, having gone through so much turbulence throughout my life.

Reflecting upon my past I am convinced that it really was another life. Who was that girl who refused to suffer any longer?
Where did she find the strength and courage to wade through an ocean of tears, loneliness, despair, and constant disappointments to finally discover the laughter, joy, and love that previously eluded her?
Is it any wonder why I feel well beyond my years yet still find it astounding that I survived whilst managing to remain mentally intact?

Separated by thousands of miles from family and friends with no one to turn to, and having given my partner many opportunities to redeem himself, he failed so I decided to end a particular phase of my life and found the confidence to start a new one with my children—
The decision I made was the right one.

My parents were post-war immigrants who decided to leave their home-land to venture forth with nothing more than their hopes and dreams of a better life in a new land. Most importantly they brought with them their values that would always remain non-negotiable.

As a consequence of these 'values', I had a strict upbringing and whist I appreciate my parents' attempts of protecting me through their love, they unwittingly placed me on a pathway of making wrong decisions at the wrong time of my life.

Thus began my long tumultuous journey through life.

Someone once said to me that I possessed all the love of a real woman and the patience of a saint. That may be so, but they don't know how much pain and agony I endured through my 20s, 30s, 40s, to achieve this patience. As for the love of a real woman—that was not enough to secure my happiness.

The 'forever' kind of love is 'forever' when it's reciprocated.
In my case, it was not…

'A woman can love only one man at a time, it is for her husband just to see that he is that man'.

Men, Women & Wedlock. (1910) London, United Kingdom: A & C Black Publishers.

To all
Who have loved and lost

Where does love go when it dies?
Where do all the leftovers now go to reside?
Is it somewhere nearby that I can visit and see
The words written,
"Here lies a love lost
Lived and died
For thee"

F.M.H.

Friday Mary Harding

BOXES TICKED? SO, IT BEGINS

AUSTIN MACAULEY PUBLISHERS™

LONDON • CAMBRIDGE • NEW YORK • SHARJAH

A CIP catalogue record for this title is available from the British Library.

ISBN 9781035858149 (Paperback)
ISBN 9781035858156 (Hardback)
ISBN 9781035858163 (ePub e-book)

www.austinmacauley.com

First Published 2024
Austin Macauley Publishers Ltd®
1 Canada Square
Canary Wharf
London
E14 5AA

I would like to thank my family and friends for their advice love and support.

I also acknowledge the following authors for granting me permission to use direct quotations from their amazing books in the hope that by doing so, will assist the reader in gaining a clearer appreciation of the 'whys' and the 'hows' of relationships between men and women and why many fail, it is also recommended that the reader visit these books mentioned below which in my humble opinion are considered an absolute 'must read'.

Special thanks to:

Carla Molino, successful author in her own right and my teacher. "Carla, your suggestions, patience and guidance will always be appreciated."
Helen Goltz, 'Fixed Term Marriage Contract'.
Dr Jonathan Livingston, 'Too Soon Old, Too Late Smart'.
Dr Michael Grayson Conner, 'Understanding the Difference between Men and Women', and 'About Love and Romantic Love' (documents included at the back of this book.)
Dr Robert J. Sternberg, 'The Triangular Theory of Love'.
Bettina Arndt, 'The Sex Diaries'.
Skye Thomas, 'Tomorrow's Edge' Every effort has been made to contact you.
Lara Clout, article on 'Can Affairs Save Marriages' Daily Telegraph, 26 August, "When Good People Have Affairs" by author Mira Kirshenbaum.
To my friend, Aldo:
Thank you for your assistance, for the feedback and for tolerating the ear blasting you received each time you asked me, "Hey Bella…How's the book going?"

Finally, to a very special person.

I have waited a lifetime for you to come into my life but it was worth it.

Thank you for your encouragement, you were and will always be my passion, my inspiration, my one and only.

You were the living proof of the 'forever love' many seek but failed to find.

Thank you for showing me how wonderful love could be.

Without you, this book would simply not exist.

May you rest in eternal peace.

Table of Contents

You have found *the one* who has ticked all the boxes.
That was the easy part as there is no guarantee that they will remain
ticked for the rest of your life together.
So now the real work begins… Otherwise there will be no
Together forever!

F. M. H.

Where does love go when it dies?
Where do all the leftovers, now go to reside?
Is it somewhere nearby that I can visit and see
The words written,
"Here rests a love lost
Lived and died
For thee."

F. M. H.

Foreword

This book is intended for both men and women and it is based upon actual events and personal experiences. Names have been changed to protect the identity of the people mentioned in the various examples that are included in the coming chapters. Some reference is also made to statistics, along with various profound quotations from a few unbelievably talented authors.

Look upon this book as an '*intervention*' an in-person discussion between you and I, because guys and ladies, you need to realise in no uncertain terms, of all the hurtful things that you say and do to each other and the long-term destructive effect it can have on your relationship. It all comes down to treating each other with the love and respect that you both deserve. It is not about control or domination towards either gender.

You will note that I may repeat some facts over and over again throughout this book; the reason for this is, though the instances and circumstances may differ, effect and outcome remain the same. Therefore, the repetition that occurs throughout this book is quite intentional.

Ladies—it is certainly not about reducing your man to a grovelling sex starved wretch: Who must be mindful of his every move whenever he happens to be in your presence for fear of upsetting you, then being deprived of any form of intimacy. Women may have the power to control the sex within their relationship, but this power should never be used as a bargaining tool to punish men. To inflict this upon a partner is not only immature it is also absolutely shameful and has long-term damaging effects.

Guys—treat your woman with the love and respect that she deserves: She is not your object to dominate, control or abuse, be it mentally or physically. She is a human being who is also your partner, how happy you want your life to be, depends on how well you treat her.

"Many studies have been conducted on couples, with apparent solutions, and in spite of the fact that the divorce rate in 2008, has dropped, according to Samuel Cardwell, AAP, there are still over 47,000 divorces granted in Australia, and 38% of these divorces are filed by wives. In the US however, it was estimated as of 2008 (by the same source) that forty per 40% of all marriages would end in divorce."

Samuel Cardwell AAP 29August 2008.

In 2009, according to the Australian Bureau of statistics, the number of divorces rose from 47,000 to 49, 448, an increase of 4.7%. This being the first increase in the number of divorces granted since 2001. (*This information is freely available on the internet.*)

Obviously, something is not working. No matter how many surveys are conducted, no matter how many experts publish their latest findings, it never seems to get any better as nothing changes and the solutions continue to evade us.

Why are marriages failing? Why are couples dissatisfied with their love lives? And, as is the case with most, why is it a given that the mystery and the passion never lasts?

Thought for you: Perhaps it doesn't last because both of you have miss treated each other over the years, hence indifference, boredom, and the over familiarity factor kicks in leading women to say "no" to sex, and in doing so, causing men endless frustration and anger.

"If it is this obvious and this simple, why hasn't anyone else written about it?" I wish I knew the answer but I do know what is in my heart, and with everything and all that life has taught me, some of the answers are starring at us in the face and yet there are so many people who don't recognise obvious solutions.

There are many questions still waiting to be answered but they need to be answered in a way that makes sense as with most things in today's fast changing world, we will need to go back to basics yet again.

Has it occurred to anyone that when things get way too hard and complicated that's when you proceed to break them down and simplify them? Sometimes the solution to a problem will become evident when one can address the problem honestly, and then proceed to simplify and rectify.

When you truly love someone and care about them and have their best interests at heart, the solutions will become evident, and it is this belief that has spurred me on to put pen to paper.

Indeed, why are couples not happy? Why are there so many failed marriages and why are men looking for love or sex outside the marital home.

If we are to function as happy and healthy human beings, we need to be honest with ourselves and with our partners yet sometimes, we are our own worst enemies.

For me, re-living the past was not easy or comfortable, but it was a healing process that enabled me to leave the sorrow of the past in the past and look ahead with some degree of clarity and excitement of future possibilities.

'*Where there is life, there will always be possibility!*'

This book was intended specifically for women, but the feedback or advice I received from Carla Molino (*author/teacher*) who's opinion I value immensely, convinced me that I should also include the '*do's and never do's*' for that of men as well, hence my original idea was suddenly on a different path. I soon realised that this path was going to be a great deal more rewarding and even more challenging.

There is merit in writing a book that will be read by men and women concurrently as men need to see and understand from a woman's perspective, and women need to understand how men think and why men act the way they do towards women's reactions.

Look upon this book as a '*tough love' lesson* and if I come across just a little overly zealous, I am not attacking either sex and it is always meant with the best of intentions because I hope that you experience the kind of love many only dream of.

You may be at a stage in your life where you are contemplating marriage, or are already married or you have just started to date. This book applies to men and women at any stage of a relationship. Most importantly, the contents of this book, does not encourage or condone '*subservience*' towards men or women, it simply encourages both sexes to treat one and other respectfully by being a little more understanding, patient and willing to compromise for the good of both.

So come on, let's empower ourselves with some good old-fashioned advice and frankness *(nothing wrong with that even though at times you will not particularly agree or like what I have to say),* in the hope that the knowledge gained from others who have weathered many a storm may prevent you from wasting any part of your life through mismanagement that could ultimately affect your future.

These are the wasted years that can never be regained, we will never get them back they are gone forever! Question is, how many years can you afford to waste? Solutions do exist but it stems right back to the very beginning of a relationship, if not *before* it even gets off the ground, in fact it begins within your very thoughts.

The first most important point to remember is that both sexes need to be in the right frame of mind for marriage. You cannot marry for the wrong reasons. Don't use marriage as a means to solve your loneliness, or fulfilling your need for anyone who can provide emotional or financial support for they are the wrong reasons. Remember, if you believe you *'need',* don't do it.

You absolutely have to be happy and comfortable with whom you are and what you are capable of by knowing your strengths, your weakness, and limitations. You should be able to function independently and be aware *(as there are no guarantees),* that if you did marry and it all fell apart, that you would survive. No one should ever act or make decisions out of desperation. When you are in desperate mode, you will be more prone to making wrong selections and wrong decisions as your mindset would be, *any man/woman will do.* No! Any man/woman will not do, you deserve to have the right person by your side, not just *any* person!

Both genders need to reach deep down within their hearts, understand who they are and what it is they desire in a partner for life and then, with eyes wide open, set forth to find that person. The timing is right, the topic always current and there is so much that needs to be exposed, discussed, and mutually resolved.

"There is a least one woman in the world for every man in the world to think the world of," quote: 1 Men, Women & Wedlock 1910 A & C Black.

Introduction

The excesses, and the disastrous management of the financial market leading into 2009, plunged the world into turmoil, and the only way to begin the recovery process meant that some banking institutions and businesses around the world had to collapse. What we experienced in the months that followed, was in effect a cleansing process, whereby, the financial world had to start again, minus the excesses.

So too, with so much material that has been written about relationships between men and woman, and who does what in a household, women's rights and men's obligations within the home, we've diverted away from peace and harmony within the home and boarded the express train to a nightmare.

The Women's Liberation Movement of the 60s and 70s certainly started the ball rolling, and while women *gained* in one way, they also *lost* in another.

What was lost was the niceties—the essence of who we are, and what we as women are meant to represent within our home. Most importantly we lost our identity within our relationship!

Before anyone gets too upset with my comments, please understand that I am making specific reference to a woman's role within the home as a caregiver or nurturer. I too believe in equal rights but not to the point where by it destroys the family. Both men and women have rights, but is it acceptable to inflict these *'rights'* against each other? Why is it a case of *'them'* and *'us'* why can't we use our rights in a positive way without hurting each other?

Why relationships break down, has been a major contributing factor to countless discussions and studies conducted by psychologists, doctors, and therapists for many years, but the same problems continue to be present—Why? Why? Why?

This is what happens when two people mismanage their relationship!

Some of the reasons have been explained to us, but is anyone paying attention? Are we acting upon the advice that is given to us? Is it even the right advice?

Psychologically and physically men and women are different no one can dispute that however problems emerge, when the significance of these differentials are not acknowledged by either gender.

Men and women act and react the way they do, because of the way we are hard wired, and when we can finally understand and accept the reasons for these differences and the impact they have within our lives, only then will we be better able to cope within our relationship by not taking each other's shortfalls personally, in turn enabling us to view each other positively, no matter which decade we live in. Given these conditions, there is no reason why both sexes cannot live in relative harmony.

It is this topic and much, much more that we will examine, as the scales need to be tipped back just a little. It has been said that male masculinity is toxic, really? Why is that? I guess strength is now seen as toxic! Not so. There is a reason for the way men and women were created. We need men to be strong because there are things in life that this 'strength' will be needed. Women on the other hand also possess qualities that are also imperative and the two go hand in hand. This should not be a competition between men and women. Both are needed.

"The year 1975 is very important in the history of Australia and the institution of marriage. The Family Law Act was passed, and this meant amongst other things, that no-fault divorce was now an option, for Australian Couples. The only grounds which were required for a divorce is irretrievable breakdown of the marriage which is determined by the couple separating for at least 12 months. Many took advantage of the new laws and in the following year, over 62,000 marriages were annulled."

"The rate at which couples divorce has certainly increased. The previously mentioned Family Law Act contributed to a large increase. But times of economic depression also show up as divorces have increased during these years. In the 1950s, the divorce rate in Australia was about 10%. It is more than four times that today."

This does not necessarily mean that marriages in the 50s were happier than they are today, what it does mean is that divorce for women in the 50s was not an easy option because women were not as financially independent as they are today. In those days, a woman would have been reluctant to leave, as it meant loss of identity, social standing, lack of money, security, fear of being alone and rejection by society.

Equality in this instance however enabled women to be rid of this stigma and this was a positive step, however I don't think it has stamped out abuse as this still continues today. No woman should tolerate this under any circumstance.

What exactly are women supposed to be contributing towards their relationships? How do women maintain balance and harmony within everyday life without turning against their partner at the first sign of discontent?

Times may have changed, but one thing should never change, and that is how we treat each other, which should always be with equal consideration and respect no matter which decade we reside in.

Of course, men and women are all equal, but men and women are also different and there is nothing wrong with being different, after all, we are *'supposed'* to be different, aren't we?

Dr Michael G Conner wrote the following—

"This paper is collection of research conclusions and observations which I have witnessed over the past 5 year that I have attempted to put into a written form that might be helpful, but more importantly stimulate discussions. The real purpose is to increase the awareness between men and women, and to help them set aside issues that are not personal but are merely manifestations of nature. To my way of thinking, it is important to honour and rejoice in both our nature and our individuality."

Dr Michael G Conner continues by stating—

"The task that faces men and women is to learn to accept their differences, avoid taking their differences as personal attempts to frustrate each other and to

compromise whenever possible. The idea that one gender can think and feel like the other if they truly loved each other is rather absurd. Sure, a man or woman could act in consideration of the other's needs, but this would not necessarily be rewarding and honest. Holding the benefit of another above our own is rewarding. But from time to time, and more often for most of us, it is important to be our self and to be accepted, and not to be the source of distress and disappointment in the lives of people we love."

Dr Michael G. Conner, Psy. D. Clinical, Medical and Family Psychology— "Understanding the Difference between Men & Women" 1999–2010.

Well said, Dr Conner!

This paper should be read in its entirety in order to better appreciate the comments of Dr Michael G Conner and gain a complete understanding on this subject. For your convenience and with the permission of Dr Conner, I have included this paper in its entirety at the end of this book.

I hope that this book will assist you in identifying potential wrong decisions, by foreseeing or calculating the possible outcome. Once you are aware of the possible outcome, you may want to rethink your decision before you proceed.

In the *'dance of life'*, where once the men took the lead, they are now being led by women to love, unity and harmony!

1

If Only I Knew Then *What I Know Now!*

Being philosophical about one's life when viewing it from a *hindsight* perspective gives most of us a somewhat enlightened feeling, at the very least, we believe ourselves to be much wiser now and quietly confident, that if we had our life over again, we would do things differently *(some of us would) "If only I knew then, what I know now,"* sound familiar?

The urge to want to change certain bad aspects of our life is a part of human nature, and given the opportunity, most of us would probably jump at the chance, knowing what we know now.

Imagine if you were able to identify just one poor choice you made way back when, that led you to the place you find yourself today, a place you don't wish to be in. Now imagine for just that one split second—to be given the undeniably incredible opportunity of altering your present, by revisiting your past—a second chance, that will remove that *'thorn'* that has weighed your life down, from your side, set you free, give you a clean slate if you will, and start again—but this time, you will do it right. Why? Because now, you know better!

By the way, the *'thorn'* I speak of could be the city or house you live in, your job, a financial investment, or even the person you selected to share your life with, for if this person turned out to be the wrong one for you, and we all know how easy that can be, then your life presently is not the way you imagined or hoped it would be, or if that financial decision you made all those years ago resulting in the huge loss you are faced with today. Now that you know better, would you make that same decision?

What would *you* change if you were given a second chance regarding your marriage?

Ladies—Would you marry the same man? If so, what would you do differently this time around? How would you treat him? Would you spend more quality time with him, would you argue less and love him more? What would you do differently if you were given a second chance with the same person?

If your answer is, *"No, I would not marry the same man,"* are you able to recognise the reason why you would not pick the same person? Could it have been some of those undesirable qualities that you were aware of when you first met, but placed little significance upon, or is it because one or both of you stopped trying to impress each other *(because everyone says that's to be expected in a marriage),* hence grew apart over the years, and if so, who do you blame for this?

What about all the occasions you said no to him, and was this the reason he felt rejected or unloved? Did your rejections ever cause him to become moody and did this constantly resurface each time you argued? If you were given another chance, if you could go back in time, right to the beginning of your relationship what would you do differently? By the way, saying no is everybody's right, not necessarily reserved exclusively for women.

Neither party should respond with a blatant no to their spouse's request no matter what it is. Remain open to compromise, not rejection, suppression, manipulation, or intimidation not to mention trickery and mind games!

Except for physical or substance abuse, which should never be tolerated by anyone under *any* circumstances *"No,"* is not meant to be used against a normal caring partner who only wants to enjoy and give enjoyment in return.

Guys—Never say **no** *to something you know she has her heart set on* something she has always wanted to do, go or see, or whatever her reasons.

If her request may appear to be unreasonable, then discuss it with her, reach a compromise, adjust, work it out, but don't just say "NO!" Ask yourself, will the consequences that will ultimately follow, be worth it?

Suppression of another human being by telling them that they cannot do something, or go somewhere and live life as a free human being is just plain foolish and wrong, it's just another form of abuse comprising of bullying through intimidation for the purpose of control not to mention the insecurity on the part of the suppressor.

The fuel that keeps us moving along the pathway to continual love is never going to be that of suppression nor intimidation, but love, trust, communication, passion and the freedom to live!

Guys—would you marry the same woman second time around—How would you do things differently and would you be willing to compromise more often, now that you know the damage your stubbornness has caused?

Would you be more understanding with her, and be there for her unlike before? Would you show her the extent of your love and communicate with her more often or just assume that she should know what you're thinking and she should be satisfied with that? Would you suppress her in any way?

Remember that your partner used to be someone's child once upon a time and that parent, encouraged their child, your now spouse, to express themselves freely. Do we not educate our children and teach them the freedom of expression and creativity? Does a future spouse, that would be you, now have the right to suppress it out of them decades later? Surely this can't be right!

You may choose to become a parent one day—how would you feel if another human being was preventing your son or daughter from living and enjoying life by not allowing them to reach their fullest potential due to their own paranoia and insecurities.

I know I would not be happy if a man was suppressing my daughter, or a woman was manipulating my son into submission due to her own selfishness or low self-esteem. Who amongst us can say that they have the right to deprive someone of their dreams? Would you want your dreams suppressed into oblivion?

Treat the other person, whoever it is, be it a friend, your sister and particularly your partner, in the way that you would like to be treated. If you value yourself, and rightly so, just remember that this right is not exclusively reserved for you alone, everyone else has that same right as well.

Life's complexities, the method of selecting a partner, planning for your wedding day and beyond, keeping your mate through freedom, and not by manipulation, staying in love by remaining young at heart and how to minimise mistakes and more, are all important facts that will be addressed in the coming chapters.

> *"Freedom means being free to be who you are,*
> *Not who you are expected to be."*

Prevention is certainly better than cure. Taking the time to think carefully means you are giving yourself every opportunity to make the right decision by weighing up your options and considering the potential outcome of something you are about to commit to which, if the end result of this thought process is not favourable, it may assist in influencing your decision and prevent you from going through with it. Give it the serious thought it deserves. This would be so much easier than trying to repair the damage an ill-thought-out decision will cause later. Let's be open to receiving as much information as possible about both sexes, in the hope that it will give a clearer understanding of the opposite sex, and the things that truly matter in life, which will prevent you from wasting some of your precious life away.

Today's trends are just that—*trends'*—they never last, they just keep changing, if you want your marriage to succeed and last the distance, placing it in the *'trend'* category is not the way to love and harmony as you journey onwards through life.

Your goal of a successful marriage begins right now, and however challenging this will be, it will pale to insignificance when compared to the next phase of your journey, for the real challenge will not be in finding your partner, it will be in learning how to retain your partner. Give yourself every opportunity to make your marriage a success, let him be the man and you the lady of the house. Don't try to be both, it will not work and if you are inclined to believe that it does work or it will work, are you willing to pay the price because payment day is surely coming!

Ladies—Did you know "You can attract more bees with honey than vinegar." In other words, be nice! You can still get what you want, arguing about it and getting nasty is only going to escalate the situation where no one wins.

Imagine having gone through so much to find that one person who will be right for you, the last thing you will want to do once you found him/her, is to now risk losing them because neither of you are treating each other with love, respect, consideration, and patience. Even more disturbing, how could you not, if you are supposed to be in love with this person?

There are many things that need to be done right, particularly in the initial stages of forming a bond with someone, but be assured that what you learn will contribute positively towards your endeavours, by showing you how to maximise your potential as an individual, for you and you alone, have the power to seek out the qualities you desire in another person, in turn enhancing each other's lives, and propelling you both within the miracle that is love and life!

"Love means the association of two beings for the benefit of one."
Quote: 113 Pg. 40 Men Women & Wedlock 1910 A&C Black Publishers.

2

You Have the Rest of Your Life *to* *Be a Wife*!

Relish the woman you are today—enjoy being you and do all the things you want to do before you get married. Why would you want to rush into marriage, to then spend your life, even if you are happily married but more so if you are not, wondering about all the things you dreamt of doing, and never did, wondering about all the things you missed out on.

"Life spent in reflection of what could have been, is indeed a waste of life."

If you dream of travelling, then do it! If you want to work on cruise ships, go for it. My point is, no matter what it is you dream of doing, make it happen, so that when the time comes for you to make that final commitment, you should be experienced and confident enough within yourself to begin the next phase of your life with your chosen one and together set forth on a pathway that will lead you to a different kind of fulfilment and discovery, in turn silencing that little voice deep within yourself that may forever have asked, *"Is this all there is to my life?"*

Everything changes once you are married; nothing will ever be quite the same again. Your life will be very different but it does not mean that it won't be good, it should be good, but you have to work at it to make sure it will be all you dreamt it would be. It will be up to the both of you to make this change happen for the better, not for the worse.

No one in their right mind enters into a relationship knowing that the union is doomed or expecting that it is going to go sour. We all enter into a relationship hoping it will be for the better, that our lives will flourish and that we grow together as a couple but even more importantly, individually as well. Giving each other space is imperative as it allows both to nurture who you are as separate individuals, this in turn will only serve to enhance both of you as a couple because growing together means staying together, growing apart means exactly that—'*apart*'.

First Basic Rule—

In order to grow old together remember vow*: "All the days of my life,"* you need to grow together…but as individuals, does this make sense? Think about it! To ensure you survive as one, you need to be able to function as two individuals while constantly adjusting to each other's growth or change but all the while retaining your individuality, as you still need to be the person each of you fell in love with.

To prevent each other from setting and reaching individual goals is wrong and resentment will follow which will eventually lead to arguments. You both retain the right to pursue your interests, not just one of you. This after all will lead to the further development of your characters and enhance your lives together as you reach *'mid-life'*. The more fulfilling your relationship is in your younger day, the easier the transition when you both reach mid-life!

This is not to say that as a couple you will never have any *'off'* days in your marriage, what it does means is by growing and developing together, you are better placed to handle any difficult situations that life will undoubtedly throw at you as you work together resolving any issues which will in turn serve to further strengthen your relationship. You don't just want to make it to *'mid-life'* you want to get through mid-life without the crisis attached to it, Right?

Don't be alarmed at the prospect of marriage, for this part of your life's journey can be the best and most rewarding but you do need to enter matrimony with your eyes wide open and throw those rose coloured glasses away.

Your dream may be marrying the right person and your greatest desire is that of a successful marriage, but it won't happen of its own accord. Just because you believe you are marrying for love, doesn't guarantee *'forever'* happiness unless you both put in 110%. Know exactly what to expect from each other, where you want to be, and how you are going to get there, and always work as a team with each other's best interest at heart. Given all of this, how can you fail? The only way you can possibly fail is if egos get in the way. There is no room for egos in any relationship. There is an old Greek saying, *"Where ever egos reside, separation follows!"*

You have the love of the man/woman you selected to share your life with so go ahead, relish and enjoy the experience of being inspired, as you discover qualities and talents that each of you will bring out in the other.

Ladies—Do the right thing by your man, treat him with love and respect— and believe that you will take care of his needs as he will take care of yours.

You no longer have just yourself to care for; from this point forward, you have your partner to consider beside yourself.

Marriage does change you, no matter what happens to you after you marry, whether it is successful or not, you will grow in ways you never thought possible for both of your lives will change forever; it's up to the both of you to ensure that this change will be in a good way. He may be your husband, but treat him as if you just met him, and keep the magic and mystery alive in order to keep the love alive.

Guys—look at your partner as if you have just met her keep that momentum, become familiar with that feeling, remember that 'feeling', if you allow it to disappear you will spend the rest of your life, looking for it, and you will not find it. Keeping the love you have for your partner alive is much easier than trying to resurrect it later. Accept that you must now learn to love someone else more than you love yourself. This will be your wife, for now and your children, if any later.

You must learn to put your wife and your children first and it absolutely has to be reciprocated by your partner as well. Each of you will have to take into consideration each other's wants and needs. Like it or not, this is the way it is, if you do not agree with this, perhaps you should put off marriage plans until you understand the concept of marriage and what it really means and even more importantly, what you are prepared to put into your relationship and what you expect in return.

Let us not forget, this may be the 21st century but men are still men, and women are still women and both need to be treated with respect and equal consideration and guess what—It's ok! Equality is meant for all not just for some.

Just because men and women are different doesn't mean they are not equal as human beings.

Ladies—You are the 'nurturers'. Do you know what it means to nurture?

It means to take care of, to protect and to love, to nourish and sustain, by being compassionate, understanding and patient.

These are the qualities your new husband needs to find in you; a loving, caring, understanding, patient, willing, sensitive, home loving, outdoor loving, fun loving, sexy woman, that is his wife.

"We can't be on a high all the time!" How many times have we heard this and it's true, there will be times when you are down but don't use your down time as fuel for arguments. If you are down, think through it and put it in the right perspective and set about finding out why you feel this way. What you believe to be bad, may not be so bad after all, seek help from family or a professional, don't allow problems to fester, do something about it as quickly as possible and snap yourself out of it, and be thankful that as long as you have your health, nothing else is as important, because without your health, you truly have nothing. You don't think it's important? I suggest you visit a terminally ill ward in a hospital, you will soon know what I mean.

Resolve any problem that is worrying you and remember, someone somewhere, would love to trade places with you. Create balance in your life by tending to every aspect of your relationship. Don't simply take care of your own needs.

You can become the woman that he can't live without, but you will not achieve this by nagging him to death!

Given that men are the *hunters*—would you prefer that he *'hunt'* for someone else? If not, then take care of business...HIM!

Turn your home into a sanctuary where he will long to come home to every night not one where he dreads to walk into. Let your home illuminate the warmth and glow that is your love when he walks in the door. This may sound a little corny in today's sophisticated world, but corny or not, this is what is required and perhaps we ought to worry less about our sophistication and more the basics of life because sophistication where relationships are concerned does not cut it anymore.

Welcome him with open arms and a kiss, prepare your dinner, yes dinner, however simple it is you can make it a joint effort, but only if he feels comfortable with this, for heaven's sake don't make an issue of it. If he does not want to cook get over it, who knows, he may eventually warm to the idea, but don't turn the whole situation into an argument because of your *'right'* to demand that he does his share in the kitchen. Give him the opportunity of deciding for himself.

He can get involved if he wants to, but don't make the mistake of forcing this upon him, it will simply become a chore he will never enjoy, and all you are successful in achieving is setting yourself up for future trouble.

Keep it fun and enjoyable. You have far more to gain by just letting it be.

"Don't nag your husband. If he won't carry out your wishes for love of you, he certainly won't because you nag him."

Don'ts For Wives. 1913 Blanche Ebbutt A & C Black Ltd.

3

When Women Were Women, And Guys Were Men!

We have been bombarded with women's wants and expectations from men for far too long. May I ask you a question—How do you wish to be treated? Are you a woman who wishes to be treated as such, or are you a woman, who wants to be treated generically? Is it even possible to be treated generically? What is a generic human being anyway? We are all human beings and we are either male or female, there is nothing generic about that as there is clear distinction, one is male and the other is female therefore if there is clear distinction between the sexes, why then must we do away with words that *distinguish* between the sexes? This book is not about LGBTQ, etc. It's just about men and women and that's it!

Could it be that it's ok to distinguish between the sexes—but only sometimes is this *'selective distinction'*? Well, you cannot have it both ways, you are either a man or a woman and together we are *all* part of the human race and that's it! If you identify as something else, it's still about being a man or a woman, is it not?

Be proud to be a woman and all that a woman stands for. We do not need to compare ourselves to men as far as equality goes, for as human beings, we are all equal, particularly when it comes to regard, consideration and respect. This is something *everyone* deserves and we should expect to get this from each other, without question.

We have our own strengths, as do men. I could not even begin to imagine a man for instance, bearing the pain of giving birth, juggling career, home, and children, but we as women are designed to multi-task, and we should handle it. Men on the other hand, have their own areas of strength—why is there the need to compete? It's almost as though we feel threatened by them therefore expect to be able to do absolutely everything that men can do.

Is it so wrong if men are better at doing some things than women? Why aren't the *men* complaining about women being better at some things?

Men and women both, have their own strengths and weaknesses, let's just leave it at that, and stop this waste of time competition between the sexes.

The majority of men want a *woman (that means a female).* As with everything, there are always exceptions, but generally a male would like to have a feminine woman at his side.

Oh, and while we are on this topic—digressing slightly, if a man wants to offer you a seat on any public transport, it does not mean that you are looked upon as a person with special needs, it's just someone being polite. Everyone knows that a woman can do just as much as a man, and we are all aware of the equality issues, so by accepting a seat will not mean that the equality level of the female race automatically drops.

Have we all forgotten about 'chivalry' do we even remember or know what it means? It's just plain and simple 'courtesy' and 'respect' extended to us by the male.)

You were born a woman, were you not? Don't you wish to be treated with respect and consideration as a woman? How can it possibly be regarded as offensive to you, if someone offers you a seat?

If someone shows you this kind of regard, the least you can do is to be gracious, welcome it, embrace it, sit down, and say *Thank you,* or are we to punish men, because they have manners, and by doing so, lose our own in the process.

If for some reason you absolutely do not wish to accept his seat, then at least be gracious about it and decline politely.

Yet, every day we are relentlessly bombarded with the latest on relationships, what's in and what's not and how to fix it, but still marriages are falling apart, *"Why?"*

The following extract, says it all, and if we are to gain a clearer understanding of why we do the things we do, and how we can overcome certain obstacles, then reading and understanding the section below will help us to accept our differences for it is the way nature always intended it to be, now let's move on from this point—

The following is an *extract* from, **'Tomorrow's Edge', by Skye Thomas,** which is explained so perfectly.

The Male—

Is the 'hunter and protector' therefore bigger and stronger?

He needs to physically move with speed and agility in order to actively conquer the object of his focus. His mind is designed for cunning and for calmness in battle. His life and the lives of his loved ones depend on his ability to be strong, smart, and stable. He approaches his relationships the same way. He loves the challenge of the chase. It makes him feel alive, the life force flows through him as he scores that first smile, the first kiss.

The Female—

Is designed to nurture and gather. She protects her family and loved ones from harm. She is responsible for the well-being of her family.

She is built with an eye for the smallest detail and the ability to verbalise. It's her job to gather the nuts, fruits, vegetables, and firewood and herd the children. She needs to be able to recognise the poison foods from the nutritious. The family's mortality rate is in her hands. She has to watch over them with a critical eye for detail, watching for the first signs of fever or sickness. She uses language and her magnetism to keep her loved ones near so that she can watch over them. She draws the man in the same way. If she can't pull him into her nest, how will she be able to look after him?

How can we apply this to present time?

Skye Thomas goes on to explain—

"He does not have an outlet for his athletic and cunning. He hunts and battles vicariously through the television remote control," says Skye Thomas.

He is lost in a suit and tie world. He creates war and battle without realising it because he has to feel that he is protecting his loved ones from an enemy. He still tends to 'conquer' his women.

She doesn't know the healing arts anymore and uses her words and keen eye to nitpick and tear down her loved ones. She overspends at the mall in order to touch that part of herself that needs to gather supplies for her family. She manipulates her man into marriage. Neither one knows what it is they're doing on a subconscious level to create the situations needed, so that they can live out their roles.

Now this is where it gets really interesting for if you have fully understood the above, read the following and think about what is being said on a much deeper level, but here's the thing, you must be willing to accept it, if you can do this, then you are on your way to a more positive relationship, one that will not be wasted on meaningless and insignificant arguments, but spent in appreciation of each other by celebrating the reasons why you are together in the first place.

Skye Thomas continues to say—

What can we do about it? We need to quit lying to ourselves by pretending to be civilised and enlightened. We are just cavemen with technology, laws and manners. The core of our biological programming hasn't changed all that much. We're still afraid of the dark and in awe of the moon. We need to rectify the world we live in today with our biological skills, drives and motivations. We need to feel useful and that our lives have meaning and purpose. Men need to find a constructive way to hunt and protect. Women need to find a healthy way to gather and nurture. Stop arguing over things like equality and whether or not we can do each other's jobs. It's not important. Both sexes are just as capable, but that doesn't mean that's where our natural gifts and talents lie and it doesn't mean that what we choose to do, is in alignment with who we really are. Move beyond stereotypes and into the core of what the human animal really needs in order to thrive not just survive.

Our relationships improve when we learn to use our gifts for something more constructive than just tearing each other apart.

Skye Thomas, Tomorrow's Edge

Herein lies the answers to why men and women are different—we were made that way, it's that simple, there is nothing we can do about it, we have nothing that we need to prove to anyone, neither sex is better than the other, each sex excels within its own world. Since when did being different have anything to do with equality?

Equality in a relationship is a prerequisite, but how we use this equality within a relationship, will determine whether or not the relationship will survive long enough to get to the next hurdle (the dreaded 'mid-life crisis'.)

"The vision of equality between the sexes has narrowed the possibilities for discovery of what truly exists within a man and within a woman. The world is less interesting when everything is the same."

Dr Michael G Conner, Psy. D Understanding the Difference between Men and Women.
Copyright 1999–2010.
(Please read Michael G. Conner's paper—'Understanding the Difference between Men & Women' in its entirety in the special section at the back of this book.)

Assuming you have a man, who cares for you, provides for you and after all, he did marry you because he loved you, then to say, no to him, when he needs you, is the first step, to the beginning of your end.

To continue down this path, you are disintegrating his masculinity and from that point onward will begin a minefield of a lifetime of problems which will only get worse as the years fly by before your very eyes.

Please re-read the extract mentioned above by '*Skye Thomas*' read it until you completely understand what it all means, for within this extract lies the solutions to so many relationship problems. Understand once and for all, that we are meant to be different, and we don't need to have to do everything that men do, in order to be considered equal.

Just because we are different does not mean one gender is more powerful than the other; we probably can do most of all that men can do, so what if we can!

We don't need to prove anything to anyone for we as women should know our worth, we don't need to physically do everything men can do in order to prove this, but we also don't need to undermine their worth either. Interesting to note that I have yet to hear of men complaining that they want to be able to do all the things women can do. Why is it the other way around? I guess men don't feel threatened by women, question is, do females feel threatened by the males and if so, why?

Both sexes are worthy in their own right, so to spend our life bickering over insignificant issues as to who does what in the home, is a waste of life, a life you will not get back again, no second chances, this is it, so, how do you choose to live it?

For too long though, this '*equality*' issue, has argued and fought its way into the majority of households because we were told that this is the way it should be. It is as if women, we were just looking for an excuse *(and now had a good one)* to not have do some of the things that women were always in charge of doing. I cannot tell you how many women I have spoken to and they all say that they have better things to do with their time than spend it do housework, but they certainly don't mind wasting their precious time arguing about it with their partners.

If a man has no problem with undertaking household duties, that's great, as long as he wants to and feels comfortable in doing household chores, I say to him, go for it! On the other hand, there are some men who have traditional values they do not believe that a man's primary responsibility is household chores.

Cleaning, laundry, cooking, and everything else associated with running the home traditionally is the woman's domain. Men used to do the outside chores and women took care of business inside the home (*remember—Hunter-Gatherer*)

Sure enough, there will be occasions when a man will help his wife out with housework if the necessity arises and yes, he may cook as well, and if his wife is not feeling well, he will clean and do the laundry.

He is not doing this because sick or not, it is expected of him, he is looking after you during this time, because he loves and cares for you and that is the difference between a peaceful home life and a turbulent home life.

When a man is pressured or pushed into doing that which he is not happy with, this discontent, over time will amount to resentment which in turn will fuel many future arguments that will lead to a huge can of worms that will be opened one day.

This being the case, what would your role be within this marriage? What happens when you have children? Will you expect your husband to get up in the middle of the night to feed the child? There is more on this further into the book.

Some men have no problem looking after themselves (*because it's their choice, not yours*) and I applaud them, but not all men share this view, if you know that your man needs your attention, he expects you to do some things for him and you proceed to ignore his wishes, you are simply asking for trouble, and by the way, no amount of '*training*' him (*assuming he will allow you to do this to him*) will guarantee that he will not snap out of it one day and either, confront you, or find someone else. Need I remind you what you have to look forward to…*Mid-life crisis!* Don't keep on adding fuel to a fire that may well ignite years down the track.

Surely you can understand and it should make sense that if you lovingly do things for each other, it draws you closer together and lessens the possibility of drifting apart by ensuring interest in each other's presence but if you simply take care of your own self with little concern for your partner expect over time, that he will find what he craves for in someone else. Whose fault will this be?

Should this possibility come to fruition? Let's stop blaming the guys for playing around if this is the treatment they are getting at home!

Priorities need to be put in the right perspective and a little of the *old fashion* values need to resurface again, unless of course you are that far gone you don't remember the way back.

Pointless complaining years from now, after you find out that your partner is seeing someone else because the balance of power has shifted, it's tipped over too much to one side and it needs to be rebalanced. Spend your life celebrating it, not wasting it by tearing each other's lives down.

"Many people are busy in the present making a past for the future."
Quote: 2 Men, Women & Wedlock 1910. A & C Black Publishers.

I say let's get busy making it a happy present, for a brighter future!

4

If He Doesn't Seem Right!
Let Him Go!

Ok, you have just met a guy, he looks great, he has a great job, he dresses well, has a nice car *(if this is important to you)* and he is about to pick you up and take you out on your first date.

Earlier on though, you would have studied your *'Preferred Characteristics'* list. This is a list of all the traits that you love or enjoy in the opposite sex, and it is these qualities that you will seek out in the person who will become your partner in life.

Ladies—is he a gentleman? Does he come to your door to collect you? Don't for one minute think that it's not important whether he does or not, because it does matter! (If he is courteous enough to do that, then he was taught basic courtesy and manners. It also indicates that he is considerate and caring and these are qualities you really do need to have within your relationship so do not underestimate the importance of these qualities at such an early stage of your relationship because if he does not have them at this point, how will you determine whether or not he has a genuine respect for women. Back to basics, remember!

Does he open the car door for you, does he pull out your chair once in the restaurant for you to sit on. Once again, don't underestimate the importance of these gestures as it simply shows you the 'quality' of man that he is and the upbringing he has received which also tells you a lot about his family (and you need to be able to get on with them as well, if you expect to be happy that is.)

He won't always have to do this, if you don't want him to, but for now, it gives you an insight into his character, giving you a clearer indication of the kind of man he is and the regard and respect this man has for women and all people for that matter.

Ask yourself, *"How do I wish to be treated now, and for the rest of my life?"* Do you want to be treated as a lady, or as one of the boys?

Could there be some hidden romantic advantage in being treated as one on the boys that we women don't know about? I think not!

Observe his behaviour, is he a neat freak, does he complain about every detail, no matter how miniscule it may be? Does he enjoy most food, or does he only ever eat the one thing all the time? Does he display any kind of obsessive behaviour? If he does, he actually has issues. If you want to take his issues on, then go for it, but why would you want to start a now *'flawed'* relationship, and expect all will be well.

That will be the very flaw you will attempt to repair later on, but it will be irreparable, you can't fix it because when someone has obsessive-compulsive characteristics, it is usually due to deeper underlying issues. This person would need professional psychological assistance. At the very least, the decision is yours, if you want to take him on, it's your choice but you must devote a lot of thought to this and be prepared to work twice as hard to make the relationship work…otherwise find someone else.

Assuming the man you chose is *normal,* proceed to find out exactly what his likes and dislikes are, who he is, and what he does for a living?

How is his relationship with his friends, parents, and any siblings he may have? Has he done any travelling? If not, is he planning to travel at some stage in his life? Is he the quiet and reserved type, or is he outgoing, ambitious, what are his ambitions? Which of these characteristics appeals to you? If you prefer the quiet type and this guy is *'out there'* then understand that he will remain that way and you are never going to change him into being an introvert.

You need to find them the way you want them to be without having to change them. If they are not right to begin with, they will not be right years down the track either, and you can be sure of one thing, what you think does not matter in the present, will matter in the future. Don't think, *"But I can change him,"* because there's not a woman alive who has not tried to change something about a man, whether it be his appearance, his attitude, his habits, etc. You cannot change a man, nor should you want to, because if you have to change him, then he is not the right one for you *(he may revert to the way he used to be only…worse.).*

41

He must be the way you want him to be now, *'in the present'*. Remember, don't waste your time or your life for that matter, trying to reinvent him to suit yourself and make yourself miserable in the process because *you cannot, and never will, succeed in reinventing a man.*

Furthermore, the same can be said for women as well, a man should never attempt to change a woman to suit himself.

Given the right set of circumstance, men will attempt to *'mould'* a woman, this usually occurs when the man is of a controlling nature and the woman he is marrying shows weakness in personality by allowing herself to be dominated by her man. This form of domination was more prevalent in some European cultures decades ago, and it still happens today.

Then again, there are instances when both have known each other since primary school, marry at a very young age, at this point it depends on which of the two is more dominant, if it's the woman, she will mould her man in any way she wants (*as men generally mature later than women, his personality will now be stunted*) and from that point onwards, she will rule him. If it's the man who is more dominant, she will become a doormat for him for the rest of her life, unless she plucks up enough courage to leave.

Given these circumstances, neither scenario will result in a happy, fulfilling relationship. Eventually one or both will end up wondering, *"What else is out there, what have I missed out on and is this all there is to life?"*

The success of a relationship should never be dependent on the premise that all will be well after a forced *'alteration'* of an undesirable characteristic has been implemented.

Some men may not have any particular bad habit, but in time, develop an annoying habit, what then? Nip it in the bud and sort it out as quickly as possible but always remembering to do so with regard, respect, and sensibility.

Do not nag him, don't threaten him, and whatever you do, don't bribe him, with you being the prize.

Be honest with him in a nice and non-hurtful, non-threatening manner by explaining to him that his new bad habit is upsetting you or the household therefore, for the common good of all concerned, you would appreciate it if he remedied the problem as quickly as possible and also assure him that you are happy to help him to do so *(and don't forget to say, "I love you darling!")*

As far as his character is concerned, be aware, that some men can present a totally different character to who they really are, you must be able to judge for yourself whether he is who he presents himself to be, or is he pretending to be someone else (*i.e. he may want to impress you by telling you things about his background or his finances, what he does for a living, that are in fact not true.*) If he is lying to you now, chances are he will be lying to you about other things in the future…you don't need this, move on!

Do the ground-work now, rather than discover something about him when it's too late and most importantly as I mentioned earlier, take your time, there is no rush.

Pay particular attention to what he says, how he says it, and does he look you in the eye when he speaks to you or is he overly nervous or fidgety.

Being nervous does not automatically indicate anything sinister, but if you do go out with him several times, and the nervousness continues, it may indicate that something is not quite right and you need to find out what it is. You don't want to find out later on, that he was hiding something from you all along or it may be that he is the nervy type, which could also herald insecurity.

How many times have you heard others say, *"I can't believe how stupid and naive I was for not seeing this in him right from the start, the writing was on the wall, and I chose to ignore it."* You don't ever want to hear yourself saying that!

Have you heard any rumours about him? There is truth in the saying, *"Where there's smoke, there's fire,"* if this happens, consider it as definitely worth investigating, particularly if rumour has it that he is a womaniser or gambler.

If it were possible to warn all women against him, I'm sure we would do so, but it is not possible, so perhaps he may be happier with someone else.

Men of this nature find it hard to stick to just one woman at any one time, it's hard enough for most men in general, let alone one who has already started the ball rolling and if they gamble—well there goes your life!

Guys—you have your own idea of the kind of woman you want—therefore you too, will look at your checklist of desired characteristics.

Who is she? What does she do for a living? How does she interact with her family and friends? Ask her to share her thoughts with you on what she thinks are prerequisites for achieving a happy relationship and once she has met your family and friends, how did she react to them? Was she genuinely happy to meet them, or was it a forced effort on her part?

The importance of this cannot be underestimated because you will be sharing these people with her should the two of you marry, if she does not like them now, she is not suddenly going to fall in love with them after you marry, if anything, she will probably try to stop you from seeing them as well and the beginning of the end has been set yet again.

Take note of the way she grooms herself; do you like the type of clothes she wears? The power of clothes is not to be downplayed for they may cover the body, but they reveal the personality of the body they cover.

If there is anything about the way she dresses or presents herself right now that does not appeal to you this should be taken very seriously, don't think for one minute that you will change her should you decide to marry this woman *(you have no right to attempt to change her anyway)* at any rate you won't succeed and even if you did it certainly won't happen without some form of resentment—so now you have allowed resentment to enter the equation—big, big mistake!

Observe her mannerisms her personal appearance, makeup, etc. What are her pet's likes and dislikes? Does she like pets? Do you like pets for that matter? This is important because if you do like them or intend on having pets in the future, it is important that your partner likes them as well or else it may one day be a case of, *"It's either me or Rocky the dog,"* or *"It's me or Jessie the cockatiel but one of us is going!"*

Who are you going to be willing to let go? Even if you got rid of the pet, the day of reckoning will come.

Does she become jealous or nasty, if you glance at other women, most of us now know *(through experience),* that there is nothing wrong with looking as long as you don't touch, right! Most young women due to their inexperience however, do not share this view. Does she phone you late into the night to say *"Hi darling"* but in fact is checking up on you?

Is she possessive or does she have some kind of personality disorder? Jealousy and being possessive or being compulsive about anything is a bad sign. These are not the qualities that will bestow happiness upon you and I promise you, at some point during your relationship, these two undesirable traits will raise their heads. Make sure that she is not into playing mind games with you.

The manner in which she conducts herself is very important, it basically tells you who she is, but it can also reveal who she may become. If she is the jealous type, then this condition, more than likely worsens once married and the novelty of the event begins to fade away.

What are her interests? It's not essential that she have the same interests as you do. It's ok to not have similar interests as long as both parties are still prepared to give each other some space to do the things they enjoy doing as individuals but also enjoy things that you both share an interest in. Life would be so monotonous if you liked the same things, shared the same hobbies, or whatever the case may be. The point I am trying to make is there is nothing wrong with having varying and different interests, as it can be complimentary to your relationship and it makes for interesting and challenging and yes *'spicy'* conversation!

Both parties must understand that you should never attempt to prevent each other from pursuing your chosen activities or hobbies simply because you are now in a relationship.

It's selfish and extremely unfair to prevent someone from doing the things that make him or her happy, which you were aware of before you began your relationship. Once again, to do so, would be setting the scene for future confrontations.

Find out all that you can about him/her but do so during the course of natural conversation, never in a forceful manner, let it all unfold in a *'matter of fact'* kind of way.

Ladies—please read the following with an open mind, and remember— *'equality' has absolutely nothing to do with it! Basic courtesy and manners certainly does!*

Your aim will be to ascertain whether or not he is respectful and considerate towards you and that he was taught these basic manners, hopefully by his parents, more specifically by his mother, who would have taught her son the right way in treating women or people in general, this in turn indicates to you that she is a caring person, which in itself is a good sign because you are going to need her at some point in your future life as the wife of her son. Yes, you will—trust me, I know what you are thinking, but there will come a time for whatever reason, that you will need her assistance, so better you start off on the right foot with her.

Is he domineering, or controlling? How would you feel about being dominated and controlled for the rest of your life? Can you live with someone like that? If you had to hesitate to think about this question simply shows a major lack of maturity, understanding, and responsibility towards your own welfare. Who in their right mind wants to be dominated and controlled all their lives? (There is a separate chapter on domineering and intimidating characters.)

To not place significant importance upon this major fault line and to fool yourself into believing that you don't mind…wait for it, because the day will come when you *'will'* mind!

If you have established that he is on the jealous or domineering side then let's move on to his late-night calls, this is the type of character who will call you very late at night, he may tell you that the reason for his call is because he is missing you, and sure, there may be a little truth in that, but it's his insecurity and jealousy, that is fuelling these late-night calls. He is checking up on you, to satisfy his curiosity as to your whereabouts. He wants to see if you are home alone, or out with someone else, even your girlfriends.

He will also seek to be reassured (hence the call to you) that you would not even think of going anywhere without him.

Does he like to play 'mind games'? Does he like to say one thing but then you discover that he means the exact opposite? Does he confuse you?

If the answers to these questions are "yes," then they come under the 'high maintenance' category and it is highly likely that you will experience problems further on into your relationship. If it's hard work now, it will never become any easier it will only become harder still. Do you need this unnecessary heartache in your life?

Life is going to be challenging even with someone you *are* compatible with, therefore what chance do you give your relationship succeeding when the negatives outweigh the positives.

Attempt to discover as much as you can about him, but it is not imperative that you find out everything about him on the first date. Each time you go out with this person, find out just that little bit more about him, and eventually you will be able to piece together his profile but take care in not appearing to be interrogating him.

Give yourself time to fully understand and really get to know this person but in order to do this, you will need to go out as many times as you deem necessary before you decide whether or not this person has the potential to be your partner. The importance of this cannot be underestimated.

Quite simply, he/she needs to measure up to your expectations and you have every right to seek out that which will further enhance your life and that of the man/woman you select.

Ladies—Research done, and you've found the one—and you think to yourself, "There is a just one or two things not quite right about him but overall he will do." What! He will do! Is this all that you are worth? You now resort to 'conforming' are you sure? Do you want to spend your life with someone on a 'he'll do' basis, really!

No way! You are worth much more than this because your life is far too important to be wasted on someone on a *"he will do"* basis. Are you willing to take a chance on betting that you can change him once you have him*? (We've already discussed the impossibility of this occurring)* or perhaps you will convince yourself that it is such a minor issue and not worth worrying about! Quite simply, if you *'think'* something about him needs changing, then you need to refresh your logic and take this as a warning sign—If his personality needs to be changed in order to suit you, then this personality is not the right one for you.

Once again, attempting to change someone to suit your requirements is wrong, it doesn't really work, don't pass it off as unimportant (*it is very important*), because one day that very characteristic that you thought was no big deal, will become that unbearable fault that you can't bear to live with anymore.

That being said, no one has the right to demand *'change'* from anyone else anyway. Men are the first to admit that no woman will change them, so what makes you think you'll succeed? Accept it, you cannot change a man, women have tried, and failed—move on! I tried to change a man once, but in a positive way, and discovered the hard way, that this was never going to happen.

I could not, and had no right, to even attempt to change someone into becoming the way I wanted him to be or in my case, think the way I wanted him to think. I did however have the right to seek out these qualities in the initial stages of our relationship, sadly though; I did not know what qualities to look for due to my lack of judgment and inexperience. We are the way we are! If someone does not suit your personality, simple solution, just look for someone who does.

There may be no guarantees in life, but at least you are giving yourself every opportunity of finding the perfect partner that will be right for you.

The point of all of this is, that while you will go out with several men during the course of your dating years, each one will have good and bad traits, do not overlook the bad or undesired traits, no matter how small or insignificant they maybe to you in the early days, it could be these very faults years down the track you could be arguing about, and this is exactly what you do not want to happen. Next on the hit list!

Ask yourself, *"Can I live with an obsessive man,"* who would be complaining about the state of your home every single day, even when there is nothing to complain about? Stubborn and set in his ways.

Do you love to cook? Do you enjoy sampling different things? Do you love to travel? Do you enjoy going out dancing? How many children do you want to have? Answer these questions honestly now and remain true to yourself.

How would you feel about never being able to cook and experiment different dishes together, because he/she won't be eating it?

Dancing! Yes dancing, if you like to dance, and you see that the man you are dating is not that way inclined, do you know what will happen? Imagine this, you have married, the honeymoon is over, and now you want to go out and show your man off. You want to begin living your life and enjoying it and you want to go out to a club. He may be obliging the first few times, but then one day he says, *"No, I don't like dancing, never have. I don't want to go, hate the party scene."* What will you do? I can tell you what I have seen. I have seen girls go out *without* their husbands—what kind of problems can you foresee happening here?

Ideally what should happen, if this is his only *'dislike',* he should rise above it and just do it, for the sake of his wife, even if it is just to keep her happy. *(I'm sure the time will come when it will be her turn to compromise.)*

That's the ideal scenario—but will he? Probably not, so once again we have one more issue that is going to be hoarded as resentment to be aired at an opportune time to make a point—*(during an argument) and* before you realise what is going on, you are smack in the middle of a massive argument. Oh, by the way, all of these situations are slow-release relationship killers.

Generally, when a person resists *'change',* they are also the ones who lack spontaneity, excitement and are pretty well set in their ways.

Could this be the beginning of your future complaints about him/her? *"He/she is boring, there is no spontaneity, and I do not feel wanted, or desired."*

Do you want a man/woman who has passion? Then go find someone who is passionate about life, food, animals, or travelling, just to name a few, find out what he/she loves about life itself. To be passionate about the good and wonderful things around us is to feel alive. To be passionate about life itself is to celebrate and appreciate it.

Perhaps opposites attract to a certain degree, but imagine a bubbly personality, one who loves to try different things and enjoys spontaneity in their lives, being with someone quite set in their ways, an unforgiving character that is argumentative within every aspect of life.

This kind of *'doom and gloom'* personality will absolutely drain the life out of said bubbly, fun loving person. You don't want to arrive at a point in your life where you begin to question, if this is all that life has in store for you.

Again, you may think that this is not important right now, but later on, it will be very important but too late. This can cause so much grief, to the point where resentment is assured.

Life is meant to be lived in the best way we can by making ourselves, our families and the people we associate with from day to day, happy. Smile and laugh more, love more, so that when problems do come along, you will be better adjusted to deal with them.

I can recall on many occasions while out having a coffee with friends (my partner (*who preferred to stay home and work...on Sunday!)* would ring me, and ask the precise time of my return. How am I to know when I am going to return? I guess when I finish my coffee and have run out of things to talk about. I mean, for heaven's sake, here I am out with friends, he chose not to come, he had no right to extend a time limit to my coffee outing. I am not a selfish or inconsiderate person but this was ridiculous.

On other occasions, I would say to him, "*Honey, let's go to the movies,"* and he would reply, *"No, we'll go next week."* Nothing would ever happen on the spur of the moment, it would always be some other night, some other time.

This is not about the movies; this is about spontaneity and the lack of it in his character, which in turn plunged my fun loving, spontaneous character into the pits of despair.

In the end I gave up my resistance, and in doing so, became more like him. To give up on spontaneity is to give up on loving life and enjoying life. It is this spontaneity and state of being happy with life, that also keeps us looking and feeling young.

I want to hang on to the qualities that make me feel alive, it's our attitude to life that will keep us young at heart this is the *'core'* and the core takes care of the exterior appearance, not plastic surgery or Botox but our attitude to life and how we live it with the people we love. Act old, and you may as well be old. We will all get there one day anyway, no need to hasten the process.

You both need to be flexible; both having the desire to explore and try different things. If he has no urge to do this in the beginning of your relationship or while you are dating, he certainly won't be spontaneous later on in life therefore no matter how nice he appears to be, it may be best to end the relationship and search for the right one. You may be happy with him now, but years on, it will wear you down, you simply cannot live with regrets and wishes of what could have been, and yet still fool yourself into believing you are living a happy life.

Your partner must be compatible with your character, the less negatives, the better, once again do not underestimate the power of that one tiny flaw, for that tiny crack could one day become the contributing factor causing an earthquake in your life. Make sure that you both complement each other's personalities.

"All men have affairs!" Steer clear away from any man who proclaims this, be it true or not.

He is revealing something to you that even he does not realise the significance of. He is a *'player'* and what he is actually telling you is that one day he too will have an affair. He has already programmed this event into his subconscious and it will happen…one day, with you as his victim. Stay away from him!

You deserve to have the love and respect of the man you chose without having such a grim prediction hanging over you like an invisible noose around your neck spending your life wondering about the waitress he's talking to or that woman at work he keeps talking about. Do you want to waste your life wondering when and where he will do this to you?

Furthermore, one has to wonder, what other weird ideas or beliefs he has concealed beneath that shallow exterior of his.

Like it or not, we must surely know that affairs are a part of life as well, but there is always a reason why this happens and most of the time, it is because something is not right at home irrespective of whose fault it is. *(As with anything of course, there is always the exception.)*

There can be no excuse for any man to say such a thing to a woman particularly one he is dating.

It simply shows that this guy is an idiot and also shows a lack of regard and respect, and you should not have to tolerate such an inconsiderate display of ignorant self-centred stupidity. Let him go!

Remember, this is the rest of your life that you are planning, the process and preparation of your wedding day ends on the last day of your honeymoon, and the marriage begins. As the reality of marriage and all that it entails sets in, you now need to get through it with your partner, both getting to the other end of it 20 or 30 40 years on, and still be able to say to each other, *"After all these years darling, I am still in love with you."*

How easy you make this, depends on you and what you are prepared to do for the man/woman you have just pledged your love to.

"Love is blind"—you have all heard of this saying, but do you know what it means? Well love really is blind because when in love we tend to turn a blind eye to the faults of the one we are in love no matter how big or small his/her faults may be. It is imperative that you pay attention instead of turning a blind eye, open your eyes and look at who is standing before you and ask yourself why you feel that you are not important enough to have someone who loves and respects you. Don't allow yourself to be fooled by anyone, if you do, you are simply confirming that they are smarter than yourself.

If you choose not listen to the alarms bells that are warning you of impending danger and you allow your heart to override your head, your common-sense capabilities will be rendered useless and you are now set on a collision course. It's all a matter of time!

Neither one of you should sell yourselves short, you should not have to *'settle'* or *'make do'* with just anyone. Make sure you find someone who possesses the qualities that you desire (*I'm repeating myself, but it's necessary.)*

Now here's the tricky part! You will, need to make your selection before you actually fall in love with this person. You can certainly like him/her, but don't wait to fall in love first, then realise their faults, but declare that it is too late because now you are in love with them. This is disaster in waiting and certainly is no way to start out your life.

If you find that you have to *'tolerate'* someone's characteristics, then that is a pretty good indicator that this relationship may not be ideal and life is far too short, to have to live it by tolerating anything or anyone, the right person will come along and when it does it will have been worth the wait.

I cannot stress enough that compatibility should be high on your agenda, the less negatives, the better and once again, do not underestimate the potential destructive power that one tiny flaw may harbour.

You must realise though, that you can do all that you can to get it right, right from the start, but still, it's no guarantee that all will be well because your relationship will be a work in progress and it will be up to the both of you. You will both have control over this, so make it work!

Everything you say and do for each other every day of your lives will either contribute positively or negatively to your life and this will determine the quality of your lives together, whether it will be a happy one, or a life scarred with tears.

There will never be just one thing that you need to do to guarantee a successful relationship, but everything you say and do, and how you resolve your problems and react to each other's actions that will determine the longevity of your marriage.

Certainly, this process will help you to zero in on a suitable partner, but it's what happens before, after and throughout your lives together, how well the two of you will treat each other and how well your communication skills develop (*by taking each other's feelings into consideration,*) that will determine whether the two of you will grow and change together as one and on the same path, or will you grow apart on different paths.

Preventing yourselves from making a mistake is far more desirable than trying to fix the mistake later. There is no joy in discovering that you married the wrong man or woman. Now is your chance to do everything you need to do, to create a wonderful and happy future for yourself and your partner for life!

"When a fellow tells a girl he will love her always, sometimes both of them are young enough to believe it."

Quote 225 pp. 65 Men, Women & Wedlock 1910 A & C Black Publishers.

5

Jealousy + Possessiveness = *Control Freak = Disaster!*

(In other words, not worth the trouble)

Many years after my divorce, I had met a man. He seemed nice enough on the surface, pleasant, friendly face but unbeknown to me, there was a very dark side to him, which was to unfold gradually.

He spoiled me, treated me to expensive dinners, flowers, long drives in his new car, he was an executive in a large company. I thought, *"Wow, how great is this, finally I meet someone who is treating me the way I want to be treated."* All I wanted to do was get to know him and for a while everything was just fine.

I did have other platonic male friends, people I used to work with whose company I enjoyed at social functions.

I remember one day, I decided to visit a friend who lived and worked about 15 kilometres from where I lived. While I was driving, my phone rang and to my surprise it was this particular man, calling me to check up to see exactly where I was and what I was doing. I think he must have guessed that I was going to see my friend so he very quickly ended the conversation and hightailed it straight to where he thought I would be.

While we were enjoying a coffee and a conversation, there was a loud banging on the door and when we opened the door, there standing before us and out of breath was one of the brothers of the man I was having a coffee with, clinging onto his torn clothes.

"What's going on?" we asked, shocked at his appearance.

"We caught a man snooping around the hotel so things got a little messy" he said while wiping the sweat from his bloodied forehead.

Turned out, the man they caught snooping around was the man I was speaking with on my phone an hour earlier. I quickly rushed outside to see what had happened, and there he was battered and bruised clutching his shattered glasses with a massive bruise on his face, demanding to know what I was doing there.

"Why are you following me, what do you want?" I asked, shocked at the sight before me.

"You just couldn't stay away from him, could you?" he screamed back, *"You bitch, you are just like all the other women,"* and he collapsed to the ground.

I knew instinctively, I absolutely had to stay calm and show no weakness or fear *(even though I was terrified)* I did not want him to sense any weakness on my part that he may interrupt as his power over me. I wanted him to realise that no matter what, I was in charge of my life, and where I go and what I do had absolutely nothing to do with him.

After this incident, alarms bells began to ring loud and clear; this was a huge, massive wakeup call and shortly after looked at ending all ties with this person.

One fine day, I requested a meeting and broke the news to him by telling him that I did not think it a good idea for us to see each other anymore.

At the time, I believed that he following me was bad enough I was very soon to realise that the worst was yet to come and could quite have been mistaken for a movie script with me as the victim.

This gentleman locked me inside his apartment, I being on one side of the room and closest to the phone, and he, on the other side of the room, closest to the door, which was now bolted. Every time I picked up the phone to call the police, he would unlock the door and say, *"Go ahead, call the cops, what are you going to bloody well tell them, look, the door is wide open."* As I proceeded to walk toward the open door, he would slam it shut and lock it again. He played this game over and over again, it seemed like forever but it must have been half an hour or so all the while attempting to stay as calm as I possibly could.

After a while, he began to break down and get emotional, and soon gave up and headed upstairs to his room weeping uncontrollably.

Not knowing what he was doing up there, I hesitated for a moment then very calmly slid half way up the steps, and called out to him, *"I'm going home now, I will call you tomorrow and we'll talk."*

Do you think for one minute that I wanted to talk to him again, absolutely not, I wanted to be light years away from him, but I knew the kind of person he was, and I did not wish to further antagonise him for fear of retribution as he was not a stable person and I was not going to take unnecessary chances with my well-being.

Every cell in my body was screaming out to me to proceed no further up the stairs, so I hastily turned back and headed down running out of the front door at which point he stepped out onto the balcony holding a gun to his head and proceeded to hysterically inform me, *"If you leave me, I will shoot myself."*

Oh, yes! This, is what was missing in my life, more drama, except this was the worst kind as now my life hung in the balance literally, I could be shot dead in an instant. I cannot begin to describe the fear that bolted through me I just stood there frozen in disbelief. Here I was, standing outside on the sidewalk, in a direct line of fire with a man holding a gun (*albeit aimed at himself),* but it would not require much for him to turn the gun onto me right there, in front of his home. *(I really believe that someone up above was looking out for me because whenever I was in this man's company, something would always tell me deep down inside to stay calm),* and at that moment, that same sensation was back again, assuring me that everything was going to be ok, as long as I stayed calm.

It seemed like an eternity, but somehow, I convinced him to put the gun down and assured him that we would talk again the next day.

Then as I was heading towards my car, he must have rushed down the stairs and out the back way to his car, for the next second, he was racing past in his car at very high speed, with the intention of slamming his car full throttle (*with him in it)* into a brick wall which lay a hundred metres away and directly ahead of him.

Was there no end to this nightmare? How could I have allowed this person into my life?

I stood there watching helplessly thinking *"Oh my god, is he really going to run straight into that brick wall,"* then all of a sudden, his car came to a screeching halt, only centimetres from crashing into the wall. Before he had a chance to come back, I quickly got into my car and was gone.

A few nights later after a night out with my girlfriend, I spotted him as I was pulling into my driveway. There he was wearing his *(wait for it)* bathrobe everyone! He was crouching behind a huge gum tree near my home, spying on me. Who in their right mind would do such a thing? I refused to succumb to his threats of self destruction deter me from what I had to do. I took heed of the warning signs and thank god I did, as I can't imagine what would have happened if I had caved in to his constant request to move in with me as this was his aim, I made it quite clear that this was never going to happen.

On another occasion, like a scene from a Mel Gibson movie, he was following me in his car, as I was franticly trying to lose him by weaving my way in and out the back streets of my neighbourhood, till one day, I became so tired of this I just stopped in the middle of the street, at which point he got out of his car, walked up to mine and put his fist right through my window.

He was an extremely lonely and insecure man, and to make matters worse, he was also insanely jealous. Remembering when I first met him, I was in the casino at the roulette table and he was opposite me when I noticed him observing me.

He made a point of walking around to where I was standing and offered me a drink, I foolishly accepted. The conversation cantered on me and how he thought I looked like a woman who was *'loved'*. When I asked him how he arrived at this conclusion, he looked at the jewellery I was wearing and said, *"There must be a very lucky man who loves you and is taking care of you."*

"I can assure you; you could not be further from the truth," I replied. In hindsight, I realise now that it was his way of finding out if I had a partner.

I look back at those days and I am still coming to grips at how close I came to being hurt or killed.

From that weak, naïve young girl, has since emerged a very, very strong woman, who can handle anything that life throws her way. I am no longer afraid of any circumstance and I know that I am just as important as the next person and possess more than enough confidence and I know that I do not have to settle for any situation that I am not happy with and I certainly have nothing to prove to anyone. I have become my own person at last. No one will ever control me again, just as I have absolutely no desire to control anyone. I thank God for helping me get through all the storms of life and finally emerge, still sane and a whole lot wiser.

"Ladies—can you understand now why it is important to beware of the man—who displays any form of jealousy? This is the type of man who feels the need to talk to you all the time, calls you and asks you where you are, wants to know who is calling you, when you answer your phone. He also wants to know whom you go out with, be it your girlfriends or your mother for that matter. He may say to you that the reason he wants to know where you are all the time is because he misses you so much and hates it when you are not around and he does not know where you are and you convince yourself that he must obviously loves you very much and this is why he wants to know where you are all the time." WRONG!

These are not the real reasons, for his incessant calls and can you hear those deafening alarm bells sounding here, Run! Run! Run!

Stay away from anyone who tries to control you in this way, no matter how cute he is, even though they may say that they do this because they love you and they want to make sure that no harm comes to you, chances are they are just lying to you and no one is that cute! It's just not worth it. Anyone who displays jealousy towards your friends and particularly your family is a sign of insecurity and this man has his own issues to deal with.

You may even fool yourself into believing that that you can handle this major fault, but imagine 10, 15, 20 years from now (*if you have lasted this long*), and he is now 10 times more jealous than before, and his jealousy now also includes violence and he wants to know your every move, from the minute you leave your home to go to work or shopping to the time you arrive home.

Will you be able to handle being shackled inside and outside your home, knowing even though you are out and about he will still be keeping tabs on you.

This type of character may also ask you to account for every dollar you have spent. Do you want to spend your life giving him an itemised account of all your living expenses?

This is his way of making sure that he has you under his control, as this is his ultimate goal—it's all about control. Don't attempt to take on more than you bargain for, if you do, be prepared for heartache later on. If you proceed to marry him, you are setting yourself up for a life of hell.

There is no '*happy ever after*' that will ever come out of anyone who sets about destroying your life through jealousy.

I speak from experience when I say that very same man (*man with gun*) I just described to you, would check my speedometer to see how far I had travelled around the city, and if he thought I clocked up too many kilometres, I would be interrogated.

Possessiveness and jealousy seem to go hand in hand. If he is possessive, he does not want to share you with anyone, at first it may be certain friends, then *ALL* friends and then he moves onto family members. If you marry him, this is what you would have to look forward to. Don't think for one minute you can change him because as we have already established, you cannot, you will not succeed! Any attempt to change him may trigger the beginning of a violent behaviour, it may well be at that point that he becomes abusive and no woman should tolerate this. No one deserves to be mentally or physically abused.

The same can be said for women as well.

Guys—women who try to control you through jealousy are very insecure women, who will make your life a misery as she eventually tries to isolate you from your friends and family and slowly take control of your life.

All you need to remember:

Jealousy + possessiveness = control freak = disaster!
Stay away from them!

6

Wedding Bells or Warning Bells!

"There is at least one good point about being married;
While you are, you can't be foolish again."

Quote: 8 pp. 16—Men, Women & Wedlock, 1910

You invest so much time and energy into planning your wedding day—caterers, flowers, limos, bridesmaids, groomsmen, wedding dress, hair, makeup, and video and let's not forget the honeymoon! Yet, when it comes to your actual life together, how much thought have you given it? Do you expect to sleepwalk through your marriage, to awaken only when a tsunami batters your life and then wonder how it happened and what went wrong?

Social psychologist, Dina McMillan says, *"When women become overly interested in the wedding day, they stop paying attention to the most important thing, their relationship. They are on a high,"* she says, *"Nobody ever thinks about, what's my marriage going to be like?"* she continues to say.

Angela Saurine, "Inside the World of Brides Who Can't Let Go"
4 April 2009, Dina McMillan. The Daily Telegraph

Knowing this, does it not make sense then, to plan your life and really understand what marriage means and how you are to treat each other, and what *'you'* need to do to achieve harmony within your home from the very first day.

You have certain expectations, and that's fine, but you cannot just sit back and expect that it will all happen in just the way you want it to unless you both make an effort, right from the start, to set the tone of your life together.

Purchasing a home or a car is no longer the biggest investment of your life. The amount of time, effort, consideration, and respect you bestow on each other that will determine the quality of your relationship should be the greatest investment of your life.

Tread very carefully when it comes to your future, and make sure you do everything you possibly can right from the beginning, to minimise wrong decisions and make sure that you have properly *'researched'* the person that you are considering investing your life and future in.

Who is he/she really? Get to know the real person, not just the *'presented'* person that stands before you, remembering all along that the one thing that can change a person is the passage of time. If you allow too much negativity to creep into your life, then he/she can change for the worse, but by treating each other with respect and by being focused on keeping each other happy you will be better prepared you to handle any problems that may arise. What happens to each of us every day of lives and how we handle it determines how happy and well-adjusted we become or how unhappy and miserable we become.

I have mentioned but I will say it again, this is the most important time of your life and your eyes must be wide open well before you develop feelings or form any attachment.

The reason for this is, you need to be able to walk away from this person if all is not right and you will not be able to do this if you are already *'in love'* with him/her. Don't be in a rush to fall in love just for the sake of falling in love, find the one who has all the desired attributes to become your future spouse and even then, proceed with caution till you are absolutely sure about them.

If you were going to invest a large amount of money in the share market, would you not research the company you were about to invest in? Of course you would, but only fools would rush in unprepared, not really knowing or understanding what it is they are investing in.

Equally, think very carefully about the decisions you make that will impact your life, because what you contribute towards your life now, should be the single most important investment for you, so where you decide to place it, and with whom, will either maximise or minimise your returns so to speak, invest in your life well and you will reap the rewards, on the other hand, invest poorly, be unprepared, and you could suffer lifelong ramifications.

Message to you: *"Don't be negligent with your life."*

Therefore use the *'dating'* period, to discover all you can about each other's backgrounds, and as mentioned earlier, get to know his friends and family as they will become an extension of *your* family one day. It will be to your advantage if you know what kind people they are and how you get on with them may determine how well you get on with each other during the course of your marriage. The manner in which you choose to treat yourself and the person you decide to spend your life with, should become your first priority.

Ladies—What's the point of spending all that time and energy—on the 'cosmetics' of your wedding day, yet devote little thought on the nitty gritty of what it actually means to get married. Are you really prepared? Do you have any idea what it's going to be like living with another person from this point forward? This is the person you will wake up next to for a long, long time (hopefully). Have you ensured that you are armed with all the necessary information that will be required to make your marriage work, to succeed? Have you laid out your plans with your partner for the future? Do you know where you're heading?

These questions need to have satisfactory answers and better to sort this out now, than later because unless you get it right from the beginning, the outcome of your marriage will be in doubt.

Consider each question and response in this book as a link, from this moment and all the different aspects of your life, the way you treat each other, the way you handle problems, how you argue constructively and not destructively, are all links that you will both need to strengthen, to ensure the continuation of your relationship.

All the people in our potential spouse's life, their family, friends and new friends to come can affect a marriage. Before you get married, take a careful look at your potential spouses relationships with these people.

Extracted from "The Divorce Lawyer's' Guide to Staying Married" Wendy Jaffe, Volte Press, 2006.

Three Important Rules to Remember When Selecting a Partner—

1. *Don't be rushed.*
2. *Be sure that your politics, religion, sexual interest and values are compatible.*

3. *Make sure that you are in romantic love, not sister/brother love. If you don't have romantic love in the beginning, you won't have it at the end.*

Extracted from "The Divorce Lawyer's Guide to Staying Married" Wendy Jaffe, Volte Press, 2006.

7

Bachelor Party, What's
He Really Celebrating?

Its origin!

The bachelor party originated back in ancient times in a place called Sparta, which is in the Peloponnesus, Greece.

It was a male ritual, where tradition had it, that Spartan soldiers toasted each other on the eve of a fellow soldier's wedding. It certainly has developed quite considerably from ancient times though.

Today, there are dedicated websites that leave no stone unturned when it comes to men planning their perfect bachelor party but even more disturbing, is the great lengths that men will go to, in order to trick their fiancée into allowing them to have their stag party.

Apparently, men or at least some men need to gain permission from their fiancée *(warden in training)* as to what he is and is not permitted to do during his night out with the boys, so they have developed a plan or strategy of all the right things to say, at least he will then have his *(as they see it)* one last night of freedom. It very much sounds like the *'warden'* is giving the future *'prisoner'* his one last night to do as he pleases *(even that come with restrictions)!* It should not be like this, anyway the wedding day has been set, and everything is ready for the big day. His male friends have organised a great *stag night* and all are excited about the coming events. Have you figured out just exactly what your man is really celebrating?

As far as he is concerned, it's all going to be in the name of good fun, he is on a high, and understandably so, he's getting married, lucky man! He has all his friends celebrating with him, but what's he celebrating? His *loss of freedom!*

As far as he and his friends are concerned, it's over, gone are the days where he can do whatever he wants to do, go wherever he wants to go and with whom.

It has not really sunk into his head yet, but his friends will, no doubt, remind him of this throughout the evening.

I remember years ago, as a young girl, I would see groups of young men, out celebrating with the groom-to-be and many times, they would be parading him through the streets on their night out from club to club, with a mock ball and chain around his neck.

Attending strip clubs was high on the agenda, and this usually involved some kind of contact with the stripper, either dancing around him or sitting on his lap, etc.

All of this was designed to tease and remind him that this was going to be his last night of such delights and he was shown one last time all the things that he would never have and '*never*' do, touch or see again. By now his friends are plying themselves and him with alcohol, encouraging him to do outlandish things, while making sure that he continually be reminded, that his days of freedom will soon be a dusty memory.

How do you feel knowing that your fiancée' is out there celebrating his most precious possession
FREEDOM!

Do you know what he is *not* celebrating? He is not celebrating the fact that he is marrying you! Once again, how does this make you feel?

Why is this entire ritual based on loss of freedom? Could it really be true that he will never, ever go inside of a strip club again (so what if he did, why does it matter?) will he never ever be able to go out and have a night with his friends ever again? Is the 'buck's night', really a, 'finality of life as he knows it', night?

This is not about strippers and clubs; the real reason lies much, much deeper. Men in general believe and women expect that once they are married, they automatically lose their freedom and will be doomed to a lifetime of having to ask for permission for most of anything they will want to do. Is this really true?

Ladies—Your call! What do you think? Are these the thoughts you wish for your, soon to be husband to enter marital life with?

You may say, "Oh but it's all in fun," perhaps it is, for now—however, if you, as his wife, sometime into the future start laying down the law as to what he can, and cannot do (and most women do go down that path) you are simply reaffirming the very clear message his friends were giving him on his stag night—Loss of freedom!

Don't make an issue about his freedom or what he can and cannot do because first of all, you are not his mother, you are his soon to be wife and secondly, you are setting the scene for much trouble in the future by dissolving the romance that just so happens to be the glue that is supposed to keep you two together in the first place. Why on earth would you want to sabotage your future?

No one wants to believe that marriage equates to loss of freedom, would you want your freedom taken away from you? Would you want your husband demanding that you cannot do this, or you can't go there?

Everyone harbours some kind of reservation when they are about to commit to another human being that said don't add weight to those fears by materialising them with unreasonable demands on your new spouse. No good will ever come of it, he will never say, *"Oh Thank you darling for turning me into your prisoner, I am so happy."* Be assured that you would be doing yourself and him a massive injustice.

The solution! Don't attempt to take his freedom way from him. More to the point, his freedom is not yours to take anyway, as your freedom is not his to take away either. Show me where it is written that woman reserves the right to take a man's freedom away once she has married him. No one has the right to take any man's or woman's freedom, married or not!

Greg Norman, one of the world's greatest golfers was quoted as saying after his divorce, *"It's an amazing thing when a burden is taken off your back; a certain amount of freedom is given back to you."*

60 Minutes, February 2009.

"Wow! His wife should never have taken his freedom away from him in the first place! Are you preparing yourself to be that *'burden'* on your man's back?"

There is nothing wrong with a bachelor party, just so long as it's not the celebration of the groom's last night of freedom rather the celebration of the next stage of life with the love of his life.

Your man can have his buck's night, but you must reassure him that his freedom is his god-given right, and that the trust you have for him is the reason you are marrying him in the first place, and it is this trust that will ensure in time, he will make any adjustments necessary to accommodate his spouse while still maintaining his own friendships. Assure him, that his friends are still his friends and you have no intention of choosing whom he can and cannot keep as his friends after you marry.

Remember—Don't badger him—"You can't do this anymore, you can't go there anymore, you're married now" or "I'm your wife and you should want to spend all your time with me."

This may work for a while (with resentment) but you would have sown the seeds for this resentment and when the novelty of being married wears off (at this rate the novelty would probably wear off a lot sooner) he will retaliate, and you can lay out the welcome mat for the "other woman."

Would you accept these restrictions, if your husband set them upon you? I doubt it, so why would you want to do this to him?

Freedom is a *'right'* and not something you can give or take.

Restricting someone from doing what they want to do (*within reason of course),* probably means that it maybe *you,* who has a problem. Perhaps you feel insecure, maybe you do not trust any man, and maybe you think that if you allow him to do what he wants to do, that you could lose him. Maybe you become slightly paranoid, whenever he is not around you, maybe! Maybe! Maybe! It's not looking very good, is it? If anything of what I have just mentioned is even remotely true, why did you marry him?

Your marriage is supposed to be based on love and trust is it not? Did he not choose *'you'* above all others, why does this not mean anything to you?

Why would you want to start out your new life together by instilling the fear of the rules that he must abide by? There are enough rules and regulations as it is, don't turn your home into a prison or somewhere he dreads to be.

Your man should feel *free* to want to be with you, and the priest does after all say, I now pronounce you husband and wife—he does not say, "*I now pronounce you, prisoner and warden."* If he did, no one would get married!

His freedom and his identity are his to keep, as are yours of course. His freedom is not yours to either take away, nor is it your prerogative to *'allow'* him to keep that which is his and it is also your right as well.

Don't become a nightmare to live with, no need for unnecessary complications, make him love being around you, by being easy to live with.

It should go without saying, that he can see his friends when he wants to, and you should trust him enough to understand and give him the opportunity to work it out for himself and he will work it out when he realises what a wonderful and thoughtful woman he has by his side, by allowing him to prioritise placing you at the top of his list but let *him* come to that conclusion. It is certainly not going to happen with you ramming your demands down his throat.

If he wants *to* spend the day playing golf, he should be able to; He should be free to do the *'men'* things with his friends if that is what he wants to do. Remember, would you want to be stopped from seeing your girlfriends?

Guys—Needless to say that your woman has the same rights as you—

Do not for one minute think that you're god's gift to her. Treat her abusively, or restrict her freedom, and your life won't be worth living. Treat her with consideration, love, patience, and understanding, be there for her and show her that you both choose wisely in selecting each other. Prove to her that you will never let her down.

Ladies—You need to be all of the above for your man as well.

You are together, but you are individual human beings and you should both be able to have full lives, together and apart. You are not his warden and he is not your prisoner and your home is not the prison! (No wonder guys are afraid of commitment I would be too, wouldn't you!) Do not turn your marriage into a prison sentence for him. He needs the freedom, to continue to be the man you fell in love with and married, and if he truly loves you, then he will reward you with his loyalty and undying love.

I have mentioned earlier that no one can change a man, actually I lie; you can but in no way that will benefit you.

The passage of time can change him as it can change you as well. Change for the better is fine, what if you both change for the worse! If you take away all that he loves and not allow him to bring some of his world into yours, and your marriage, then he will change—he could become moody, resentful, argumentative, defensive, and it is this, that will scar the personality of the man you married.

If you were asked to describe your man the day before you married him, what would you say? *"I absolutely love and adore him, he is gorgeous, he is kind, and fun loving, sexy, thoughtful, and he loves me so much."* Would you have married him if your description of him was, "Well, he is a son of a bitch, he is disgusting, he is mean, selfish, he is moody, argumentative and he only cares about himself…" would you have married him? Of course not!

Don't make him become like that by your treatment of him and your unreasonable demands.

Knowing all this, why would you want to erase the wonderful characteristics of your man, this is why you married or are marrying him—now add to the equation, *you*, taking away his freedom and this is what you will be saying about him years down the track, *"He is distant, he hardly ever smiles, he never compliments me, we don't seem to go anywhere together, he never buys me flowers,"* he never says, *"I love you, we never go dancing like we used to, we hardly ever have sex, I don't feel sexy, I am bored with my life and I can see that he is as well, and worse still, we sleep in separate beds."*

Trying to convince him to visit a therapist is futile, if the love is gone, it's gone, if you could miraculously turn back the clock, would you do things differently so that you never reach this moment? Here then is your chance right now!

You do not want to be saying to yourself, *"I can't go on like this anymore, there must be more to life than this."* Whose fault do you think it would be?

The blame does not lie solely with you, but if you have over the years slowly stripped him of his freedom, whereby he has to ask you if he can do anything and everything, then you, have become his *'mother'*, and he your *'son'*, and like sons who are constantly told no continuously, get resentful and do the exact opposite.

You are his wife, not his keeper, you are not in charge of him, and he is a man, who needs to act like a man not like a child. Would you have married him if he were a weakling, a puppet, *'a yes dear' or a 'no dear'*, kind of man? I am willing to bet that the answer to that is *"No,"* this being the case, don't change him into an unhappy or bitter man, you would not be marrying him if he were like this to start with, would you?

When he comes home in the evening, don't immediately pounce on him with your problems, give him a breather, he probably had a very hard day at work, and coming home for him should be like entering a sanctuary. Make it pleasant for him, so that he looks forward to coming home to you. Don't place forced boundaries on each other. You will both know instinctively what your boundaries should be; you will accept them more freely as you each set your own. Each of you must love unconditionally as there can be no substitute for freedom.

For centuries now, the desire and need for this one basic human right has been the reason why wars have been fought and lives have been lost—all in the name of freedom! Freedom is a basic human right and it is instinctively within all of us.

We need air to survive
And our freedom—to live!

8

Marriage = Mt. Everest! You Need to Acclimatise to Both!

Have you any idea how much work and planning are involved in preparation to climbing the highest mountain in the world—Mt. Everest?

It is essential to be fit in mind and body, but you also need to have practiced climbing smaller mountains, you need to be prepared with all the equipment that you will require along your journey, you need to trust the people you will be climbing with, because it may get to a life or death situation where their assistance will save your life, you need to be able to get along and share the same determination and passion of attaining the goal you have all set out to achieve, to get to the summit!

Above all, you need to have the utmost respect for the mountain itself, if you don't you may not make it to the top or die while descending.

Once the necessities of this climb are all intact and you now find yourself at base camp, the climb will commence and as you commence and begin to reach higher ground, you will need to stop and acclimatise to that particular altitude, then you proceed to the next camp, higher altitude again, you will have to stop and acclimatise yet again as you continue to forge ahead to the summit.

The sole purpose of this acclimatising is to not die, while in the process of achieving your goal that being, reaching this summit.

Marriage is exactly the same thing, except in this case the journey you have both undertaken will teach you how to acclimatise to each other's personalities *'the good and the not so good',* in order to reach the next level of your lives together.

Your priority should be in learning to trust each other while respecting your marriage; you do not need to conquer it immediately as it will be a work in progress.

You must be prepared mentally for what you are about to enter into which is why experience in life will be handy, therefore consider this as your training for the climb of your life.

You will know what it is that you admire in the other person by first understanding exactly what you are getting yourself into and what it means.

Trust is imperative as it will be each other you turn to for assistance when you need it. The person you are about to share your life will be there for you as problems emerge in your relationship, you should rely on each other to work together as a team while acclimatising to the different altitudes your marriage will take you through and by communicating with each other every step of the way, this will enable you both to be better adjusted to handle the *'lows'* that are inevitable in life.

The sole purpose of this is to reach the summit of your marriage, which is equivalent to being together 40 or 50 years on, but even more importantly to still be in love with the person you married, now that's a summit worth conquering, don't you think?

The single most important point to remember is you both need to respect the institution you have entered *(assuming you married the right person that is)* because if you fail to do this, you will not survive the long climb to the summit.

Remember, have an understanding of where you want to be within your marriage *'before'* you get married, and make a point of setting time aside to discuss your life together, before you announce your intention to the world.

If something does not feel right, discuss it, and reach a mutually accepted resolution. Make sure that you are both travelling on the same path and that you both know what to expect from each other, and both know exactly where you stand now, and to where you are heading in the future.

When you both fully understand the concept of marriage and what it really entails, then, and only then, should you consider marriage because if this marriage is to survive, you need to build a strong foundation, right in the early stages of your relationship for this is the foundation that your future will rest upon and flourish, how strong you make it, depends on you and what you are prepared to sacrifice for your man/woman; *compromise, and respect and consideration*, just to name a few.

Would a builder build a home on weak foundations? Of course not, just as you would never attempt to build your life on weak foundations either. In both scenarios the only result would be *collapse.*

71

These qualities are worth fine tuning because they will serve to benefit both of you, so get used to it, there is simply no room for egos, stubbornness or temper tantrums, they are all negative forces that will simply prove disastrous to both of you.

The more you fortify your marriage with these essential elements, the more it will be able to withstand any change in the future *weather forecast of your life.* You can easily navigate through a little choppy water in a small vessel but you will need a very strong boat to survive a storm.

If the bond between the two of you is water tight, nothing will sink it, if your relationship is weak, at first sign of a leak (*if not repaired*) expect at some point, that it will sink.

No one can actually put their finger on the exact moment that a couple decide it's over. It's like a plane crash, it's never just one mistake that brings a plane down, it is a series of mistakes, so too it's a combination of a lot of bad decisions that lead to unhappy moments that destabilises a marriage as it begins to disintegrate.

You *can* have a happy relationship, you just need to put in the effort and work at it to set about in motion the actions that will take you down the long, loving path of your life together.

By learning to put your partner's well-being before your own, you strengthen your marriage and ensure the happy continuation of your relationship.

Example 1—Dominic and Cheryl—True Story!

Dominic *(not real name)* and I had been friends for some time when one day he asked to see me because he was distraught. We arranged to meet one day, and before too long, the misery and distress he was experiencing was too much for him to bear, so I asked him what was going on in his life.

Very quickly his story began to unfold and I was beginning to understand why he was feeing the way he did. He told me how he had been seeing a young woman, *Cheryl (not real name)* for a few years, now she would have her bad days (*which lasted weeks*), then have one or two good days (*which lasted a few hours*). He could never really rely on her, she was hardly ever available to partake in the normal activities that couples do, like dinner or movies with friends.

He would have to wait till the last minute to see if she *felt* like appearing then, low and behold, on one of her *'good days'*, he asked her to marry him, to which she replied yes. However, the engagement had to be kept a secret by her own request and still she would rarely see him, then one day my friend discovered that she was about to get married…to someone else! All this, while wearing his engagement ring.

He was absolutely devastated, and could not understand why she would do this. The how and the why, is irrelevant, what was shocking was the fact that he accepted her behaviour without question, even though he had all the warning signs, he failed to see them, and for two years he was walking blind, totally oblivious to her true motives.

Could he not see that when one has to keep one's own engagement secret that it's just not normal there is something very, very wrong?

Could he not recognise that she had her own agenda and that when someone is hiding something as significant as an engagement secret it's obvious there must be something quite sinister lurking in the shadows.

Love truly is blind. It blinds us to major faults that the one we *think* we love may have. Our common-sense faculties fly out the window, when love enters through the door.

Dominic was truly blinded by this love he felt for her, even though it was not reciprocated, he was prepared to make do and in doing so had just wasted two years of his life on someone who was not worthy of his affection.

Don't ignore the warning signs. If something does not seem right, it's probably not! Don't expect that the problem will just disappear you must absolutely find out what the problem is and resolve! Resolve! Resolve!

Had he taken the time to look just a little deeper into why she was so *unavailable* all the time, he would have discovered the truth about her and saved himself the trouble of proposing to her, thus saving a whole lot of heartache for himself.

Example—2 Jennifer and Thomas—True Story!

Jennifer (*not real name)* had been seeing a young man by the name of Thomas *(not real name)* and had fallen head over heels in love with him. He, on the other hand was always quite distant with her, but she placed little importance on this and just ignored his behaviour. They too, would have some good days, followed by some bad, but she always made excuses for his lack of interest, because she did not want to believe anything else other than they were in love and all was well.

As the wedding began to edge closer and closer, word started to filter back to her that he had been seen socialising with another woman on more than one occasion, and word also had it, that his reputation as a womaniser was growing but still she would not take heed, refused to listen to anyone as her heart was ruling her head.

Finally, the day arrived and they were married—one week into their marriage, he cold-heartedly announced to her that he did not love her he was in love with someone else and that he was leaving her… One week after the wedding! She was absolutely devastated.

She had her chance, she was warned, but she chose to ignore the obvious; because she did not want to lose what she had, and what was that exactly?

She just wanted someone to marry, someone she believed she loved. Perhaps she was in love with *love* itself! She played Russian roulette with her future and lost.

Before you embark upon the journey this book will take both of you through, you will need to throw out any pre-conceived ideas you may have regarding relationships. Clear your mind, and set your inner self-free by being open to other avenues that may just possibly help you, in establishing a long, contented, loving relationship with the man/woman you've chosen to marry.

Look upon this as a '*reawakening of life*' experience, so that when you reach the end of this journey, you will be able to tell yourself, *"I met my man/woman half way in all things I cared for him/her the best way I knew by sacrificing just a little (acclimatised) and we both made it to the twilight years of our life together," (you've reached the summit)*

Remember to take your roles seriously and to not put too much emphasis on, "*it's your turn*" or "*it's not my turn too, 'cause I work late just like you do,*" etc. Work as one, resolve as a team!

Real love means, to love unconditionally, you obviously must be compatible, and of course, sacrifice, respect and compromise, go hand in hand, as these are the ingredients that are required within a marriage and while you're at it, fine tune your skills on forgiving as well, you will probably need it someday.

As I mentioned earlier, there is no room for stubbornness or egos in any relationship, let alone within a marriage.

Having a modern approach to towards your relationship is fine, but not at the expense of your marriage breaking down. Reinstate just a little of the definition that has been bled out of the roles of husbands and wives. Give yourself every opportunity to make your marriage a success, let him be a man by being *'the'* man and what about you? Why you are the lady of the house of course!

Don't try to be both; it will never work and the proof is in the number of unhappy marriages that end in divorce.

You should be able to talk to your partner about anything you want, need, or wish to do without turning it into a major drama. Besides, common sense should prevail at all times, the good of your home and family should also be at the fore of anything you want to do.

If what you want is going to put your family in financial strife, then I strongly suggest you listen to the other party and seek professional help if you cannot reach a compromise, but then again, this is the key word, compromise, find a way to achieve your desire without breaking the bank and plunging your family into financial turmoil.

Can you see and understand that the key to a happy life is not in the planning of the perfect wedding day with all the trimmings—they key to a happy life together begins the very instant you met, and the second you walk down the aisle or the microsecond you come back from the honeymoon.

What happens when you both return? How you will treat each other in the beginning and how you go about your lives together every single day as reality sets in, will play an important part towards how the rest of your lives together can be. It will be up to the two of you to make your marriage work by becoming more loving, patient, understanding and considerate towards each other all the time, every day. No one is saying you will never argue, of course you will, but it's how you argue and how you resolve issues that will play an integral part in the longevity of your relationship.

The wedding day and the honeymoon may be over, but capture just one snap shot of the many that were or will be taken on that day and carry it around in your heart for the rest of your life to serve as a reminder as to the reason why you both chose each other over everyone else.

Every time you have a tiff, look into your heart and re-acquaint yourself with that picture of the two of you and remember the love you felt that day for him/her and by doing so you will hopefully never allow an argument to escalate to a point when resolution becomes unattainable.

This is your time, this is your life, you have this chance to get it right, therefore if you really feel that you have found the love of your life then do all that you can for each other, remember, no need to trivialise about unimportant matters, because as sure as the day is long, you will have enough to worry about during the course of your everyday lives. Reserve your energy, and apply it to something worthwhile—your marriage!

Ladies!

'Art is a hard mistress, and there is no art quite so hard as that of being a wife'.

Don'ts for Wives
Blanche Ebbutt A & C Black Ltd 1913

Guys

"Don't forget to be your wife's best friend as well as her husband. True friendship in marriage does away with all sort of trouble."

Don'ts for Husbands Pg. 24. Blanche Ebbutt A & C Black Ltd 1913

9

Don't Tell Him You Love Him
Tell Him You Adore Him!

Times have certainly changed from when women stayed at home with the kids and husbands worked to provide for their families.

Today, these men are still providing for their home, some look after the children and the women have just as much input financially as well, and it certainly is an effective way of living comfortably and affording a home particularly while there are no children as it offers a couple the opportunity to do all the things they want to do together and be in a better position to save as much money as possible before children enter the picture.

While this is a good thing, let's not allow the concept of equality rule our lives to the point where it begins to destroy it.

If you really want to keep your man happy, ask him in what way he would like to contribute physically towards the running of the home. If you are really smart, you will keep him out of the kitchen *(unless he absolutely loves cooking)*, and make that your domain. He may suggest to you that he will take care of the outside of the home and that's a good thing, isn't it?

Some men have absolutely no desire whatsoever to neither delve in the kitchen, nor do they want to be washing dishes or doing the laundry or any of the things that primarily was a woman's chore and honestly, how much of a chore is it these days? It all goes in the dishwasher, or the washing machine, right?

Like it or not ladies, make it your responsibility and as for the men, well they do other things around the home. Cooking and cleaning or doing the laundry should be a no-no for your man *(unless of course you are sick, and not because it happens to be his turn to do it.)*

Example 3—Julia and Jack—True Story!

Julia (*not real name*) lives in another state, but she shared with me a very sad but true story of a family friend who is related to her husband and after listening to it just left me reeling with disbelief.

She began by describing what this very unfortunate man (*Jack*), is expected to do each and every day. He is a professional man *(doctor)* who has been with his partner since their teenage years. *(Now, this is the perfect example of being together since teen years where the woman is of a stronger personality than the man and she, begins to mould him the way she wants.)*

Eventually, in their late teens-early twenties, they marry and have been together ever since, but this man has absolutely no say about anything, he gets up in the morning and before he goes to work, prepares the kids for school, their breakfast, their lunches while all the time, his wife is still in bed.

Her belief was that she should not have to do anything inside the home, outside the home including holding down a job, so she spends her days lounging around the house or out shopping for her own self. This woman also proceeds to wait for her man to come home so that he can, *'wait for it'*…wash the kids, tend to the household chores and cook the evening meal! She does absolutely nothing for her husband, except issue orders as to what, when and how she wants things done.

This poor man receives no respect or regard, no consideration for his position and all from a wife who sits around the house all day feeling quite precious! This man has no freedom as he is not permitted by his wife to enjoy himself if they are out with friends; he must ask her permission to drink a glass of wine, this man is not even allowed to laugh unless she approves. Can you believe this? Don't get me wrong, if one is fortunate enough to be living within a wealthy environment and the wife does not need to work or she chooses not to work, that's fine, there's nothing wrong with that.

What is troubling is that this woman does not work, but also refuses to take part in any household contribution. She does absolutely nothing. Surely you can all see how wrong this is (at the very least, hire a maid), it isn't as though they can't afford it.

She has so much control over him, it really is a sad story, but one day, this man will surely wake up and when he does, he will realise what he's been reduced to, which is a housemaid and when this happens, I would not want to be in his wife's shoes. This kind of treatment is not that of love, but control that in itself is a form of abuse.

Do you think that this man actually feels like a man, I would imagine that his state of being would have to be the equivalent of the *battered wife syndrome?*

I realise that there are some guys, who like to be *'stay at home dads'*, but this is not quite the same thing as the example above. If your man is a stay at home dad, that's ok, but if it is not and he begins to resent you forcing him to do all the chores in the kitchen, ask yourself seriously if this is going to be worth all the trouble that is surely coming your way.

There comes a time in every man's life when the need to reassess his life becomes overpowering. This usually happens when the children have grown up and left home and how well you have treated him and each other will become a crucial factor in his determination of just where your lives will be heading. If you have been forcing him throughout your lives to do things against his will, and he obliged just to keep you happy all the while resenting you then you had better hope he has forgotten about it or forgiven you.

It's at times like this (*heaven forbid*) he feels that he has missed out and looks to *'the other woman'* who may treat him the way he has always longed to be treated by you, in which case I'm not too sure of your chances of ongoing joy.

Thought for you—don't turn him into a puppet, to be there simply for your use.

He will more than likely turn this into a weapon one day to be used against you.

It does take two to run the household, there are some chores that he will have to do, and then again, there will be other chores that you will have to do.

With this in mind why don't you do the things that a wife is supposed to do (*unless you are ill*) and let him do the tasks that men do, and focus on keeping home life simple.

Forcing or badgering him to do something that goes against what he wants, is asking for trouble. If you do, you will end up arguing and the culmination of all these arguments won't be delivering a positive outcome for your marriage in the future.

Ladies—don't we always say how good we are at multi-tasking—so multi-task—there is no reason to tell your husband that it is his turn to do the laundry, while you sit there and watch television. I am all for equality, but only when appropriate and always with respect.

If you begin your evening with an argument, you can forget about the rest of the night!

Make it your responsibility to prepare the evening meal where possible. This is where the nurturing comes into play. I know you would like to be pampered, but you do it for him first, don't worry, your turn will come too!

Think about it, you come home, he knows you have been working all day as has he, but you come home, you tell him to do whatever he likes to do to unwind and relax, while you prepare the meal that you will soon enjoy with the man you love.

To the newly wed couples—It's what you do right now. How you conduct yourselves at the beginning of your relationship and how well you maintain continuity of your treatment toward each other, that will determine how the rest of your life with your chosen one will turn out. You won't know whether or not you have a successful marriage, as it's a continual progression, till you reach the other end and you both have a long, long road ahead of you, so why not make it a happy and loving road.

It's the little things that you do for each other along the path of your life that will matter in the end, after all that is what love is—all the little things you do for him/her that will make the difference in the end.

Do not set yourself up for trouble and heartache. He/she will love you even more for pampering them and they will reaffirm their appreciation of you. If they don't, you need to find out why and quickly!

Don't underestimate the power of the words, "I love you" in fact, I'll say it again, tell him you adore him verbally, and then show him as well. Why not have a John, Peter or a Paul night, set the scene, with soft lighting and softer music, run a bath for your partner, and kneel down by his side, try scrubbing his back, give him a facial, go ahead and fall into the tub with him and have some fun! Give him a relaxing massage, you won't be sorry you did.

Guys—Now it's your turn to do the same for your woman. Treat her to her own special night and pamper her in every way you can. When you are both doing this for each other, you are creating a 'mood' within your relationship, and this mood will continue to set like concrete where there will be no room for arguments or bickering to enter your lives.

I guess what I'm saying is if you fill your lives with romantic love and intimacy, you leave very little room for negativity to manifest itself. By the way, these *'nights'* to be set aside should be spontaneous, do not make the mistake of designating certain nights that you will do this, if you do, then you are turning this pleasurable experience into yet another 'routine' and that's the last thing you want to do. Make her feel like she is the only woman in the world for you.

If there's truth is, *'one reaps what one sows'*—sow some love and spontaneity and then sit back and reap the rewards.

These are the things you should do, to show your partner how much you love and value then, because once the children come, you may not be able to do this as often, so cement the foundation that your love is based on now.

Marriage is a work in progress while you learn how to share your love and your whole being with the one you love.

I have said this in previous chapters—it teaches you to put someone else's needs ahead of your own and by putting someone else's needs ahead of your own, you grow in ways you can never imagine and more to the point, you grow together, let me repeat this, *"you grow together,"* as you grow together, you are constantly adjusting yourselves in every way to fit in with each other. Have you any idea how seriously important this is? If you grow apart, you end up growing indifferent towards each other, ending up in different directions which makes staying together impossible.

While marriage can be the most wonderful experience in life, it can also be the worst time of your life.

If the person you married is not compatible with you, your marriage will not be heading in the right direction. You both absolutely have to not just love each other you need to *'adore'* each other and try very hard to never take each other for granted and foolishly believe that they will always be there no matter what, because if you continue to hurt each other the pain will become irreversible, they won't be there for long.

Life can change dramatically when the children arrive and you will spend the best years of your life raising them, then one day they're gone and it will be just the two of you again. What then? What will you have left if you have both spent the formative years of your relationship *(which are the most important)* tormenting each other.

It will be the communication you have maintained throughout your life, and those early foundations that you have set in place, that will now get you through the rest of your life and this part of your life could be the most exciting if you have taken care of each other along the way but it can also be the worst time of your life, if you have not had a happy life together. If anything bad is going to happen to your marriage, now is the time it's going to happen.

It's all well and good to read books that depict case studies and quote statistics; however this is you we are taking about. Sometimes, the things that appear the hardest can be the easiest things to take care of, by being honest, respectful, loving, caring nurturing etc… Be the woman you presented him with when you first met and allow him to be the man you fell in love with and married.

What's the point of mistreating or ignoring your partner all year and then telling them Happy Mother's or Father's or Valentine's Day. Those days should be the culmination of how you have treated each other all year not just on that one day. Don't wait for Valentine's Day to tell your partner *"I love you,"* tell them, *"I adore you baby"* today, right now, put this book down and if you are both homes, go and tell your partner you love them and throw in a kiss for good measure.

When you say this, you need to feel the love and when you do, the rest is automatic. It is not something that you can manufacture or pretend to feel, either you do or you don't, and if you do, it won't be difficult.

Your love for each other and your future should be the most important thing in the world, don't tear it down with unnecessary squabbles.

Guys!

Don't think that it is no longer necessary to 'show' your love for your wife, as she "ought" to know it by this time. A woman likes to be kissed and caressed and to receive little lover-like attentions from her husband even when she is a grandmother.
'Don'ts for Husbands' Blanche Ebbutt A & C Black Ltd 1913

Ladies!

Don't quarrel with your husband. Remember it takes two to make a quarrel; don't you be one of them. Lovers' quarrel may be all very well, but matrimonial doses are apt to leave a bitter flavour behind. The quarrels of spouses are not always the renewal of love.

'Don'ts for Wives' 1913 Pg. 12 Blanche Ebbutt A & C Black Ltd.

10

What's Love Got To Do With It?
Absolutely Everything!

There are many different variations or categories of love and in order to gain a clearer understanding of which category your relationship fits in; it is imperative that you be able to distinguish between them. Whether your relationship is a happy one or an unhappy one, it will assist in shedding some light on why your relationship is the way it is (*be it happy or unhappy)* and how it got to that point and what it is that keeps it there in that mode.

For instance, if you are sharing a happy marriage, ask yourselves what it is that you are both doing right, that keeps the two of you happy. Ask yourselves what else can you each do for the other that will take you to a higher level of love and happiness.

If on the other hand you are not happy, then you need to take some time to really look at your life, your partner and only by being honest with yourself, ask the necessary question of *WHY?* What is it that you are doing that is causing so much stress, pain, indifference, because if the cause of your problems is inside the home, then you have the power to fix it, as long as both parties are willing but you must be brutally honest with each other.

If you want to repair your relationship but are not quite sure where to begin, seek the professional assistance you both require and trust each other to believe that you will get through this and transport your marriage to a much happier place as long as the damage is not too deep.

If the damage occurred over a long period of time, chances for repair are reduced because there is too much to forgive, too many things that need to be forgotten and somewhere in between, you both need to fall in love with each other all over again. It will be difficult, but not impossible so long as you are both willing to do whatever it takes to make your relationship work and as long as you both care about each other and there is still a flicker of flame left in your hearts, you can reignite your love once more.

Is it any wonder then, when asking someone on their thoughts on true love, that the immediate response is—*"No such thing as real love,"* or *"Yeah, it's there for a short time and then you get married and the love's gone, it never lasts. I've been with my partner for years and I'm not excited anymore, I'm just comfortable (or maybe not) bored or indifferent"* whichever the case may be, or *"Don't believe what they say, fact is the passion never lasts, and that's the way it is. Marriage kills the romance?"*

No, marriage does not kill romance it's the people involved and their attitude towards marriage and how they've treated each other that kills the romance. Don't accept this as the 'norm' nor is it the natural course of a marriage. It is whatever course you put it on. Do all that you can to ensure that this does not happen to you by feeding your marriage all the right elements necessary for survival.

OK let's look at this from another angle, the outcome of 'love' (in most cases, not always) is marriage but then the outcome becomes the catalyst in destroying the love, the same love that brought two people together. If you do not want your marriage to destroy the romance in your life, then do not allow it to.

How do you do this? By the loving and considerate way in which you treat each other, that's how!

At the risk of sounding like a broken record, I shall repeat myself yet again, treat the person you are with respectfully, for if they deserve your love, then they also deserve to have your respect, care, and consideration.

I have spoken to so many people about this, and the second I say that romance does not have to vanish after marriage they look at me as if I have descended from another planet. To this I say, *"Well, if romance lives on within marriage on this other planet, then I think I like it better there."*

Seriously though, the answers to why they do not believe in love, would lie somewhere within the torn and tattered pages of their everyday mundane boring lives, which leads to an equally boring, non-passionate interaction with their partner taking in all the big issues, the small issues, absolutely everything that occurs to them during the course of their day *(which in turn will affect their night)!*

Certain changes, some subtle some not so subtle, would have taken place over the years.

Consequently, changing some of the components that determined the quality of their love, be it positive or negative, hence taking them out of one kind of love, and placing their relationship onto a different path which may or may not be, where they wanted to be. It is at this point we can uncover the reasons why love, passion and communication are no longer part of everyday vocabulary, for somewhere between picking the kids up from school, doing the washing and ironing cleaning drudgery, boredom and monotony sets in. This is the silent killer of romance.

I understand there is nothing exciting about the normal every day routine but try to retain the right attitude so as not to become complacent by not caring about yourself or your relationship with your spouse, your job your life, because once complacency gets a foot hold, within your life it will be the beginning of a downward spiral for your marriage.

Fast forward to the present time—and we have women pretending to be asleep when their husbands come to bed, leaving them to sink into their frustration or off to find *'connection'* elsewhere—and so the pages of your downfall are being written while you pretend to be asleep when your partner comes to bed.

Can this *'cancer'* spreading into every aspect of life, be stopped? I think it can, but there are many, many factors that absolutely must come into play in order to achieve this, and an enormous amount of effort from both will be required, if you are to succeed.

If you keep throwing up the old excuse of, *"I'm tired,"* and make no attempt to compromise, then you obviously care little about your own well-being and even less for that of your partner.

Of course you are tired, you may be a working mother and raising your children as well, or some women don't work but have other responsibilities as well as children, the reasons are not important, what is important is that you are tired, now, what are you going to do about it. If you leave this major problem unchecked, it will only become worse as time goes on and by allowing it to worsen you are damaging yourself, your partner, your marriage, your life!

You must be willing to find a solution, but also understand that no one said that marriage and all it entails *(children, etc.)* was going to be easy.

You will get tired many, many times over, both of you will be. Question is what are you going to do about it? Attacking each other is not going to solve this problem. Believing in and trusting that your partner will be there for you when you need his/her assistance is paramount.

Remember, the children will grow up one day, and they will leave home. If you cannot get along with your partner now, imagine what it's going to be like when the children leave and it's just the two of you left. Sure, you sacrifice yourselves for the sake of your kids, but you must leave something of *you* for each other as well, because in the end, that is all you will be left with, *each other!*

The fact that you are raising children does not mean that you have to stop living a full life in every sense of the word—*your needs and your partner's needs* are just as important as that of your child's needs. Would you tell your children that there is nothing for dinner tonight because you are too tired to cook? Would you send your kids to bed hungry day in day out? Of course not, so what makes you think you can use the same excuse on your partner, tired or not, reach a compromise, but don't just turn him away.

Bettina Arndt's Sex Diaries: has revealed some startling but true results as far as men, women, and bedrooms are concerned.

Andrew from Queanbeyan, New South Wales, writes to Ms Arndt, revealing the state of his marriage—

"What makes women think that halfway through the game they can change the rules to suit themselves and expect the male to take it, if. If we started to abuse them or treat them badly, that is totally unacceptable, but for them to do this to us is a part of life and acceptable. I JUST DON'T GET IT! What about the male? The new world expects the male to be a provider, Father, understanding husband, considerate and everything else. Well that is ok but if he does not get his needs met, who gives a shit?"

Bettina Arndt, "Fifty Thrusts and Don't Jiggle My Book"
The Sex Diaries, University Press, 2009

Ms Arndt has exposed what is going on in the bedrooms across the country—women just don't want to have sex, leaving their husband's wondering what ever happened to the woman that could not keep her hands of him.

The *'Sex Diaries',* should be a huge wake up call (*both men and women should read this book,)* but how do you, as a woman feel when you read this. Do you just read it, then put the book down, and think, *"Well, I'm not alone, there are millions of women out there, all feeling the same way, so I must be normal."* If this is all you do with this priceless insight revealed to us by Bettina Arndt's Sex Diaries, then you are simply contributing to the cause, instead of finding a solution.

Think twice before you reject your man. Reject them and you may as well tell these poor souls (*men*) that they are not allowed to breathe anymore, because sex, as far as men are concerned, is compared to oxygen—they need the oxygen to live, in order to have sex!

Acknowledging that there is a problem, is a good start, but now, let's search for possible causes, and no doubt, there are many that we will examine in coming chapters.

Guys—you need to be a little more 'there' for your woman, acknowledging— and appreciating her and understanding that once children enter the picture, life does not need to change for the worse, life needs to be readjusted for the better.

This means to accommodate the new baby, but what is even more important, your new life needs to support the two of you as well, you need to be there for each other just a little more, you need to say, "I love you" a little more often, you need to make time for each other even more.

By making these readjustments, you are ensuring the survival of not just your marriage, but you are also setting a pattern that will allow your love to continue to grow.

If you don't want the desire for each other to vanish, then don't allow 'familiarity' to set in through indifference and complacency.)

Re-adjust your lives to suit each other and not just the baby, for now you have two very different forms of 'love' in your life and believe me you absolutely need both.

You will be thankful as the results of these 'readjustments' done by the two of you, will become evident every day of your lives, and wait until you have been together for 20, 30 odd years, for that is when you will really appreciate these readjustments you do now, today!

Try not to be so demanding of her when you can clearly see that she may be stressed out, offer her assistance in any way that you can, even if it involves you doing something that you do not particularly enjoy doing, you can 'just do it'.

This is what it means to 'love' another person, so do it because you care about her, and not because you are looking out for your own interests (sex)!

Women can see right through this and that being the case I don't like your chances of getting lucky any time soon!

Once you find love, you then have to nurture it, and it is this nurturing that turns the love into *'real'* love.

So you see, real love does exist but only if you provide the necessary environment for this to thrive in. If this is not happening then you are not doing the right thing by your partner, by this I mean that you are not treating each other the way you should and therefore what becomes apparent is that neither of you are pushing the right buttons that could have set about the continual chain of events that would be required in order to fuel on going passion and love.

You may begin with one argument, then it leads to another and gradually it spirals out of control to the point whereby you begin to resent each other, say things that are hurtful, and you know a woman does not forget hurtful words spoken to her by her husband, she will remember them only to be aired the next time you have an argument.

Similar scenario for men as well, what it all means is, it's far too easy to go down this pathway of pain and hurt. Once the damage is done, it's a little late to try and take back the pain you may have caused. Each time you do this, you weaken your relationship. Instead of trying to fix something that has broken, how about you try not breaking it in the first place. You don't want the one thing that is keeping your relationship intact; to be scar tissue, do you?

The Triangular Theory of Love

Robert J. Sternberg developed the theory, "The Triangular Theory of Love," which characterises love within the context of interpersonal relationships by three different components;

Intimacy—encompassing feelings of closeness, connection and bonding.

Passion—encompassing drives that lead to romance, physical attraction, and sexual consummation.

Commitment—Which encompasses, in short, the decision to remain with another, and in the long term, the shared achievements and plans with that other?

Combinations of intimacy, passion, and commitment

	Intimacy	Passion	Commitment
Non-love			
Liking/friendship	X		
Infatuated love		X	
Empty love			X
Romantic love	X	X	
Companionate love	X		X
Fatuous love		X	X
Consummate love	X	X	X

No love is the absence of all three of Sternberg's components of love.

- **Liking/friendship** in this case is not used in a trivial sense. Sternberg says that this intimate liking characterises true friendship, in which a person feels a bonded ness, warmth, and a closeness with another but not intense passion or long-term commitment.
- **Infatuated love** is pure passion. Romantic relationships often start out as infatuated love and become romantic love as intimacy develops over time.
- However, without developing intimacy commitment, infatuated love may disappear.
- **Romantic love** bonds individuals emotionally through intimacy and physically through passionate arousal.
- **Empty love** is characterised by commitment without intimacy or passion. Sometimes a stronger love deteriorates into empty love. In cultures in which arranged marriages are common, relationships often begin as empty love and develop into one of the other forms with the passing of time.
- **Companionate love** is an intimate, non-passionate type of love that is stronger than friendship because of the element of long-term commitment. Sexual desire is not an element of companionate love. This type of love is often found in marriages in which the passion has gone out of the relationship but a deep affection and commitment remain. The love ideally shared between family members is a form of companionate

love, as is the love between close friends who have a platonic but strong friendship.

- **Fatuous love** can be exemplified by a whirlwind courtship and marriage in which a commitment is motivated largely by passion without the stabilising influence of intimacy. A relationship, however, whereby an individual party agrees to sexual favours purely out of commitment issues, or is pressured/forced into sexual acts does not comprise Fatuous love, and instead tends more to Empty love.
- **Consummate love** is the complete form of love, representing an ideal relationship toward which people strive. Of the seven varieties of love, consummate love is theorised to be that love associated with the "perfect couple."

According to Sternberg, such couples will continue to have great sex fifteen years or more into the relationship, they cannot imagine themselves happy over the long term with anyone else, they overcome their few difficulties gracefully, and each delight in the relationship with one and other.

However, Sternberg cautions that maintaining a consummate love may be even harder than achieving it. He stresses the importance of translating the component of love into action.

"Without expression," he warns, "even the greatest of loves can die" Thus, consummate love may not be permanent. If passion is lost over time, it may change into companionate love.

Robert J. Sternberg, Intimacy, Passion, Commitment, "Triangular Theory of Love" 1986

Perhaps consummate love changes into companionate love, because we allow the magic to vanish and we cease trying to impress our partners. Perhaps we become too complacent and begin to believe that we do not need to try any more, we have achieved our goal of *'getting'* the one we wanted, and now believe that no further effort is required, thus over the course of time, that initial passionate love we felt has ceased to exist.

Which category would you place your relationship in? Can you imagine then, that even the strongest and most complete form of love in the beginning of a relationship is no guarantee that it will succeed if both are not prepared to do all that it takes to keep the flames of love stoked and still burning.

There are so many different stages that a couple goes through during the early years of their relationship, finances, children, parenting responsibilities, career, etc, there are too many obstacles that could get in the way of the concentration and focus that is required on each other in order to fulfil each other's needs and desires.

Ideally, it would be great, if we could have our children, raise them, be there for them and do all that we can for them, have no financial problems, careers are on track, the wife never tires of her responsibilities, never says no to her husband when it comes to sex, the husband is never grumpy, and both have all the time in the world for each other.

I guess under those circumstances, passion would be retained by both but we don't reside within perfection, what we can do is try to create our own form of perfection.

What is perfect for each individual couple, what suits them, what works best for them as a unit, because women do get tired, and they do say no to their husbands and one thing leads to another and after years and years of this, what chance does love and spontaneity have of surviving. Don't nurture the kind of hostile environment that will allow the above to materialise.

Perhaps after ten, fifteen, or twenty years, the once passionate love *(consummate)* has now turned into companionate love (*minus the passion)* or worse still, the love has died altogether.

What does one do under these circumstances? Sometimes couples carry on in a companionate relationship and they can be reasonably happy, but if one partner still has the passion and the other has let it die, the relationship may end, as living without passion (*for the one who still craves it)* can be a fate worse than death because they need passion in their lives to *'feel'* alive and can never be content with anything less. More than likely they will end up going their own separate ways, perhaps after the children are gone, or at any time of the relationship.

We are told that love can be fleeting, it may last months or years and then it ends, or at other times continues into a kind of *'love bond'* whereby you spend your life, with the usual highs and lows, but overall happy in knowing that you have a good connection, love and care about each other, some aspects of your life may have changed, perhaps spontaneity is not as it used to be but still care for each other very much.

If you fall in this category, consider yourselves very fortunate, at least you have found the level of love *you* are content with.

Then there are couples that *imagine* they found love, only because they are in love with the *idea* of being in love, perhaps they have seen one too many romantic movies, born romantics or they are afraid of being alone or never finding *'the one'*. Therefore, first man/woman that comes along, they fall in love with, without really understanding what love is supposed to mean and have even less idea of what they are getting into and with whom. What success rate would you give a couple such as this?

Chances are, this relationship is going to begin to disintegrate slowly and in the process it will be this very same couple that will confess that there is no such thing as real love, because they thought they found it and it all fell apart, so obviously real love does not exist, however their love was more a *'let's fall in love for the sake of falling in love', kind of love* which is why it was doomed right from the beginning. It is quite possible that they were probably never right for each other, more than likely had nothing in common, not much of a connection other than the notion of the idea of love.

None of these qualities will provide the necessary building blocks to build a foundation for a marriage to survive on because you cannot build a relationship on a notion.

Don't fall for the first person who comes along without questioning who they are, where they come from and what do you have in common with you—what do you like or admire about them. Can you see yourself spending the rest of your life with them? More to the point—what are you prepared to *sacrifice* for this person?

Are you prepared to put that person ahead of yourself? If you do not know the answers to these questions, don't marry that person. Find the person who by their presence or their quality of love for you, will unlock your heart and allow those questions to be answered automatically, and without hesitation—that's called love!

Having said this, there is however another kind of love that only very few get to discover and experience, this is a whole different ball game, the *'Rolls Royce'* of romantic love, if you will.

Now this is the kind of love that truly blows you away, it keeps you young, it makes you feel like you can take on the world, it makes you want to stand on the highest mountain and tell the whole world how happy you are, your heart skips a beat when you see him/her not just at the beginning of the relationship, but for years to come.

This is the love that makes you feel that anything is possible. Your heart feels as if it's going to burst with so much happiness, you feel as if you are walking on air. Nothing can compare! This love inspires you; it reaches deep inside of you and reveals strengths and talents you never knew you possessed.

It is *this* love that truly sets one and other free, free to live, free to breathe, free to love, free to be the person you are, free to dream, free to forget your age and free to be any age you want to be and to be fortunate enough to have this kind of love and connection in your life is truly a blessing, and if you find it, never let it go for that flame of love will keep on burning because it is permanently fuelled by your love and passion, unlike anything you will ever experience again.

This is the *'forever'* love that some people hear about but do not believe in its' existence. This is the kind of love that can fuse two hearts that will forever beat as one.

It is also the kind of love that can never die, only thing is, you never really know when you will find this love, will it be in your youth, or in your later years. Perhaps the later on in life one finds this consummate love, the better the chances of it surviving.

It's food for thought anyway because true love is not exclusively reserved for the young, it can come to us in later years, because as we mature, we learn more about life and ourselves and know and appreciate the qualities we seek in someone else.

Michael Grayson Conner, Psy. D explains the two different types of marriages, in his paper—'About Love and Romantic Love' he says that:

'Utilitarian'—*Marriage is one that shows an absence of mutual passion or involvement, he goes on to say that this kind of marriage is primarily held together by social, financial or family considerations. In fact, the relationship is made tolerable by long separations, community activities and usually infidelity.*

Then there is the other kind, 'Intrinsic' marriage, this is the one that will hold all the passion and emotion and sexual involvement.

"The experience of life is shared," says Michael Grayson. **"The relationship is more fulfilling and interesting than any social activity and in this relationship, there is a tendency to avoid activities resulting in separations."**

Michael Grayson Conner, PsyD 'About Love and Romantic Love' © 2001
(Please read paper in its entirety located in the back of this book.)

This love needs neither rules nor boundaries. This love needs total freedom; it is the freedom of choosing to be together, freedom of expression that keeps the two together in the first place. Notice how, *'trust'* has not entered the equation, the reason being is that *'trust'* is automatic, it's a given, two people who feel this kind of love, have moved beyond *'trusting'* for that word belongs back on earth where mere mortals reside, as these two lovers have skyrocketed into the stratosphere.

This is the kind of love that makes you forget the rest of the world and sees just the two of you in it. You can't buy it, you can't coax it, you can't tempt it and you can never substitute it, and it weathers the test of time, it just goes on and on and it accelerates in the process—this is what absolute real love is, and the good news is (*in spite of what anyone may say to you*) it really does exist!

This kind of love is experienced only once in a lifetime and you can never love another person in this same way again. It does not mean that you can never love another person, what I am saying is, you can never love another human being in this same way again.

As we have already established, there are different levels, different kinds of love.

The *'forever'* love that I speak of only happens once in a lifetime, and some people go through life, never finding this *'forever'* love, in spite of this they have their own version of what love means to them and are quite content with it.

You will never know what you're missing, until you experience it, and once you do, you'll never be able to love another in the same way again.

The following poem is dedicated to all the couples that feel they have found their 'soul mate' or the 'love of their life'.

I have written the following poem and I dedicate it to each of you to read this to your partner.

ROMANTIC LOVE

Is eternity
Beyond all time
Romantic love is 'your' love
A power so divine
Romantic love is the ocean
The moon and stars combined
Guiding light to heaven
To ultimate love sublime
Romantic love is to hold you
And to dream of what could be
To live within your halo of light
Shining eternally over me
Romantic love means to stay in love
Till all our days are through
To stand by heaven's gate one day
To forever be with you!

F. M. H.

11

The More You Do You Will
The More You Don't, You Won't!

"Just do it," explained Bettina Arndt, "Once the Canoe is in the water, they do paddle happily" Bettina Arndt was absolutely correct—but why then did these comments unleash such furore on logging sites and apparently landed Arndt "in deep schtuck" as Shelly Gare, who is a well-respected journalist and editor, points out to us in her article, "What Men Want is More Complex Than You Think" appearing in The Advertiser, 27 March 2009.

Shelly Gare also explained, "Arndt has unashamedly gone in to bat for men trapped in sex less or mostly sex less, partnerships where physical intimacy is doled out like Meaty Bites to a dog; relationships where men lose a sense of their masculine selves."

Bettina Arndt, "Just Dot It," 'The Sex Dairies'.

This book was based on the feedback received from the ninety-eight couples that emailed Ms Arndt the daily diaries kept on their sexual activities or lack of.

Why is it that we as women are always ready to accuse men about either the things they do, or don't do, or the things they say, how they say it, the things they don't say and why they never say it, what they do, where they go, etc. We are first to tell men how we want things done, what we want to hear, how we want to be treated, but as soon as men make their own 'wants' heard, they get hen pecked by their partners and accused of being thoughtless, selfish, uncaring. Why is this so?

Men have just as much right to want the things that they expect from their women just as the women have their list of 'wants', well guess what—So do the men! Is there something wrong with the *'give and take' principle*, is this not what relationships and life is all about?

Ladies—Do you want to know what men want? Well, here it is—they want the woman they fell in love with to love them back…always, not just for now or only on Valentine's Day or just during the honeymoon, but long after the honeymoon is over and reality sets in. It's up to you both to make this reality a good one.

They don't want to have to tread carefully around you—in fear of upsetting you (no matter how trivial)

They want to be themselves after all—you did choose them. Why is this even an issue, if you are both doing your part to keep the marriage on the right track, why then is it necessary for the guys to have to be cautious or they may lose their privileges this being having 'sex' with their wife. (Would you prefer he have sex with someone else)! No, I thought so.

They want to be able to pat their woman's butt—while passing them in the kitchen and not be reprimanded or accused of being "interested in one thing only."

They do not want to have to ask permission—to participate in their favourite pastime be it golf or whatever else (so long as it is all above board.)

They want to be able to discuss their intention with you—and you should be mature enough to understand that if he wants to go and play golf with his friends then he has the freedom to do just that, just as you have the same right as well.

They don't want to be mothered, they want their wife—their partner in life to do things together but also apart, to be there for each other and to nurture your relationship.

They want a woman who can turn the house they bought for you—into a 'home' one where they look forward to coming home to every night. You both need to eat, so learn to cook (or at least learn together) they don't want you to nag them, they want you to take care of yourself and always make an effort to look good, they want you to be their best friend, their lover and their wife.

They want to feel like a man is supposed to feel—in other words, he does not want to feel as though he is kept on a leash. I'm sure there are probably a few more wants I can add to this list, but you get the picture. It's not rocket science, this is what men want, there's no mystery.

Bettina Arndt was correct in making the comments above, what is extremely disturbing is that some people cannot see the point that Ms Arndt was trying to make.

Men have lost a sense of their masculine selves because we, the women, have taken it away from them. We demand equality at home, but then resort to treating our men like children, so where's the equality for men? Why is it so wrong for men wanting to make love to the woman they married, that's you by the way, the lady he fell in love with and promised to love and cherish, and by the way, did you not promise the same to him as well?

After all, this is what marriage is all about, there is a certain *'unspoken word'* on both sides, that cannot be ignored and it has absolutely has nothing to do with women's rights or the right to say, *'no'*. You can't say *'no'* to your partner unless of course you are ill, or he is abusive, under the influence of alcohol or drugs *(in which case you need to seek professional assistance ASAP.)*

If none of those conditions apply and it is just a matter of *'you don't feel like it'* then you had better dig up those wedding pictures or your wedding video and replay it till you remember why you both married him in the first place.

Recall that day and remember how every little detail of your wedding was so important, remember your wedding dress, the bridesmaids, the cake, the food, the colour of the flowers and how you believed if the colour was not the right shade, or if the main course was not just right if would have been the end of the world.

How important is all this today, what relevance do all the things that you believed mattered back then, have in your life today? How could you have put so much emphasis on unimportant things, and they are, when compared to the *'big picture'* of life and yet have no regard for your life with your partner now.

Do you remember that snapshot from your wedding day that I suggested you carry around in your heart because it may come in handy one day? Well, this is the day? If you have turned your husband away from you, recognise the reasons why this might have happened and if you care about him and yourself, you must talk to him and set about finding a solution together before this escalates.

To simply say, *'no'* is so wrong, it's almost criminal, you should never allow a situation to fester and get out of control.

There are many reasons why you may be feeling the way you do towards him, and it is your business to find out why and work through it so that you can continue your lives together, but if the reason is because you no longer love him and feel that no amount of intervention or counselling will benefit, then you owe it to him to tell him *(and leave)*, don't just be there making him and yourself miserable. You both deserve to be happy, if you simply cannot make each other happy, then it's time to call it quits and stop wasting both your lives.

Assuming that you wish to make your marriage work, you must understand the process of growing together never ceases, it's a work in progress for the duration of your marriage, and you need to stay on top of it all the time, as soon as you feel something is not right—*FIX IT!* If you don't fix it as a problem develops you can now better understand how and why you have arrived at the place you are in today and that is saying *'no'* to your man and still expect that everything will be fine or that you and he will just carry on within the confines and boredom of this marriage *(because that's what everyone says happens to a marriage)*…wrong!

Your marriage will be whatever you want it to be, depending on how much effort and care you apply, refer to it as, *'maintenance of marriage'*, by maintaining the quality of your relationship *(everyday)* also improves the quality of your relationship every night. By maintaining the continuation of this state, you stand a better chance of being happy. To infuse negativity with marriage— well you may as well open the door of your home and push your man out on to some other woman. If that happens, who are you going to blame, him, the other woman, or yourself?

If you don't want your marriage to suffer, tell him you love him *(before you lose him)* reassure him, don't make him feel rejected by blatantly diminishing his masculinity either, just go ahead and do it, or at least promise him that you will make it up to him on another night.

You can't just disregard his desire which is *you*, with degradation and rejection. Can anyone honestly blame a man for seeking comfort elsewhere; when this is the treatment he receives in his own home?

Hormones play a major role in our lives and by understanding how they work will give us a clearer understanding of why some women feel the way they do and the reason for their disinterest in sex. Oxytocin is a chemical produced by the hypothalamus in the brain and released by the pituitary gland. This chemical is responsible for *'pair bonding'*, i.e. between mothers and infants or between males and females.

Without going into too much detail, oxytocin is released during sex, which in turn promotes bonding between sexual partners, particularly when it is with the same sexual partner.

This hormone is responsible for our need for attachment and assists in the choices we make and why we choose one partner over the other. This is the hormone that lays down the foundations of lifelong bonds.

The moral of the story is, women may not feel like doing it, but if you take heed of Bettina Arndt's suggestion and, *"Just do it,"* you will begin the process of releasing the hormone oxytocin into your system, and the more you do it, the more you will want to do it, because of the release of this hormone.

On the other hand, the more you don't do it, causes your body to cease releasing this hormone, now the absence of said hormone decreases you desire to make love to your man. Hence the more you do—you will, and the more you don't—you won't. Does that make sense?

Ladies—How much do you care for your man, your marriage? Please think about the damage you are doing, not just to him, but to you also, by denying him, you are also denying yourself of a loving and nurturing relationship and a future. You are denying yourselves the right to happiness.

Still not convinced? Ok let's look at this problem from a different aspect.

When he proposed marriage to you, did you pre-warn him (before you accepted his proposal) that once you are married, at some point you will be turned off sex and most likely not have sex for a very, very long time if any at all? Did you also make mention that you will achieve this by pretending to be asleep when he comes to bed or stay up later than he does so he's asleep by the time you get to bed? No?—Well, there you go!

Knowing this, do you think he would have married you, if you had revealed this little bit of non-essential about yourself? Do you honestly believe for one minute that you can deprive your man of sex, and think, "Well he just has to accept it, end of story."

Yes, it is the end of the story for both and the beginning of a nightmare, for you. The one that you have started, but whatever happens, never blame him, for what will inevitably follow.

"Many a man has fallen in love with a peach only to discover that fate has landed him a lemon."
Men, Women & Wedlock 1910 pp.18 Quote 16 A & C Black

12

Oh Baby, Baby!
What Are You Going to do
When Bubs Arrives?

It is important to note, that the content written below is directed towards women who have no apparent medical condition after baby is born, and that a reasonable amount of time has lapsed since the birth of the child. It is not intended for the new mothers who suffer from *'postnatal depression'*.

Women who do suffer from postnatal blues, depression, or psychosis are not at fault and have done nothing wrong. Guys if your partner is suffering from postnatal depression it is *imperative* that you be there for her 200% and make absolutely sure that she is provided with professional medical assistance as soon as this becomes apparent.

I have said many times throughout these pages that there needs to be balance within a relationship as with life itself and particularly when baby arrives. This is where further readjustment is necessary in order to maintain the balance if your desire is to lead productive and enriching lives because your baby is going to be demanding most of your time.

Your husband will of course assist you when he is home, but it is essential that you both make whatever adjustments you both feel are necessary to accommodate the new arrival, as well as yourselves.

As a woman, you must accept and also understand, that you cannot delete your man *(or the love you have for him),* from your life, by replacing him with your new born child in other words it is inconceivable to think that you can replace the love you share with your husband with the love you now have for your child.

Remember, earlier, we talked about the different kinds of love, you now have *two varieties of love (the kind we have for our children, and the kind we feel for our partners) and both* need to be nurtured in order for your marriage to continue successfully. To allow the love for your man to wane, or die, in order for the love of your child to live is unimaginable but there is one more kind of love revealed further on in the book!

Honestly, there can be no *'ifs' or 'buts'* about this (*I am not a doctor but unless there is a medical reason for this (I know they exist, in which case medical attention needs to be sort out immediately)* it is simply unacceptable to believe that your husband no longer needs to be loved or to be shown love by you, his wife, the woman he married.

If we were to reverse this situation, how would *you* feel if your husband, for whatever reason, no longer felt love for you because he can only love his new baby, how would you feel? Would you be able to function within this kind of environment?

Not only do you not *decrease* your love for him, if anything, he will probably need even more love than ever from you, in fact you will both need more love if you expect to maintain a healthy mind and body not just for yourselves, but for your child as well.

Imagine now a different scenario, what if we reversed this situation again, and instead, *you* continued to love your husband (*after baby arrived)* and proceeded to abandon or neglect your child.

If you rejected your child in any way by not providing the necessary love and nurturing, you would probably have your child taken away from you by the Child Protection Services.

So too, starving your man of your love and attention is not a good idea, for it simply serves to make him vulnerable to the attentions of the *'other woman'* whom you have now inadvertently (*due to your indifference toward your man)* invited into your life, and why?—Because you decided that you have no more time for him, no love and no longer interested in sex.

This will be the consequence of your actions should you decide to ignore him; do you want this to happen to your marriage?

Surely you must now realise that you cannot reject a man in this manner, and expect that it will be ok, it won't be ok, it will never be ok, and there will be a price to pay one day.

Men may be able to get by without sex for a while, but in the end, they will cave in to the *'need'*, and make no mistake, if you continue to refuse him, he will turn to someone else. Do you want to share your man this way?

Once this happens, there's no point in blaming the third person who now has your express invitation to *'take care'* of your man because you initiated the first move by rejecting him, and your husband has reacted by seeking elsewhere, that which you refuse to give—intimacy or sex.

If you are going to act negligent towards your marriage, don't then try to shift the blame onto the *'other woman'*, by labelling her the *'home-wrecker'*; the person to blame is yourself for your contribution towards the downfall of your marriage.

There are not two, but *three* certainties in life—death, taxes and men needing to have sex!

(It may be an old wives tale, but in my day, we were told a new mother should abstain from sex for at least 6 weeks.) No doubt there is a medical reason for this in which case—guys you need to back off a little and show a little patience during this time and do not force your wife or upset her in any way regarding you wanting to have sex.

If you love your woman, give her the time she needs for her body to return back to normal and the more patience and love you show her, the faster she will be able to recover.

Guys—Be aware that a woman's body goes through hormonal changes, after the baby is born as she did when she first became pregnant, however these hormone levels should correct themselves within a short time. If there are complications, seek medical attention.

What can you do to help? You can give her your full love and support and be there for her. This is a perfect opportunity for you to show her how much she means to you by putting her needs and her well-being above and ahead of your own, and if that means that your sex life is going to be interrupted for a while, then so be it.

You are in this together—yes? Your life has changed forever, but you are still you, your body has not changed, neither have your needs. She on the other hand, has gone through 9 months of carrying another human being inside her, now she has given birth and her body has gone through massive changes. This does not mean that she will not recover, she will, but it all takes time, so go ahead and reassure her with love and understanding and above all patience!

Postnatal depression is a condition that should never be underestimated and should this happen, you must ensure that she receives immediate medical assistance. You and your entire family should be there for her, if she needs you to be.

Ladies—just because there is a child in the picture, does not mean it's ok to neglect your man, your child needs you, but so does your husband, you still have to find time not just for him, you have to make time for yourself as well.

Never forget, that you both need to 'reward yourselves'. By this I mean that neither of you can afford to ignore the other's needs. You both have needs and dare I tell you both have an obligation to each other to meet those needs.

If the scales tip too much to one side, the other side will consequently suffer.

Guys—Don't forget that women, birth, hormonal imbalance equals turbulence—be patient, it will pass soon enough. Be there for her, comfort her, and give her all the support and love she requires.

Allocate *'together time'* this gesture will clear the path for you to have 'me' time. There is no need for examples, I'm sure you get the picture.

Don't complain about it, make the effort to meet his needs, if he needs a little intimacy from you and if you love him then, just go ahead and do it. Unless of course you are exhausted or ill, then at least be understanding towards him. If he desires intimacy and you are tired and feel you must to say "No" to him, let him down gently, don't degrade him or make him feel rejected in the process but show some sensitivity about his feelings as well, it's not just about you and the baby, it's about him as well, don't make him feel guilty, selfish or left out. He should not feel as if he is on the outside looking in, he is part of the picture of the life that the two of you created.

If you really are tired, tell him that you will make it up to him when you feel better, because if you keep refusing him, eventually he will find someone else who won't refuse him. How do you feel about that?

Guys—why is your woman tired? Offer her assistance around the home— it's more effective if you offer this assistance, rather than wait for your partner to ask for it. Show her your consideration, and she will be more considerate towards you as well.

Ladies—Ultimately, he needs to reaffirm his position within this new family-portrait as well, so rejection should be the last thing on your mind. Show him the same consideration that you expect for yourself and let him know of your feelings, let each other both know where you each stand so that there are no surprises later. Trust one and other and be good to each other, because there's lot of life to get through.

Communicate! Communicate! Communicate!

Guys

Don't let your wife devote herself so exclusively to the children that you are left out in the cold. She doesn't put you there on purpose, but you must show her that you are still her husband and lover, and expect to be treated as such.

"Don'ts for Husbands pp. 69–70 Blanche Ebbutt
A & C Black Ltd, 1913"

13

Till Divorce *Do Us Part!*

Every aspect of your relationship is extremely important, and it needs to be nurtured every step of the way in order for it to grow and survive. How can your family function in a positive manner, if your home is one filled with tension and stress, creating an unhealthy and unstable environment for your baby and yourselves.

Becoming complacent within your life is not the solution. Your relationship does not have to be this way, if it is set about fixing it by talking to your man/woman in a calm manner. I don't think men react too well to an aggressive or angry woman, by being loud and abusive you may end up escalating an already inflamed situation, making the prospect of resolution even more distant.

If your man is in an angry state, you must be the one to stay calm, don't *'dare'* him to say or do anything, because he probably will which in turn makes the entire situation quite ugly! One of you needs to stay calm, if it's not one, let it be the other.

The message here is to never escalate an already bad situation. That's not the solution, that's not the way to sort out the problem.

Your life does not have to be this way, but it will be, if you don't attempt to make the necessary changes within yourselves, by changing any bad attitude either one may possess and by doing so, you automatically change the manner in which you attempt to solve your problems.

Don't just accept a bad situation, because it is considered as *'normal'*. Normal is whatever you want it to be, take yourselves out of this self-inflicted jail cell called *'boredom',* and turn, your relationship around. Live your lives to the best of your ability by loving your partner, yourself, your family. In other words, LOVE YOUR LIFE!

You know what they say—what goes up, must come down! Life poses all kinds of obstacles, and you certainly can't expect to be on a high all the time, but at least when there is a low period in your life, you will be in a better or healthier frame of mind to make the necessary decisions required to move out of this *'low'* mode a lot faster.

If you are an unhappy stressed-out person to begin with, what will happen when a major problem enters your life? If you are already in a bad place, you will only fall deeper into depression, your mental ability becomes clouded, your family will suffer, your job may be threatened, and all along, you are doing untold damage to your relationship.

Remember one of the certainties I mentioned earlier on, the one I am referring to this time is *'death'*. One day it will be over for all of us, no one lives forever, at least while we live and breathe, anything is possible, live life the best way you know how, so that when that time comes, and we reach that part of our life, we won't be bitter or twisted and by the way, there is nothing worse than the regret of lost opportunities, of what could have been, and the realisation that there is absolutely nothing you can do about it would be devastating. Imagine how desperate and devastated you will feel, knowing that you had a chance to make life better and you did nothing about it.

Re-introduce unconditional love back into your heart, and then let it seep on to the one you love through your actions, your words and even your thoughts.

Revisit the love you felt when you first met, recall that feeling of love once again but this time, do it like there's no tomorrow, put that smile back where it belongs (*on your faces for each other*) love your man/woman the way you used to and allow respect, patience and trust to permanently reside in your heart and home once more.

If you have been having problems but still feel that you both have a good chance of reconnecting with your partner on an emotional level, make sure that the feeling between the two of you is still one that is good, in other words, you are both on the same page and that the desire to make one and other happy is still a priority and if this is the case then you both stand a good chance of achieving success.

It won't be an easy road, but if you are both determined and still feel that the love has not gone perhaps just temporarily pushed to the side, then you will get your relationship back to where it should be. If either one has doubts as to the level of commitment that will be necessary into reviving this relationship, then a lot of soul searching is required, you absolutely have to do the above for the right reasons, don't do things half-heartedly, it's like flogging a dead horse.

Look forward to seeing each other when you both get home. Treat your home as though it were your sanctuary, a place where you both *want* to be. It may sound idealistic but it is so important that you both have your space to come home to where you can shut the world out, if only for a short time, and just be there for each other.

Having quality time should be automatic, the minute you both get home, should be considered as quality time. How to achieve this will be discussed as we go along and it will be repeated in other chapters.

***Passion*—Did I mention passion?** An abundance of this is required if you are to get through your lives together and still be in love, years from now. Only problem is, you cannot manufacture it, you can't go out and buy it, you have to be born with it. How do you know if you possess this quality? You should be able to ascertain this by just looking at your life, the things you enjoy doing; what makes you happy? Do you enjoy the work that you do?

How about sport? What about cooking—do you enjoy cooking? There are so many things out there, what gets *your* motor running?

If you live an active life and generally enjoy what you do, then chances are you possess some passion as well, bring this to the fore, and multiply it 100 times, now apply this energy to every aspect of your relationship.

Endeavour to do all that you can to not take each other for granted and perhaps if you make the effort to realise and accept the fact that just because you *'have'* him/her, does not mean you own them and they can never leave you, because they can!

You can certainly keep your partner, but not by trickery, manipulation, or ground rules, house rules or any other kind of rule invented by mankind.

You keep your partner through *unconditional* love, trust, and respect. This in itself is a challenge however if you really love each other, your determination and combined efforts will ensure the desired result.

If you do not want to lose your partner, and still retain the mystery in your relationship, love like you've just discovered love for the first time. Love your partner the way you wish to be loved, speak to them the way you would like to be spoken to, and show the same trust, consideration and respect that you wish to be shown yourself by placing your partner and their needs ahead of your own.

Which of the above are you guilty of not doing for him/her, once you have identified the problem, initiate the process of pushing the right buttons to set about the continual chain of events that is required, in order to achieve on going love and harmony within your lives.

To love means to be selfless, and that has absolutely nothing to do with equality, both must put each other's needs first, now if you are both doing this for each other, where is the problem? You may or may not agree, but the fact is, this is the way it should be—embrace it!

Once again, if for some reason the desire is no longer there and one or the other is truly unhappy and cannot go on any longer, then only you can decide what is best for you and follow your heart—talk to your partner first and tell them how you feel and why you feel the way you do. Tell them what you feel is missing in your life that you simply cannot live without.

To stay within an unhappy, mentally or physically abusive relationship is an intolerable situation that no one should have to endure. Within a normal caring relationship, you should not be depriving each other of anything, least of all sex. No excuses!

Marriage and life are indeed about balance, depriving each other of love *(sex)* and not paying enough attention to your partner is wrong as it can destroy the romance, which leads to the next two destructive forces, boredom and monotony, which can one day spell the end of your marriage.

Let's look at a few hypothetical situations.

Your man has just arrived home and he is extremely tired or has a serious concern about something; it may be that *he* does not feel like talking, eating or even having sex *(it's not just the women's prerogative)* he just wants to be left alone with his issues, how are you going to react?

If your man comes home in this state, whatever you do, don't harass him and don't insist upon knowing what his problem is. Of course, you may ask him if he is ok, but if he reacts by telling you he has problems at work and needs some time alone to think his problems through, then leave him alone and go about your business.

He will appreciate your consideration by giving him the time and space to himself. Allow him to sort out in his head, whatever is ailing him just assure him that you are there if he needs you. Learn to read your man's body language and act accordingly, know when to back away rather than full on attack. There is a right time to say or do things, and there is a wrong time as well.

Some women may think, *"Well, I've had a hard day as well, and I need peace and quiet or I need to be left alone,"* etc.

This may be true, but this is where your consideration for him, and your love for him, will come into play. If you proceed to push your point across at this time, and demand that you too need time to yourself, what you are doing is setting the scene for a major argument to erupt and even worse, your relationship will one day be at stake.

It is at this point that you need to put him ahead of yourself. It's not a matter of who's state of mind is considered more important, it's a matter of why would you want to be at loggerheads with your husband, he needs to be left alone, so go ahead and leave him alone. Sure, you may be tired, but he may have a major problem at work and perhaps his job is on the line, so how important do you think it is that you happen to feel *tired* on this particular night, or maybe you won't mind if he comes home in a few nights and no longer has a job, how will you feel then? Get my point? Of course, you are important and you matter as well, but there are varying degrees of intensity within problems, some are not as important or urgent as others.

He will come to appreciate you and love you even more when you show him the kind a level of understanding that only comes about by really loving and caring for someone.

The day will come when he will do the same for you as well. Putting someone else ahead of yourself occasionally is not going to spell the end of life, as you know it. You are simply saying, *"I love you darling and I will give you space to do whatever it is you need to do."*

So, forget about nagging him and by the way keep the kids quite as well *(if there are any.)*

Give him the peace and quiet he needs to sort his issues out and what better place to do this than your home, better this, than some bar somewhere, or worse still, some *'other'* home.

Don't take it personally, show him you care by assuring him that you are willing to listen if he wants to confide in you, otherwise give him a cuddle, and leave him alone.

Guys—you should be prepared to show your partner the same courtesy— as she too may require it someday, which means, bath the kids, feed the kids and clean up the mess in the kitchen and most importantly, don't complain about it, they're your kids and you love her, remember!

The point I'm making is; don't take it out on each other because one or both of you is tired. We all get tired, that's normal, but just because you are tired, does not give you the right of way to neglect your partner, you still are a couple and if you use your continual state of being tired as an excuse for lack of intimacy, you will end up drifting apart—is this what you want to happen to you?

Ladies—Sometimes your man will do the same for you as well—by doing so, he too will be showing you just how much you mean to him, each little thing you do for each other becomes the cement or glue that will keep your relationship intact throughout your lives.

Back to the 'sex' issue—If you do not feel like having sex because you are angry at your partner due to unresolved issues—resolve them!

If you have a headache, don't just say *"No,"* show a little understanding, and explain to him that you are not feeling well, but *"Let's see how I feel in the morning, darling."* No need to be nasty, just because you do not feel like it, because this is not a perfect world we live in, and you may not feel like it, but he does.

Question is, how much do you *'feel'* like your partner seeking affection elsewhere—It's a sobering thought, isn't it? Don't be angry I'm just showing you a little of the *tough love I spoke of earlier!* Therefore, by blatantly saying *"No"* or *"I'm too tired, not going to happen tonight,"* *(which also means it will probably won't happen the next night either because unless something changes, you'll be just as tired tomorrow night as well).* What you can do though, is show a little understanding, tell him you love him. You can still make him feel loved and wanted because down right rejection is not going to stoke the flames of passion—it will extinguish them.

Guys and ladies—If either of you is too tired for sex or anything else—for that matter, acknowledge this fact in a caring manner and endeavour to make time another night, rather than allow this scenario to continue day after day, night after night.

Set time aside and calmly, voice your concerns, and inform each other of all the possible problems that the current situation may lead to and together work out a solution that will benefit both.

Ideally, this should be done as soon as these signs appear, again I stress, don't allow unresolved issues to fester, they will become bigger and cause greater and possibly irreversible damage to your relationship. Never forget the words, "I love you" say them more often, you won't regret.

You need not live in each other's pockets, give each other room to breathe because everyone needs a little space, but never, ever allow yourselves to drift apart through neglect.

Who will you blame once your life begins to fall apart when you discover that your partner is no longer interested and he is cheating on you? Don't court trouble, then look for someone to blame. If you have done something to hurt your partner, try to make amends, whatever you do not turn a small problem into a major marriage breaker. Whatever the situation is, sit down together and work it out.

The flip side of this story could read as follows—Your man comes home often later than normal, is in no mood for you, walks in the door and goes off into another room, or maybe straight into the bathroom, he tries to not look directly into your eyes when he talks to you. He seems always on edge and most of the time is moody. He is forever criticising you and although he loves his children, does not spend enough time with them.

When in bed, he complains he is very tired and is not in the mood for sex, says very little, then turns his back and goes to sleep.

Does this scenario sound familiar to you? If it does, you have a major problem on your hands, and you must work very quickly to find out what is going on because something is definitely happening.

It could be, that either your man is *'bored'* at home, meaning, he loves you, but there is no desire for intimacy, or excitement, or he could be coming down with an illness, in which case you send him off to the doctor, or there could be deeper problems developing—he may be in the early days of having an affair.

Talk to your partner about this, find out as much as you can (*in a constructive manner if possible)* because if you want to work this out and you do not want to lose your partner, then screaming and yelling is not going to achieve the desired result. You may well need to seek out professional help and if you feel that this will help you, then by all means, do everything that you can to save your marriage—as long as this is what you *both* want.

There is no room for stubbornness or ego trips within a relationship as you are both major contributors towards the common good of your family and your home. Reaffirm this by reminding each other of why you are together in the first place then and once again, Resolve! Resolve! Resolve!

Of course, if you discover that he has been unfaithful, but you both still love and care for each other and you both want to make amends, then forgiveness will be needed on your part.

If you decide that you will forgive him *(and that's a good thing),* but now you need to make sure that you never bring it up again.

If you do, you are not allowing the wound to heal as you keep scratching it every time you have an argument no matter how large or small, this will build up as resentment, possibly on both your parts. If you are going to forgive then do so, and now for the hard part...*you need to forget!*

How many ladies are feeling angry about what I have written? Someone needs to tell it like it really is, if we as women are doing something that is hurting our men and robbing them of their masculinity or manhood, then accepting that there is a problem but doing nothing to resolve it, is even worse than the problem itself. If women are hurting their men, they need to be told that what they are doing is wrong and they need to fix it.

If men are hurting their women and are inconsiderate towards their needs, then they need to be told that they're wrong and they need to fix it as quickly as possible. Men are nowhere near being perfect by a long shot, but then again, no one is perfect, we can only achieve our own form of perfection by openly discussing concerning issues and jointly working out a suitable solution.

Life does not always have to be perfect in order for it to be perfect! Some imperfections can work perfectly if both parties are accepting of this, which in turn becomes their own form of perfection. Re-read this...it does make sense!

The situation between the sexes will only improve, when there is a shift in attitude, which will come about when our understanding of what makes men and women *'tick'* is accepted. Each and every one of us is capable of making our life as easy or as difficult as we want it, to be and what appear to be the obvious solutions to some are anything but to someone else. What should be obviously clear to everyone, is actually not the case, there are so many people who know so little, about the obvious *(what needs to be done to keep you both happy.)* We are advised on how to remedy an ailing sex life, but where is the information coming from?

Do the answers really lie in just going off to some holiday resort with your partner, in a last-ditch attempt to reignite an ailing sex life...what happens when you come back to reality?

Or perhaps some retail therapy, in the form of sexy lingerie, may well fix the problem.

Sadly—the damage to the relationship was done long before the need for new underwear or a *quickie* holiday.

Marriage is a very serious business. When you marry you enter into a very powerful legal contract. It is the biggest financial and personal transaction of your life. You need to look at the other person and realise that you are not going to change them. Ask yourself this: Does this individual have the basic qualities that matter to me, characteristic traits that aren't going to change over time? It is not all about the cake, the wedding planner, your gifts, and your dress. It takes a lot of work to make it work.

Mabry De Buys, Seattle, WA 'The Divorce Lawyer's Guide to Staying Married'
Wendy Jaffe Esq. Volt Press, 2006

14

Affair-Proofing a Relationship
Oh Really! How Exactly?

How many of you actually believe that this is possible and how many of you think that the way to prevent this is by keeping tabs on your partner's whereabouts by making him accountable to you at all times…wrong!

The idea that one can affair proof a relationship in this manner is absurd and an illusion, dreamt up by women who like to give themselves a false sense of security and control over their man's actions. It allows women to continue with their relationship, believing that they can reel their partner in, if he steps out of line or whenever she deems it necessary, but ladies you are sadly mistaken and if you don't already know this, then marriage should have been the last thing on your minds.

If there is any way of ensuring that neither party strays, it is never going to be by sneaking around checking up on them because while some, particularly guys, may be careless and get caught out, the majority of them have learnt how to cover up their tracks, not to mention the sad state of your marriage if it all comes down to this kind of behaviour because if this is what you need to do to ensure your man does not stray, then I would question if this marriage is worth anything to start with.

*Guys—we know that you have perfected the art of concealment—*it's known as 'deception perfection'! Some men have perfected the art of deception.

*Ladies—don't even waste your time checking up on him—*because there will be no trace of anything at all. He now knows to pay cash for any expenses relating to him and the 'other woman' and he knows the exact perfect time he will see her, probably when you are at the gym or lunching with your friends or during business hours, where he has the freedom to move around unhindered by you.

Go ahead and keep your eyes and ears open all you like; you will see nothing and hear nothing because he has perfected the art of deceiving you.

Prevention is best, but not by being vigilant as to his whereabouts, who he talks to, who his friends are, etc. This kind of vigilance never works unless of course you have nothing else to do with the rest of your life but be his keeper and follow him every hour of every day of every week of every year!

Where there's a will there is always a way, if he really wants to play up, the second you ease up on your *'vigilance'* of his activities, is when he eases back into his own activities and he will be out there doing exactly what you think you are preventing him from doing.

The whole point to this is, he should not have any cause to want to cheat on you in the first place. If he is cheating, find out why, is it something you did that made him unhappy, is it something you both have done to each other that needs to be addressed. Whatever it is, if you care for each other, then take some time off together and work it out. You need to find out what it was that prompted him to do this to you.

Don't be hasty in blaming him, or the other woman, for it may not be entirely his fault, and certainly not the *'other woman's'* fault therefore you need to do some soul searching. It does not necessarily mean that the relationship is over, as we have already discussed, no one is perfect—you are not perfect, everyone makes mistakes. Re-evaluate your relationship and if you do decide to forgive and start again, that's great, but this time, make sure you both have learnt from your mistakes and never make the same mistakes again.

When men are first confronted by their partner, the first thing they do is deny the whole thing anyway, then when that ceases to have effect, they then proceed to profess that it was just a one-night stand or the other woman is nothing special, or they will tell you that "*She threw herself on me, and the temptation was too strong,*" or maybe he will say to you, "*You are never there for me, all you do is nag me and treat me like a kid.*"

Then, in order to appease you, he may say that she was not that attractive and she didn't really *'do it'* for him anyway! He's lying to you! Men will say anything to save their backsides!

Of course, you are going to be angry and devastated, but as I mentioned in the previous chapters, you both need to sit down and communicate with each other and openly discuss, why is this happening?

Both of you need to be open and up front and if you feel that you both need to go to a marriage guidance councillor, then do so, but honestly, if you both look inside your hearts the answers to your problems are there, bring them out, sort them out. The kind of vigilance that *is* effective is the kind that resides within your heart.

Guys—You can be vigilant too by addressing any issues that may arise— between to two of you as soon as possible. It's not a case of 'out of sight out of mind'. Problems won't just disappear they go underground for a while and you can bet your bottom dollar these problems will re-emerge. The only way you can get rid of them is by resolving them.

Be vigilant in attaining resolution, vigilant in ensuring that your partner is loved by you and knows it. Vigilant in ensuring your actions do not cause her unnecessary pain. Be vigilant in your continual support and trust and vigilant in always having her best interests at heart.

Ladies—you can be vigilant by providing a warm, loving home— environment for your man, vigilant in the way you treat him, and vigilant in the depth of love and trust you place upon him. Be vigilant, about being vigilant! This is the only way and the best way, to affair proof a relationship. How about all the couples out there that have not been confronted with this problem? How would you attempt to affair proof your relationship?

15

Controlling Your Man Through Paranoia and Manipulation
Dream On!

I was visiting a bookstore one day on a research mission as to the *'why's and how's'* of happy or unhappy relationships, when from across the room, my gaze became fixated on a book titled, **'You Can't Have Him, He's Mine'** by co—authors **Marie H Browne, R.N. Ph.D. and Marlene M. Browne, Esq.**

The book is aptly subtitled, *A Woman's Guide to Affair-Proofing Her Relationship.* Well, for one thing, the title certainly did what it was supposed to—attract attention, I mean, honestly, how many women could read such a great title and not be slightly curious as to the content of this book?

Without wasting one more moment that could well have been spent devouring the contents of this book, I purchased it and literally ran home breathless with book under arm.

Eagerly, I raced through the pages, in great earnest and anticipation. I had to know what the solution to this age-old problem *(affair-proofing a relationship)* was but after a short time, I suddenly began to slow down and felt the need to digest exactly what I was reading. This slow pace however, soon came to a screeching halt—I backtracked and re-read the pages.

At first, I thought there must be some mistake, or this must be some kind of a joke, simply designed to add a little light and frivolity to this very serious subject.

There was no mistake, this book for all intent and purposes could have been written for me as for the millions of women alike, but what was alarming and very disturbing were the suggestions made on how one goes about preventing a spouse from having an affair.

I am neither a sex therapist nor a psychologist, I am one of the millions of women who have been through divorce and learnt the hard way, and therefore we can relate to the pain associated with affairs. Yes, I know exactly how it feels to discover that hubby is seeing other women and back then; I too, wanted to know why, hence my reason for purchasing this book besides curiosity got the better of me, great title!

As I began to leaf through the first pages I began to wonder, if I had this book before my husband began his *'other life',* would this book have helped me? Would I have handled matters differently? I wonder, had I scrutinised every female friend and relative who entered my home and then proceeded to banish them because of my insecurities, would that have stopped my husband in his tracks regarding the other woman, and would I still be with my husband?

In other words, the closer the proximity your mate has to stimulus—your neighbour, your pal, your sister—the more favourably he will view her.

Marie H. Browne, R.N., Ph.D., Marlene M Browne, Esq. 'You Can't Have Him, He's Mine'
ADAMS Media Avon, Massachusetts.

Does this mean that suspicion already exists within this relationship? Should I have prepared for, *'just in case'* and proceeded to banish all my pals, or at the very least, all the ones that looked as though they could pose a threat (*including my sister*), from my home.

"Recent studies have shown, that when it comes to protecting your mate from the designs of a same sex friend, neighbour, relative, or colleague, you are best to, select better company," warns Dr H. Fisher.

Marie H. Browne, Marlene M. Browne, "You Can't Have Him, He's Mine."
ADAMS Media Avon, Massachusetts.

In another chapter from the same book, it is suggested, *"Many marriages are broken by interlopers within the couples' inner circle of acquaintances."*

Marie H. Browne, Marlene M. Browne, "You Can't Have Him, He's Mine." ADAMS Media Avon, Massachusetts.

I guess this would also include the workplace environment and any special gathering at anyone of our friend's home, particularly if it is within a 5-mile radius of home or work.

Does this mean, that if my friends live further afield, then the chances of anything untoward occurring are greatly reduced? It just does not make sense to me. Am I correct in understanding that I am to examine every single person, be it friend or a relative? Can anyone one of them really be able to poach my man away from me, and will my interrogation of all these would be *'poachers'* prevent this from happening?

Should I introduce dress codes before someone enters my home, do I screen them to determine whether or not they are suitably attired before they walk into my home?

What happens if we were having a pool party? Does this mean that only I and my man would be wearing swim suits while my guests look on fully clothed or that laughter coming from the backyard where my sister is laughing while chatting to my man is supposed to be viewed as a direct attempt on her part to steal my man? Does it mean that she is trying to steal him from me, just because she happens to be laughing with him?

Imagine, not allowing a friend or relative into your home, because they look a little too attractive and the husband may be attracted to her, so she is now banned.

The whole idea seems to me to be utterly absurd. I am not saying that a friend or a relative cannot steal a partner, what I am saying is, is he worth keeping if he allows himself to be *'stolen'*?

To pre-judge my friends and put them through some kind of screening process for the express purpose of deciding who is to remain a friend and who is to be banished is a very tragic way of ensuring that a marriage continues. If such are the extremes that one must go to, then just how much is this man worth keeping? Just what kind of an unstable fool is this man who lacks all self-control over his actions. Who is this man anyway? If a man cannot be trusted then that man is not worth having. If I cannot trust the friends who come into my home, then there is something wrong with my ability to have selected these friends in the first place.

If I have to fear sisters, cousins and all female family members, then there is something wrong with my family, and if my man does not have enough scruples to interact with female family members in general and be aware of the unspoken boundaries, then, I don't want this man. I will certainly not spend my life controlling *his* life and waste my life by selecting suitable *(safe)* friends. No thanks!

What kind of man would just sit back and allow his partner to pick and choose who will be his friends and who will not, oh and by the way, is his backbone on holiday? Perfect example of treating a man as a possession or a child. He is neither, he is your husband/partner, a full-grown adult, treat him as such, by having some faith in him.

How does one sack their friends, then go about the business of selecting a new group. Can you imagine deliberately seeking out less interesting people to be friends with so that the husband won't be tempted to stray from the marital home?

Looking for boring, unattractive people to become our new friends actually makes the mind boggle because I struggle to understand how one goes about actually finding these people. Where would one begin looking?

Solid friendships don't happen overnight, how do you throw friendships away and replace them with just anyone?

There are the casual, fun friends, they are our friends because we have things in common, we may enjoy the same sports, similar hobbies, food, music movies, how do we replace them with people we have nothing in common with, I know I would die of boredom within 5 seconds and for what? Just to give myself the false sense of security that my man won't betray me. No, I don't think so, because if I have to go to such extremes of throwing out my family and friends in order to keep the man then this man is not worth having.

There are different levels of friendships and some of these have taken years to develop, they're the ones, you confide in, cry, and laugh with, how do you replace these friends?

However, this is not the end of it, for the next place to be conquered is his work environment.

Can you just picture going to his work place and making your presence felt by openly displaying your authority over your man in the hope that females in close proximity *(and in fact everyone in the office)* be made aware that you are never far away and a clear indication that you—the wife is alive and well and, in their midst, who may appear unannounced at any given moment.

Would you insist that photographs of you and the family be posted in his office or workspace? Again this is intended to ward off any females within close proximity and yet again reiterating the message, *"Move on honey, this man ain't going anywhere."*

To demand that your man display photos of your entire family in his workspace is ludicrous.

If anything, it will be an open invitation for a female colleague to make a comment such as, *"Oh what a cute dog, or cat or child."* Initial contact has now been established anyway, but then again, they all work together so the *'contact'* has already occurred.

Where does it end? Where do you draw the line? Can you picture yourself at home, wondering all along what he may be up to, or reassuring yourself, *"It's ok, no one will approach him, because they can all see how happily married he is, because his workspace is full of photos of me."* Honestly, do you *really* think so?

You may be able to get away with showing up at the office unannounced once and twice, but continue to do this and you will become a source of embarrassment to your husband and it will simply alert everyone else in the office that your husband cannot be trusted. Not to mention all the arguments you are going to have night after night at home if your continual unannounced presence in his office becomes a distraction for everyone else.

Let's assume that the office in which your husband works in has at least thirty married men working there as well. What would happen if the wives of these 30 men also decided to heed the advice given and decided to make their presence felt in your husband's office as well and they too take it upon themselves to post pictures of their entire family history in their husband's cubicle as well, can you even imagine a workplace whereby wives are arriving at different days and different times constantly to *'check up'* on the husbands.

This is no longer a workplace; it is a circus! Can you see now how impractical it is to believe you can *'affair proof'* your relationship in this manner?

This is no way to "keep" your man?

There is nothing more unattractive for a woman, than to display her jealousy by demeaning other women because of her insecurity and paranoia. You should not have to stoop this low for any reason and more so just so that you can keep your man. I for one would not want him anymore for if I had to spend my life worrying about his every move and about the other women he talks to through the course of the day and our life, then that *'life'* would not be worth living! I would be more inclined to take a good look at myself and how I treat him at home, and if I treat my man the way he deserves to be treated, then I will fear none of the other women he encounters on a daily basis, because he would never find another to replace what he has at home.

You certainly don't have to resort to trickery either and oh! By the way, where is this very precious man through all this hiring and firing of his friends and relatives, does he not have a say at all? (Yet again, where is this 'equality' for men)?

I think we have already established that we simply cannot attach ourselves to a man's sleeve and follow him around all day every day in an attempt to avert potential poaching. It just does not happen this way so you may as well come to terms with the fact that you will never be able to stop him with trickery, suspicion, threats, or psychological manipulation. Even if you could, what good would it do, how could you live your life this way?

"Mate Retention Tactics." These tactics are designed to ensure that your man goes nowhere and in order to achieve this, what is required is vigilance—keep eyes and ears open at all times, and along with that comes 'Concealment of mate'. It is suggested that you keep your mate at home, and dress him like a happily married man.

Marie H. Browne, Marlene M. Browne, "You Can't Have Him, He's Mine." ADAMS Media Avon, Massachusetts.

I guess this means to dress my man in boring clothing will contribute towards an unflattering appearance so that woman won't look at him. I don't think I'd want to look at him either.

We are then encouraged to monopolise his time, which means to keep him busy, plan his every free moment so that he has no time to fool around.

Moving right along to—

'Infidelity Punishment', *this is meant to scare him into staying within the confines of marriage as the losses and isolation would be great, not to mention the regret he would feel, coupled with 'Emotional Manipulation'—to brainwash him into believing that only the spouse is the worthy love object, followed by* "Commitment Manipulation, Derogation of Competitors, Resource Display and Sexual Inducements, Verbal Possession, Physical Possession, Signal and Possessive Ornamentation."

Marie H. Browne, Marlene M. Browne, "You Can't Have Him, He's Mine."
ADAMS Media Avon, Massachusetts.

The implied suggestion here is—the wife has the right to control every aspect of her husband's life be it at home, socially, work place, even, without him having any say whatsoever. Not forgetting the place where the now *'over controlled'* husband happens to work. Furthermore, the husband must be discouraged from attending work functions and the spouse must accompany him on any out-of-town seminars. *(This gesture would simply convince staff that he is not to be trusted and may even get him fired).*

Wow I'm lost for words! I can only say that I feel absolute pity for the poor man who has to live his life this way for it appears that he absolutely has no say in his life, he is simply a puppet who has no mind or reasoning power of his own and can only move when his partner pulls the strings in whichever way she sees fit.

Having now transgressed through enough paranoia and suspicion to re-sink the Titanic, the shock of what I had read was only slightly softened by what was revealed in chapter 5 of said book.

We are also reminded that:

Your husband should not be keeping his feelings secret. Remember a marriage requires trust and open constructive communication.

Marie H. Browne R.N. Ph.D. Marlene M. Browne Esq., "You Can't Have Him He's Mine"
ADAMS Media Avon, Massachusetts.

Eureka! Finally, some sane advice! This is correct, that is how it should be, but now I believe this to be a direct contradiction to what was said earlier for when taking into account all of the above, where then was the love and trust on the wife's part during all the suspicion, paranoia and manipulation?

If you trust your man, then you won't need to plaster pictures of the entire family around his workspace. If you don't trust him, then you need to question, why because all the family pictures including that of your ancestors will not prevent your husband from another woman's clutches.

Are you prepared to become your husband's keeper; this means spending the rest of your natural life monitoring his every twitch? Are you prepared to embarrass yourself and humiliate your husband by utilising his workspace and time and in the process make your husband look incompetent and untrustworthy to the rest of the world?

I cannot even begin to fathom the possibility of any marriage lasting even ten years, let alone thirty nor forty years under these conditions, can you?

The need to resort to trickery and manipulation is not the way to promote love and trust within your home. If this is the only way to keep him, then how did you land him in the first place? Did you not trust him in the early days? You must be very insecure within yourself and your capabilities of conducting a relationship and need to resort to 'hanging on' to your man through manipulation, rather than retaining him through love and trust.

If you feel threatened by every female that comes within a stone's throw of him you need professional help, someone will help you identify why you feel this way and assist you in gaining confidence within yourself and your ability to have and keep a man because *he* wants to be with you, not because you are monitoring his every movement.

Hey baby! This is a lifetime we are talking about, you need to get through this life and you have the right to live as well, you deserve to enjoy your life, how are you going to do this if you have to spend your waking hours wondering where your man is, who he is talking to when at work, who he is having lunch with, who he is talking to on the phone, etc., you simply cannot live this way and he does not deserve to be treated this way either.

Can you imagine the side effects of such paranoia would have on you and your health not to mention your family? It all boils down to this—your man married you because he loves you, he found you attractive, sexy, wonderful, loving and caring woman to share his life with. By the same token, you married him because you saw in him, a wonderful, beautiful man and together you embarked upon life enhancing each other's lives.

How could you now set about destroying this by turning him into a puppet to be deliberately, overstuffed (*fattened*) and manipulated, for the purpose of ensuring the continuity of your marriage? What does this say about you? Perhaps it shows that you are an extremely insecure woman, it's either this, or you two are simply not meant to be together.

I thought it was all about *'trust'*, but it is a pity not enough emphasis was given to *'trust'*, had this been mentioned much earlier on in the book, then the remainder of the contents, would have been obsolete.

You cannot use trickery or force in order to keep your partner, even if you have managed to convince your other half not to leave, your relationship is now an accident just waiting to happen.

Not all *'other women'* are out there to get your man, maybe your man is out there to find someone who will give him the love that you are failing to give him because just maybe, one of his issues may be that you have turned into a control freak, obsessed with every other female within a 5 km radius.

Yes, there are the different types of *'other women'*—there is indeed the:

'Part-time lover',
The *'flinger'*
The *'lifer'*.

"You Can't Have Him, He's Mine" Marie H. Browne R.N. Ph.D., Marlene M Browne Esq.
ADAMS Media Avon, Massachusetts.

The explanation that we are given is that the *'lifer'* is a woman who has a low self-worth, this being the reason for the need to cling to your husband. There are many different types of *'lifers'* but my point is, why blame the *'lifer'*, why not blame your husband or even yourself as to why this *'lifer'* has now a foot hold in your life.

It's not necessarily the *'other woman's'* fault if there is a problem, look inside the home, not outside the home the problem may be inside *(which is why the 'outside' was allowed to gain access.)*

Think about it for just a minute it may not have nothing to do with some other woman wanting to *'cling'* to your man, has it ever occurred to you that maybe your man may want to *'cling'* to someone else because of the neglect he is receiving from you?

Perfect example of a *'lifer'* that stayed with the love of her life not because she would not let go of him, but he would not let go of her either, remember Katherine Hepburn, famous movie star from the 40s. Katherine was a *'lifer'*, she and Spencer Tracy, also a movie star from the same era were very much in love. The problem being, that Spencer Tracy was married.

Theirs was a true love story that endured for 27 years, albeit in the shadows, as divorce in those days was definitely frowned upon.

To live in fear of our man wandering off with some other woman, good time girl or whomever, really only proves that it is the wife who has the self-worth issues, not the other woman.

She is the one who fears losing her man due to her, oh I don't know, perhaps fear, inadequacy, thus compelling her to use every form of manipulation and trickery, into securing the false belief that he can be prevented from leaving or straying.

Dr J Gottman's *suggestions on "Good Marital Habits" are all the right things that couples should do like—"Remembering why you fell in love with your partner, being grateful for one and other, care for your spouse's emotional health, resolve differences by being respectful, helping each other reach your potential into building a positive life together," are exactly the qualities required within a relationship.*

Marie H. Browne, Marlene M Browne, "You Can't Have Him, He's Mine" ADAMS Media Avon, Massachusetts.

The above being the case, the question begs to be asked, why would anyone need to resort to manipulation and trickery in order to keep a man as a permanent resident in the marital home?

Reinhold Niebuhr's serenity prayer.

God, grant me the serenity to accept the things I cannot change, courage to change the things I can, and the wisdom to know the difference.

Marie H. Browne, Marlene M Browne, "You Can't Have Him. He's Mine" ADAMS Media Avon, Massachusetts

Thankfully, this prayer made no mention of using any form of manipulation and threats into keeping this marriage alive, for if the husband of this marriage was not happy with his wife's compulsive controlling personality disorder, intruding into every aspect of his life, it would take more than a prayer to save this marriage and keep this man at home.

If there is a need to resort to such manipulation in order to keep your mate, then does this not scream out that there is something wrong with the marriage itself! If one must resort to tactics and manipulation in order to maintain a relationship, then I question the reason why this relationship needs to be kept alive.

If your man/woman loves you, never allow that love to die and have the confidence and belief to know that you are more than a worthy partner and your mate is so fortunate to have you in his/her life. Don't waste your time and energy worrying as to what your husband could be getting up to when he is away from you.

This kind of negativity will only serve to wear you out. Honestly, if this is what you had to concern yourself with every time he left the house, I think there would be a more pressing question like what's the point of being married if you have to worry to such an extent. *I don't know about you, but I have no desire to be any man's keeper…how about you?*

If a man loves you and wants to be with you, there won't be anything any other woman can do to take him away from you.

By the same token, if a man wants to cheat on you, all the *'checking up on him'* in the world is not going to stop him from doing what he wants to do.

Do you honestly want to waste your life managing and controlling your husband's life *(in order to guarantee survival of your marriage)* while living in a state of constant fear lest some *'home-wrecker'* steals your man, I think not!

It is heartening to read that this same author, Marie H. Browne also explains to us how happily married she currently is, and still in love with her childhood sweetheart, which is wonderful, but does this mean that her marital bliss was achieved by following her own suggestions on how to keep a man from straying *(trickery and manipulation)* or was she just lucky enough to have married the right man whereby love, trust and all those other good elements were just second nature?

It is rare, but it does exist, as is the case here. This is the kind of union we all deserve and should strive for, right from the beginning of a relationship.

If you are lucky enough to be spending your life with your childhood sweetheart or the love of your life and still be *'in love'* many years later—that's great, it simply proves that real love does exist and more importantly, it can survive the test of time.

There can be no modern or fashionably trendy way of treating a man. Just remember this, if this is such a great idea, why are marriages still failing, why are men *(and women)* not happy and why are men looking for affection, or this elusive *'connection',* in another woman?

If there is any possible way of affair-proofing a relationship, then it has to be the one and only way and that is *(as I have already mentioned many times,)* it will only ever be through, unconditional love, patience, warmth, understanding, freedom, trust, resolution, communication, and the burning passionate desire to want to be with each other. That's it!

Once again, prevention is indeed better than the cure; however, it won't be easy so how much do you want your relationship to succeed? How much do you love your partner, I mean honesty adore him, do you adore your partner?

If your answer is *yes,* then work with your partner, not against him and this will allow both of you to grow together not apart. Nurture your relationship, and allow it to be one where you both relish and look forward to being in each other's company. Develop your communications skills and learn to read each other's body language and just be there for each other.

"While it takes two people to start a relationship, it only takes one person to end it."
Too Soon Old, Too Late Smart—pp. 27 Dr Gordon Livingston.

16

Life is Too Short
And Forever is a Long Time!

It should be obvious now that you cannot stop a man from leaving, if he no longer wants to be with you, unless of course you are going to blackmail him or threaten him with finances or your life. Threats like that do not have the makings for a great life together.

A couple should be together because they *want* to be, not because they have to or one has forced the other to be.

Ladies—as his partner, you should have the faith, trust and belief—that he loves you, would never deliberately hurt you.

What kind of life do you think you will have with a man whose only reason for remaining with you (even though he loves someone else) is so that he does not lose all his money, do you really want to make a man stay with you, knowing all along that he does not want to be with you.

Then again, some men do end up leaving in spite of the consequences, even if you managed to change his mind, it would only be a stay of execution, it will always be there just under the surface, then when the first sign of an argument looms in the horizon, he will bring it up again, and eventually, he will go.

Failing that, how does the idea of 'sharing' him grab you? Would you like to share him? Could it be that you are so desperate for him that you are prepared to sell yourself short? What does that say about you—don't you deserve to have love in your life as well?

The very same can be said for that of women as well. If a woman has decided to leave her home, no amount of coaxing will make her stay, why would either party stay if they are not happy because their heart lies elsewhere.

Statistics do show that more and more women are also leaving their marriages.

This being the case, can you, as a woman, now imagine your husband telling the *(other man)* the one you want to leave your husband for; "*You can't have her, she's mine,*" is this going to be enough to chase the other man away? Do you believe that your husband can *'hang on'* to you, if you have already decided that you want to leave him? Therefore, what makes you think you can keep a man who no longer wants to be with you?

What a waste of a life it would be to have lived it within arguments and disillusionment or violence. Violence should never be tolerated and under these circumstances it is best to call it a day, and let this relationship go, and find the strength and courage to start again.

As I have consistently mentioned in previous chapters, if there is a chance to mend the relationship, that wonderful but prepare yourself, for now you have a troubled, damaged relationship that needs to be made whole again and to do this, it must be a mutual decision and double and quadruple the effort that you will both need to put into this damaged relationship, if you want to give it any chance of surviving.

If his heart lies elsewhere, or simply wants his freedom because you spent a lifetime taking it away from him, or if the woman wants to leave because her husband has spent his life making her feel worthless, inadequate, unattractive, or whatever the reason. If she/he has decided to leave, they're gone!

*Ladies—you got the man you, just didn't know how to keep the man—*Look within your home, does it feel like a home should feel or is it just a house? Did you take the time to turn this house into a home? One that he will look forward to and want to come back to each night, so the first thing you must do as the lady of the house is create a warm, nurturing atmosphere, one where he relishes coming into each night, hence you need to finetune the art of turning that house into a home—for the both of you, not just for him.

Each new day will reveal one more thing you did not know about your partner, but this is ok, this is the only way you will learn who he/she really is and in turn enable each other to grow together, I will repeat that—grow together! (That's the secret!)

It is important as you get through each day, to remember that even if you do have disagreements the manner in which you resolve them, will determine how the rest of your day is going to pan out. And what about the night?

What do I mean by this? Imagine that you have had an argument over an issue and you insist you are right, he insists that he is right, you don't resolve this, one party storms off in a huff, the other slams a few doors and you both go to bed angry. What do you think is going to happen that night or the next day?

You will either ignore each other, go about your business in silence, this may then trigger off another argument and off it goes again till one day, 30 years later you both find yourselves in a place where millions of couples find themselves today—Don't join those ranks and end up reciting the same story.

"I can't remember the last time she/he last said love you," or *"My partner is no longer interested in sex, hasn't been for the last 10 years."*

Resolve grievances, always be respectful and considerate of your spouse, and never ever lie to them. You will get caught out in the end and you will lose the trust.

It is so important right from the word go, to nurture the man you call the love of your life, assuming that he is, he must be, you hope he is because you married him, treat him the way he wants to be treated and in turn he will love you even more for the wonderful woman that you are and in doing so, he will treat you the way you wish to be treated.

Why then would he want to mess around, he would have to be an absolute fool to risk losing his greatest asset—*YOU!*

Give each other the space to grow because growth and change is inevitable, so I say to you, grow under the same roof and change and develop together, that is if you wish to stay together. It doesn't mean that you live in each other's shoes though.

If you're really smart, you will know to do this right from the beginning of your relationship, in fact insist upon it and never stop.

Example 4—Mike and Wife—True Story!

Mike (not real name) for many years was not happy at home with his wife. He tried many times to leave, but each time his wife would ply herself with alcohol and then proceed to collapse on the floor, and each time he would unpack his suitcase and stay put.

One day, she drove herself down to a cliff top and called him on his phone and threatened to throw herself off the cliff if he was going to leave her. This was emotional blackmail so he came up with a better solution. He informed his wife that he had to leave on a business trip overseas so he packed his suitcase and left...and never returned! Did she throw herself off the cliff? No, she did not!

Today, I am happy to say that she is happy with someone else, and he has married another woman, what is important is that his now ex-wife is happy and he is too... *(I think)*...but that is another story.

What kind of life do you think you will have with a man whose only reason for being with you is because he doesn't want to risk losing his financial assets! Do you really want to force a man to stay knowing this, and of course you know that at the next argument the whole *leaving* issue would resurface like a ticking time bomb—eventually he *will* go.

If he wants to leave, and you feel that the marriage is beyond salvation, the best thing you can do for yourself and for him is to let him go, don't threaten him, just let him go.

Perhaps if he has his freedom, he may realise that he does love you after all and you can both try to work through the reasons for the breakdown in your marriage and if you both desire to make an effort at attempting to rebuild your relationship, you may just have success second time around.

It can happen, but you both have to absolutely want this and all your energies must go into acknowledging the mistakes you both made and rebuild your relationship by using this knowledge to your advantage.

Ultimately, the best way to stop a partner from leaving you is to never give him/her cause to do so in the first place.

"What gives love its power is that it is shared."
Too Soon Old, Too Late Smart—pp. 93. Gordon Livingston, M.D.

17

Must All Lessons be Learnt
Through Our Mistakes?

As much as I love my parents and knew that deep down, they always had my best interests at heart, they were very controlling and I came to believe that marriage was the only way of escaping the control that my parents held over my life.

Dating was never going to be an option, it was totally unacceptable to my parents and there was no way their teenage daughter (*me*) was going out with boys, because of this, I was denied the opportunity to date, or meet young men, hence I was never in a position to compare personalities, to come to know what I wanted, what I liked in a man so that I would be able to choose a suitable man to share my life with when the time came.

What they *'did'* do, is organise for the son of one of their best friends to visit one day, in the hope that we would instantly fall for each other, and be married within the month. That was never going to happen!

I do not blame my parents for being overprotective, they like many other families left their home lands and moved to a new country, new life, new everything, and with them they brought the ways and traditions of the old country. This was the only way of life they knew; therefore, they did what they thought was best for their daughter. My parents were tough, but they loved their children.

Over the course of the next few years, life was just work—home, with nothing much in between, till one day (my very early 20s) I was introduced to a young man by a friend of mine, whom I proceeded to date, if you can call it dating, it was during lunch times within working hours, and within 6 months, we were married, 6 MONTHS!

He was nice enough in the beginning, I was attracted to him, he was a good-looking guy and I thought that mattered, but as the relationship progressed, warning signs began to emerge, but my inexperience prevented me from recognising the magnitude of damage these warning signs would lead me to.

All I could think of was marrying this man *(who wasn't so bad after all)* who was going to be my passport out of my parents' control and into freedom of enjoying life with my partner. Already, I am considering marriage for all the wrong reasons.

Example 5—Anthony (not real name) and Wife (me)—True Story

Anthony *(not real name)* was young, handsome, and full of life, seemed to know where he was going. *(What I did not realise at the time was that it did not really include me.)*

By this is I mean, when two people get married, they do so with the intent of living their lives as one, that they would have a normal relationship whereby the wife now takes precedence in the husband's life and no longer the parents *(even though parents will always be there)* and they would do and enjoy all the things that couples do as they share their lives.

For me, though it was going to mean a life of being, *'seen and not heard'*, and so for the next twelve years, I found out what it felt like to live life as a piece of furniture on the other side of the world far away from family and friends.

The only *'sharing'* that occurred was that of our *'home'*, with his parents and sister, and thrown in for good measure, were his uncle and aunt and their young son, who were at our home more often than not. This was not a normal situation for a young married couple in any universe that I know of. This was not the ideal situation that a married couple would thrive in, let alone survive.

For me it was twelve years of mental abuse, the kind of psychological brainwashing, whereby I no longer believed myself to be worthy of breathing, let alone living, and this becomes the norm. It was the kind of despair that wracked my mind was destroyed my very soul.

I longed for those days as a single girl, with just my parents over controlling nature to deal with. Suddenly that seemed like heaven. I will say though, that my husband never ever physically abused me. Watching your man ready himself for his *'girlfriend'* is something I would not wish upon anyone. Worse still, I was prohibited from approaching my husband and confronting him about his behaviour as I was instructed by my mother-in-law to, *"Just let him go, he's a man, wherever he goes, he will still come home to you!"*

Was this remark meant to ease the heartache? Was I supposed to think, *"Oh, that's ok then, he's going out with another woman, but he is going to come home to me, so it's ok."* Sure, maybe in some alternate universe!

During my marriage, the only blessings I received were my two beautiful children, but I couldn't endure my life any longer and after so many years of separation by thousands of kilometres from family and friends, I found the strength and courage to call it a day, and collected my babies and headed back home to Australia.

I fought long and hard, I gave my husband every opportunity to redeem himself and during the course of those 12 years, I gave him 3 chances to change and embrace me as his wife so that we could continue living together, but each time he failed.

I remained with my husband during those tragic years for many reasons, the most important one being, I wanted my children to grow up with their father in their lives. I also wanted them to have their grandparents (*both sets)* in their lives as well. I did not want them to be deprived of any member of the family on both sides, but there was another reason for my staying, I simply could not imagine my life without my husband.

Divorce was viewed quite negatively during the 70s and I did not want to be tagged *'divorcee'* or worse still for my parents to be ashamed of me nor did I want them to be humiliated within the community.

I stayed in this marriage for the well-being of everyone else, and always put myself last. Perhaps it was fate, perhaps it was meant to be this way for me, who knows.

I wonder who I would have become, had I held on to these ideals, and as a result, to have spent the last 35 years in an unhappy relationship, who would I be today? Would I have lasted the journey? Would the stress have taken its' toll on my health and would I be a shadow of the person I could have been? Would I have written this book?

"To live in a state of constant distress is to die slowly within."

I had no intention of throwing my life away and finally one day, I scraped up enough courage to end my marriage.

That was a long, long time ago and I have forgiven my ex-husband; I hold no grudges against him or his family, in fact after all these years, and all the pain and tears, we are now on friendly speaking terms.

Why am I telling you this? If I had been given the opportunity of dating young men during my teenage years, I would have had the chance of getting to know what the opposite sex was really like and come to understand what I liked and didn't like in a man.

I would have been better equipped to make decisions affecting my life and my future. Had my parents advised and taught me what to look out for and be aware of, who knows where my life would have taken me, perhaps I might have handled my life differently. I guess what I am saying (*without intending any blame towards my parents*) is that as we mature, this maturity allows us to see life through our parents' eyes and I know they did what they thought was best for me at the time, however because of the overprotection I received, I was rendered handicapped as far as life's experiences were concerned. I was totally oblivious to life outside my comfortable cocoon.

If only there was some fool proof way that that would enable us to find the right person, all you can do is go by your gut feel and lots of common sense, in other words, do not let your heart rule your head.

When you chose the one you wish to marry because you love them, it's equivalent to taking a leap of faith into the unknown. You can only hope that when you first meet a man/woman that you will be able to recognise all the qualities that you desire in the person you choose to spend your life with. The selection process is so important and not to be taken lightly.

The younger we are when we tie the knot, the greater the chances that this marriage is not going to last or that we may be marrying the wrong person.

You will discover this as you travel through life together, through your interaction with this person and how you cultivate the ability to problem solve, while maintaining a loving relationship.

If you ever reach a stage in your life where things are not working out, and are having big problems with your spouse, talk to him/her and work out why you are having these problems. On no account should you let this drag on and on and ask yourselves if you still love each other enough to fight for your relationship (bearing in mind that the other party must want the same things you do), you both must want to fight for the survival of your relationship.

Be careful whom you allow into your life to offer you solutions or try to problem solve for you. Sometimes, friends could be meaning well, but in fact give you the wrong advice, sometimes they encourage you to leave your spouse by telling you that you can do better or they don't deserve you, etc. but beware, some friends may have a little jealousy mixed up in this advice, and sadly, some so called 'friends' can rejoice in your downfall. I am not implying that all friends are like this, I am saying, *some* may not who you think they are and may have their own agenda. Be mindful of this and proceed with caution.

Ultimately, only the two of you can decide what is best for you, and provided there is no physical or substance abuse (*which should never be tolerated),* look into your heart, and ask yourself, *"Can I live without this man/woman in my life?"* answer it honestly and know if your heart that you will make the right decision, at least then, you will never have any regrets.

As for me, I had definite warning signs, but as I mentioned earlier, I had no one to point them out to me, if only to explain to me, what the ramifications would be if I chose to ignore these signs.

To single out an important life task about which most of us could use some instruction, we might look at choosing (and keeping) a mate. The fact that upward of half of all marriages end in divorce indicates that collectively we are not very good at this task. More often, those whose parents are still together, describe them as living a boring or conflicted coexistence that makes economic sense, but lacks anything once could describe as excitement or emotional satisfaction.

Dr Gordon Livingston, "Too Soon Old, Too Late Smart"

When a man announces to his future bride, *"I think it will be a good idea to live with my parents after we marry,"* is a pretty clear-cut indication that something is not quite right and this would have to be the last thing any bride would want to hear, from her soon to be husband.

"Why not live on our own for 6 months, let's just try it, and if in 6 months' time you are not happy, then I guess we can move in with your parents" I said to my husband, all along thinking to myself, that if I can get him to agree to this, then I will make those 6 months the best 6 months of his life, I will make him so

happy and show him all the things we can do when we have total privacy that he won't want to move in with his parents.

It sounded like a great idea at the time, because I honestly believed I would be able to change his mind—"*Ah! Ignorance is truly bliss.*"

How wrong was I! For the next 6 months, I cooked for him, I prepared myself by looking as seductive as I possibly could, the apartment was spotless, and the scene was set…for six months!

He in turn would stop by his parents' place on his way home, and would eat to his hearts content (*his mother was an excellent cook)* then upon his arrival home, he would announce that he has called by his mother's home and has already had dinner. He was constantly critical of everything I attempted to do to please him and of course within a blink of an eye, the six months had been and gone and so we gone to live with his mummy and daddy!

The plan failed, and for the next 12 years my life was spent in total despair and disillusionment. If I could have saved all the tears that I had shed during those 12 years, I believe I could have sailed away back home to Australia. I have never cried so much in my life. What did I do wrong? What should I have done? What was I supposed to look out for or be aware of? WHAT!

My first big mistake was in believing that I could change him and his ideas. My second mistake was in believing that I would achieve this by trickery—how young and foolish was I.

I had no experience with men, I had absolutely no idea what it was that I wanted from a man or from a relationship and knowing that my parents wanted me married, they were not about to pick fault with him and to top things off, I believed I could change that which I did not like about him to suit my own likes and requirements.

I was wrong and I paid the price—I devalued myself by compromising the very essence of who I was. I had paid the price for my sheltered life for here I was, on my own and two young children that I had to raise on my own.

Having gone through this experience did not automatically make me street smart. I was not the party girl type, I did not frequent nightspots on a weekly basis, I did however venture out occasionally with my girlfriends and one day I as introduced to another man who was to become my second husband.

Now he seemed to fit the bill but still I had no one to advise me. I thought I knew what I wanted. I believed a professional man, running his own business reasonably well off just enough to live comfortably and there he was, all of the above, but there was just one issue, the one issue we really did not talk about (*because I did not think it was necessary*) I thought we could always work it out later. I honestly thought this time I would get it right but I was so very insecure and I really believed, *"Why would anyone want to be with me?"*

I guess I thought as long as he looked nice and spoke eloquently, that should be enough—no it wasn't!

I tried making a mental list of what I thought would be considered as desirable traits in a man, and this man came close to all the characteristics I looked for in another person, taking into account of course the very limited experience I had.

Everything seemed fine, his parents approved of me, I liked them, his sister was a nice lady, everything seemed to progress just nicely, but there was one issue regarding my children, which at the time I did not think it necessary to discuss at that point, after all I could sought this out later, after we marry, or so I thought, *"2 out of 3 ain't bad,"* and we were married!

9 years later though, this one issue I did not address when I should have, became a monumental problem that led to a few more disagreements and we parted ways.

The point I am making here is this one issue that I chose to not put too much emphasis on, turned out to be the cause for many arguments during our marriage which eventually chipped away at the love till there was nothing left.

Our problems stemmed from the fact that while he too had been married before, he had no children, thus felt disabled around my children, he did not know how to act around them or react towards them.

Rather than just focus on simply going out and having a good time with him, I should have had deeper more meaningful conversations with him to find out as much as I could about him, and what his dreams and desires were. I did not do this. I just made sure that I looked like a million dollars each time he came to collect me in his Porsche. He had no idea what to expect because we did not talk about what we expected from each other or our life together before we married.

The fact is, he was not comfortable around children and he did not know how to react towards them. I believe he would have been happier if they were not there. Unfortunately, when it comes to my kids, the matter is, *'closed and not negotiable' therefore the* marriage ended, and several more years of each other's lives were wasted!

What was the lesson I learned here? Never overlook any issue, no matter how small, discuss the matter and reach a resolution, or in my case, if no resolution could be reached, then *"Good bye and good luck"* would have been more appropriate than marriage.

I would not have wanted to waste his time or mine, he was a good man in every other respect, but we were not really suited to each other because we had different ideas regarding *'family'* but we have remained friends over the years. He has had his own misfortunes in life and I respect and admire his tenacity and fortitude of being strong enough to pick himself up, and make a success of his life. I have the highest respect for him, as do my children.

Sure I learnt my lessons, but at what cost? By losing twenty-five odd years of my life, that's gone, forever, and I can't help wondering, knowing what I know now, if I could have my time all over again, where would my life have taken me had I done things differently? We need to stop and take a really good look at ourselves and re-acquaint ourselves with the things that truly matter in life.

Aim at making the lives of our loved ones and for us, a much happier one. Life is stressful as it is—we do not need to contribute towards our own downfall by ill-thought-out decisions.

I, like many millions of other people have learnt lessons the hard way; for myself at least, I hope that any mistakes I make in the future will not impact my life to the same extent as in my younger day, because the time I have left now, has to be spent in as much happiness and calm as possible.

I would much prefer to spend my life being happy, instead of being miserable over insignificant and trivial issues and to then continue the damage with polluting my life by carrying grudges or past hurts into my present, this is a waste of energy and life.

Forgiving all the people who have caused us pain throughout life is a good start. Wish them well and set yourself free and in doing so you place your life on a much happier path. I value every second that I breathe, I relish in the simplest of things life has to offer by valuing the things that really matter in life.

My family's love and well-being is at the top of the list. Sometimes it is best to just let go of issues that have been too difficult to resolve, better that, than carry it around as excess baggage, which in time will become a dead weight, which would only drag you down. Move forward with life and live it the best way you can.

Each new day brings different opportunities into our lives, different circumstances, and different choices requiring appropriate decisions; thus the learning process continues.

It is what we learn, and how we apply it within our lives, that will shape who we become, in turn bringing out the best in us and making us more understanding, tolerant and more compassionate. It teaches us patience, forgiveness and most importantly, unconditional love.

Wouldn't it be great though, if we could know everything that we are destined to learn over the next thirty years…*now, today!* How much easier would our life be if we could avoid some of the mistakes that we are destined to make.

We need to figure out what we want out of life and what kind of person we want to spend it with, therefore making the right choices in life is pivotal.

How are we going to achieve this goal though, when it is preordained, that we can only learn by making mistakes. After all isn't this the way we have been taught by our parents? What our parents did not tell us was how much of our *life* would be wasted by making these mistakes.

My question is—why must everything be learnt this way and at what cost?

Perhaps we can begin by changing the way we think and instead of thinking, "We learn by mistakes," let's assert the notion, "Not everything has to be learnt by making mistakes, sometimes we can learn through the wisdom of others."

Figuring out what we want out of life, and making the right choices is never going to be easy, but if we keep an open mind and gain as much information as possible before making major decisions, then just maybe, we may not have to pay the penalty by having to learn everything through mistakes. So much time, so much energy and so much of our life is lost. If only we could have known, if only someone could have warned us. The old adage— *'If only we knew then, what we know now',* has never been more accurate, bear this in mind as you continue to read on.

There is no reason why you can't take all the precautions necessary *now*, so when you are ready to select a mate to be join you in life, you will at least give your relationship every chance to succeed and move forward within your relationship and never have to look back with regret and wish that you had handled things differently.

You would not wish to live with regret, it is a 'soul destroyer', it's a slow death, if you don't let it go, it will devour the love and the passion in you, till there is no more left.

To have the man/woman of your dreams by your side is the greatest gift. However, getting the *'man/woman'* is sometimes easier than keeping the man/woman, and finding the *'right man/woman'* is harder still.

Making life-changing mistakes is a luxury that no one can afford anymore, especially in today's age when everything happens so quickly.

We just don't have the time to have to suffer through everything. For instance, no one will come along and say to you, "Here you go, here's the 5 or 10 or 20 years you just wasted, but just make sure you do it right this time."

It would be wonderful if we really did get a second chance to do it right but those precious wasted years of our youth are gone forever. What price are you prepared to pay, all because of that one bad choice or wrong decision you failed to place importance on way back when, when you held your fate in your hands and did not recognise the value of this power. To think it could have been prevented but for a few words of wisdom, the kind of wisdom that only comes about by the passage of time that provides the experience.

Take the time to handle your life carefully, even if you learn just one thing from one person, take me for instance, I did it the hard way, and I learnt alright, but it cost me all the best years of my life.

"A safe bet, was the one you were going to make, and didn't."

pp. 58, Quote 191, Men, Women and Wedlock 1910 A & C Black Publishers.

18

Meet the Jealous Mother-in-Law,
Who is Jealous of You!

Believe me, they do exist. Let's look at the profile of a jealous mother-in-law. This is the woman who gave birth to a son and from the minute she laid eyes on him, like all mothers do (*or most mothers),* fell in love with her baby boy. I did, I love my son beyond anything I can imagine.

Now imagine this mother, who may or may not be also be a little on the domineering side (*heaven help you if she is)* who feels she knows it all as far as her boy is concerned, so there she is having spent the last or 20 or so years, loving him and looking after him like he is her prince. Anything he wants, Mamma gets for him. He is her pride and joy and she wonders which woman is one day, going to take her precious son away from her. Or she may even imagine that he will never be able to find any other girl to look after him the way she does.

Then one day it happens…her pride and joy is bringing home '*her'* to meet you and the father of course!

A mother's immediate reaction could be one of feeling threatened thus immediately erecting a barrier between the two of you, then proceeds to tread very cautiously as she approaches you, the woman who dares to imagine that she can take her son away from her.

Bear in mind also, that his mother probably thinks that you may not worthy or good enough for her boy.

What will you do—or more to the point, how are you going to get this woman on side with you? Do you even believe it's necessary?

Firstly, ask yourself how much do you love her son? If you are absolutely sure about him and his love for you, then all you need to do is win his mother's heart and you're in.

If at this point you feel that you don't care whether or not his parents like you, and you are still going to marry him believing that it's not necessary to do anything to win her over, you are now heading on the wrong path, turn back quick!

You should care if she likes you and don't for one minute think, *"I am determined to go ahead with the marriage no matter what!"* Heaven help you if you feel this way, I actually feel sorry for anyone who has this mindset, as they are not thinking logically, and I fear for your prospective husband, yourself and the in-laws, not to mention your future.

Not only are you starting out on the wrong foot, but it is also saying something about your character. You show a lack of respect, no flexibility, and little love for your man, and that's just to name a few. If you have no desire to show some form of patience now, in the beginning, then you surely will not acquire it later on.

"Marriage is hard work. The decision to marry should not be based on a single factor. People need to stop underestimating the importance of family relationships and religious differences."

Marshall Wolf Cleveland, OH, "The Divorce Lawyer's Guide to Staying Married. Wendy Jaffe Esq."

Life sometimes places us in certain circumstances whereby patience needs to be exercised, in order to achieve a certain goal. This lesson enables us to become better human beings, but the desire to want to learn must be there, if that desire is absent, so too will be a very important lesson that could have been learnt and this being the case, getting married should be the last thing that you would want to do, because guess what! Patience is and always will be one of the necessities within a marriage, amongst many others.

It all comes down to this—Do you want your marriage to survive? Now that you understand the importance of family, let's go back to winning the mother in-law over. Before we do so, I would just like to point out that I too am a mother-in-law, but I always made it clear to my son and my daughter, that I would never take sides against my son and his wife, or my daughter and her husband. If I thought that my son-in-law was right and my daughter was at fault then my daughter would be the one who would be advised to get her act together. The exact same applied to my son and his wife, I was never on his side, or her side, *I WAS ON THE RIGHT SIDE* whomever that happened to rest with.

I can see both sides of the story, because I have been on both sides. I know what I want to hear from my son and daughter-in-law, but I also know what it's like to be the daughter-in-law who is not appreciated or respected or even loved by her husband's family and because I know what that feels like, I would never want to put another mother's daughter through that.

Winning the mother-in-law over may or may not prove to be easy but if you love her son and you want to live happily with him you have to find the strength and determination to see this through and show her the kind of woman you are and why your son loves you.

I make reference about his mother first, because it's usually the mothers who tend to feel threatened about losing their son, more so than the father, but you can show them both how much you adore their son and how your only desire is to make him happy.

One excellent way of winning over his mother is to show her how much you will be depending on her to teach you how to cook some of his favourite dishes, even though you may already be a great cook.

Tell her how much you admire her strength and how much you appreciate her parenting skills by having raised such a wonderful man that will be your future husband and what a wonderful job she did of him.

Tell her that you love her and his father and you want them to be in your lives, particularly when you will one day have children and reinforce the fact that grandparents play a significant role in the children's lives. She will need reassurance from you, she wants to know that she will still be in his and your lives perhaps to a lesser degree, but she will still be there and if you make it clear to her that you will both want her in your lives, how can she not love to you?

Always present yourself by being in the right frame of mind and attitude. Just be your wonderful self and try to put yourself in her shoes, and understand why she would feel the way she does, it's all part of character building on your part, who knows, you might feel this way one day, so be diplomatic and disperse any fears she has about *losing* her son. Reassure her that she is not losing a son, but gaining a daughter and if she is a genuinely good-hearted woman, she will embrace you.

If on the other hand his mother is a mean-spirited woman, who no matter what you say or do for her, she is relentless at her disapproval of you, then I have to say, proceed with great caution. Are you prepared to have his mother as a negative influence in your future lives together because make no mistake she will be there in all her glorious negativity! What will you do if your husband takes his mother's side, leaving you on the outside? Can you see potential problems with this scenario?

It may be that his parents, one or both do not like you for a particular reason but you may not know why. Make it your priority to find out why they don't like you and if it is something that can be resolved then aim for this and do it quickly, but if his side of the family are just unreasonable and have no particular reason that is immediately obvious, yet still disapprove of this union, I can hear alarm bells sounding loud and clear, can you?

Speak to your soon to be husband, and try to find out why, because entering into a family that does not like you is not wise. No point in saying, *'But I am marrying him, not his whole family',* if he loves his parents, then you *are* marrying the whole family.

Do you want him to be influenced by either his mother or father against you? Is this how you want to start your future lives? Surely not! Ultimately, it is your decision, but bear in mind; you have no one to blame but yourself if things do not work out in the long term for reasons already stated above.

It would also be noteworthy to mention, that his, and your parents should get on as well, you're getting married, do you really need to have one more headache as to where you are going to place his and your parents for fear if they are sitting too close, they will begin a war. You don't need this hanging over you like a dark cloud.

Your wedding day, is supposed to be the happiest day of your life, and yet we clutter that day up with some much unnecessary negative weight. Give your partner and yourself every opportunity to start your lives off in the right direction, with the love and the blessings of your families.

Make your wedding memorable for all the right reasons so that when you look back at your wedding videos, you won't see your family, or his sitting long faced in the corner of the room. Nor do you want to catch a glimpse of either party arguing in a corner somewhere, or heaven forbid in front of other wedding guests. Surely you would not want your wedding day to be marred in this manner it should be a day to remember the love and the joy shared by all.

His family has now become yours, and your family has become his and while as within any family there will always be some disagreeing about one thing or another, how well you work through these issues will ensure the survival of your marriage. Remember, patience, respect, understanding and love should always be present and if you work through any problems with these components close to your heart you will be reinforcing your marriage, making it ever so stronger and the love and respect will flow freely within your lives and for all concerned.

I have seen such regard and respect in action, and believe me it is a joy to behold. I was a guest on a friend's boat some time ago and while I was discussing some of the contents of my book, I began to observe the interaction of another female guest, towards the rest of her family, her husband, teenage son, and her in-laws.

My first observation was that of the respect she showed towards every member of her family and this became evident in the manner in which she spoke to them. I could sense the love she had for them and they for her simply by the way she spoke to them. The manner in which she addressed her husband and her boys was admirable, to say the least.

I take my hat off to her, she obviously is doing it right, she does not have a problem loving her husband and taking care of him the way she should be taking care of him, and the way he wants to be taken care of. Her two boys are respectful, and her in-laws love and respect their daughter-in-law as well. This is what I am talking about I wish I could have had a similar relationship with my in-laws!

19

Future In-Laws,
Do Your Parents Like Him and Vice Versa?

You may think that this too is not important, for as long as you both love each other, he is not marrying your family, he is marrying you, right—wrong! Your goal should be to ensure that you do all you can to at least have half a chance at a successful marriage, and this means that your parents should like him, as his should like you, this *liking* period, should then progress on to *loving, and* eventually as your relationship progresses and marriage is in sight, both sets of parents should *'love'* the both of you.

Why is this important?

You are marrying this woman's son, she gave birth to him, she raised him to be the man you fell in love with, you need to have her on your side and the list could be endless as to why, but the main thing is, if your man, who we assume is a good man and loves his parents, wants to know that the woman he's chosen to marry will also love his parents.

If his mother has been a good mother and has taught her son to love and respect the woman he marries and all people for that matter, then you need to show that you too have this quality, and after all, his mother moulded him and made him into the person you fell in love with.

If the man you are considering having a relationship with is right for you and he is compatible with you, then your parents, and his will see this as well and they will be accepting of both of you. If one or the other set of parents does not like either one of you then you both have a decision to make or as I mentioned in the previous chapter, you must set about fixing it as quickly as possible. Before you arrive at any conclusion, you can try talking to the party that is not happy and find out what is the cause for such concern.

If a solution cannot be found straight away, keep the communication lines open, don't give up, be patient and understanding, show that you care about how they feel and show them how important they are to you and of your desire to resolve this. Tell them how important it is for you and your future husband that everyone be happy.

On the other hand, if the party concerned is totally unreasonable and reluctant to discuss and resolve any issues they may have, then you have a major decision to make, as this is certainly is not an ideal way to begin a marriage.

You can still go ahead and marry if you wish, but their dislike of you or the dislike of your parents of him, will hang over your lives like a dark cloud, it will filter into your life and create havoc. Like a time bomb, just waiting for the right moment to explode, so in effect, the foundations of your life are already on shaky ground and you haven't even begun yet.

One cannot tell another whom to marry and whom not to marry, but one *can* bring to your attention of possible outcomes, be they favourable or otherwise, thus enabling you to arrive at a suitable conclusion.

Listen to what your parents have to say about the man/woman you are considering as a partner. If they have any doubts, let them tell you exactly what troubles them about him/her. They have a wealth of experience behind them.

They come from an era where getting married was more about the union of two people, and most likely placed less emphasis on the trivialities of the actual day and more weight on the future life of the couple.

They may see something in him, that you, being so close *(and in love)*, cannot see, hear them out, ultimately it will still be your decision as to whether or not you proceed.

I am not suggesting, that if your parents don't approve, not to do it, but if your mother and father bring to your attention a particular trait he has that they deem unfavourable, take it on board, and check it out, there is no harm in that.

Your future spouse may have a jealous streak that you don't seem to place too much importance on, and if this is the case you should be thinking very seriously of what you are about to do, and ask yourself just how much you want to take on this problem, that will inevitably more than complicate your life. I discuss the jealous type in the coming chapters.

Ultimately, only you can make that decision, only *you* have a right to take a chance with your life and your happiness and no one else, but don't dismiss what your parents have to say either, after all they are concerned about your welfare and they too want you to be happy.

Our parents did not get this far in life without having learnt something along the way, don't blame them if they try to save you some heartache, it's only natural for a parent to want to protect their child from any pain. You too will one day want to protect your children from pain as well. Life will be anything but stress free and there will be plenty of opportunities for you to learn some of life's lessons the hard way, but if there is any possible way that your parents can protect you from heartache, or the unnecessary waste of part of your life, at least hear them out and do not condemn them for simply caring about you and loving you.

Both sets of parents will more than likely become grandparents one day, wouldn't you want your children to know and love both sets of grandparents, and what about birthdays and Christmases and all those family functions that a lifetime brings along.

Now imagine that you are not on speaking terms with his/her parents, imagine the arguments that you will be having with your husband/wife, *"You always take their side, you never support me on anything,"* can you hear yourself saying this? Or how about, *"If you can't live without your mother, then why did you get married? Time to cut the apron strings or it's over."*

By the way, just because your future husband cares about his parents does not mean that he is tied to his mother's apron strings. It simply goes to show that he is a caring, sensitive man and does not want to hurt you any more than he wants to hurt his mother or father, so do yourself a favour and don't use that line on him because it's not going to do you any good whatsoever. Threatening your partner is never a good idea as they will remember this and bring it up the next time you both argue and so it goes on, and on, and on.

If this should occur, can you see what would be happening now, it would be the beginning of a pattern forming, and what you are actually doing is slowly accumulating toxicity which will increase as you go through life, to one day be used against you.

This kind of toxicity will only poison your lives. Try to be kind, loving and understanding to your future husband's desires as far as his family is concerned. Of course, he too should show you and your family the same consideration.

Can you understand why it is important to have both sets of parents love the both of you, and any children you have together will be able to enjoy the benefit of having both sets, loving them and spoiling them and making for *memory making* family gatherings you will all cherish in years to come.

Having loving parents can be a blessing in your life, they have been through many tough times and have learnt so much, tap into this resource and extract from that what you need to apply within your lives.

They know more about life than you do, how can they not! They are more than twice your age, they have lived longer and experienced more, so assuming they are the normal, loving and caring parents, what they can offer in the way of advice, could be priceless and should be appreciated.

If the alarm bells sound, then set about silencing them in a positive way. You do not want to hear anyone saying, *"I told you so,"* or *"I warned you about him/her and you did not listen."* or *"You made your bed, now go lie in it."*

Don't allow this to happen to you, set about dispersing any doubts that may arise and ensure everyone is happy, you really do need to have their love and their blessing if you want a happy future. How important is this on a scale of 1–10, I would have to say 20!

All of the people in your potential spouse's life, their family, their friends and their friends to come, affect a marriage. Before you get married, take a careful look at your potential spouse's relationship with these other people.

Pamela Pierson, San Francisco, CA, Divorce.com *"How to Stay Married,"* Wendy Jaffe, Esq.

You may be blinded by love, but your parents can see clearer, because of love—the love they have for you!

20

Domination and Control
Run! Run! Run!

Domination and control within a marriage may as well be considered as the *'resident evil'* of that marriage, consider it the beginning of the end. There can be only one outcome for this and that is absolute misery. For a man to dominate and control his wife is the most despicable act and can be labelled as cruelty in its highest form.

For one human being to prevent another human being from living a life of freedom, the freedom to live and learn in order to grow and develop, should be punishable by law. Anyone who denies another human being of his or her freedom is a cruel, insecure, and unstable individual that seriously needs help, be it male or female. In most cases, it is the usually the male who tends to dominate and control the female, if this in fact is within his personality.

I am not suggesting that only men are dominant, because females can also be dominant towards their partner. What I am saying is that between a male and a female, if anyone is going to be the aggressor, it is usually the male and to a lesser degree, the female.

While both scenarios can be devastating, it is far more severe when the aggressor is the male directing his abuse toward the female. This form of mental, verbal and physical abuse is much more common and if you are the person being abused you must without question seek immediate professional help or at the very least speak to a close relative but under no circumstance should you allow this abusive treatment toward yourself to continue indefinitely, even if he apologies to you later, it's already too late, because nearly always, it happens over and over and over again.

Most times, when a woman is asked, *"Why do you stay and put up with this abuse?"* Do you know what she replies?

"Because I love him!"

She loves him? How can you love someone who abuses you this way? Even worse, is when they then announce *"He loves me, I know he loves me, he's just angry I did something wrong that's why he hit me."*

I hate to burst the bubble but a man who loves his woman/ wife/ girlfriend/ lover, who physically abuses her due to the overwhelming *"love"* he is feeling at the precise moment he is beating you black and blue, that is not love, never has been and never will be—abusing a woman is not love, it is the end of love!

Guys—I have a question for you—Have you ever abused your partner— in any form? Do you try to control her and manipulate her into doing the things you want her to do? Do you intimidate her? Have you ever hit your partner? If the answer is yes, I say this to you. Who on earth do you think you are that you raise your hand to a woman, any woman for that matter! How absolutely dare you think that you can do such a thing to a woman! Who's next, your child?).

Here's another question for you. How would you like it if one day, let's say, your daughter (if you have one) grows up and goes off into the world, after you have spent a lifetime of blood, sweat and tears raising her, to then discover one day that her husband is abusing her, hitting her, and using your little girl as a punching bag, your little girl! He, making her life unbearable or what about your sister, how would you feel if some man was bashing the daylights out of her? What would you want to do to that man?

Don't you in turn, become 'that man', is this clear to you? Do not become the man that you would annihilate if he were bashing your daughter/sister.

If you suffer from fits of uncontrollable rage and take this out on your partner, then please seek immediate attention, before you hurt your wife and the mother of your children.

The above is an extreme example of domination and control fuelled by abuse. Not all dominating men are abusive but they are very controlling and just as damaging to a relationship and the mental state of their partner.

You are not her *'keeper'* to determine where she can go, what she can do, how long she can stay, what she can buy, how much she can spend, and who her friends are or will be. You are her husband, not the almighty *'ruler'* where life begins and ends with you. Do you have any idea the untold damage you are inflicting on the one you claim to *'love'*. Do you understand the mental anguish you are selfishly inflicting on this person. Is this what *'love'* means to you?

How would you feel, if someone dominated and controlled *your* every move and prevented you from reaching your full potential as a human being for the simple reason that they felt threatened by your possible success.

I think I can safely say that you would not want to be in this position, so why then, would you want to mentally terrorise your partner by inflicting this pain on her. Some men think that by yelling at the top of their lungs to their partner, that they will intimidate them into submission and usually that's exactly what happens but already your life is now in a very sad place and it's all downhill from here.

From a women's perspective, let me inform you dear Mr X—that the louder you shout, the less of a man you appear in the eyes of your woman and society and you ought to be ashamed of yourself. If you sir, have insecurity issues, then you owe it to your family to seek professional help, don't punish your woman and frighten your children, who will undoubtedly grow up to hate you and because kids usually mimic their parents, they too will become *'screamers'* because this is what their father did to their mother. Is this the kind of future you wish for your children?

Of course, there is the other kind of mental abuser as well, one who uses cold calculating calm to achieve his goal. On the surface, this type of character appears to be just perfect. In front of family and friends, he appears to be by all intent and purposes a wonderful and devoted husband by, treating his wife and children (*if there are any children)* in a calm but cold manner.

The wife responds in a reasonable manner, she does not have to work, because he provides more than enough, the children are respectful and very cooperative, and everything seems great.

What the rest of the world does not see is that, behind closed doors, this man is a cold, emotionless control freak, he determines how long his wife can stay at any given place and he marks the end of the visit, by going to the friend's house and proclaims that the visit is now *'over'.* He is also the one who sees no purpose in his wife working, for no other reason other than to *'control'* her and know exactly where she is at any given time and not because he wants her to be a lady of leisure. He is the kind of person who robs another person's ability to enhance their personality by diminishing their self-worth by not allowing them to explore their potential.

Ladies—this is not the kind of situation you want to be in—I'm sure he would not have presented himself in such a way when you first met him, I wonder though if there were early signs of his sickness, that perhaps you may have missed, or perhaps you chose to ignore it.

Could this controlling behaviour have been evident right back in the beginning, was he perhaps calling you up incessantly all hours of the day and night under the guise of "Hi honey, just wondering where you are, if you're ok cause I miss you," could this have been responsible for pulling the wool over your eyes and not see him for what he really was, an insecure man with low self-esteem.

If a man is domineering, controlling, abusive or the jealous type, and has a woman who may be attractive to the opposite sex, she is an outgoing personality who attracts attention wherever she goes and is quite popular, the jealous man will feel threatened by this and it is this man who will pull the reigns in on his wife by verbally abusing her by calling her demeaning names, by hitting her, and generally making her life unbearable. Do you know why he is treating this woman in this way?

He does this to make her feel worthless (we know who the real worthless one is) because of his jealousy and the fear of possibly losing her one day. This is how this man controls his wife and places her exactly where he wants her to be. He wants to remind her of *"who's the boss,"* this is not the right kind of boss for anyone. A marriage that does not comprise of fairness, respect, unconditional love and consideration for the other person's needs and desires is not a marriage, what it will become is a kind of *'hell'* for all parties concerned and leads to a violent, empty, emotionless and a meaningless existence which will only lead to destruction for all concerned.

This is the kind of domination and intimidation that can lead to stunted personal and relationship development and which could lead on to different forms of depression for the abused.

Reaching one's goals and expanding one's knowledge is meant for everyone who seek it, it is not just meant for one gender or the other. Their life is not yours to destroy as you see fit.

Simply because we marry, does not mean we automatically forfeit the rights of one individual over the other, and just as the saying goes, our children are *'gifts'* to us, they are only lent to us, we don't own them, so to within relationships, one gender does not own the other. Each party has lent themselves to the other, if you do not treat the person who has given themselves to you with love, respect, kindness and consideration than this person, if so desired is free to leave and divorce you.

Don't think you can live your lives apart under the same roof and still be happy. Marriage is a joint affair, and cannot be worked along separate lines. Pp 19—Don'ts for Husbands 1913 Blanche Ebbutt A & C Black Ltd.

21

Who's the CEO in Your World?
You, Me—Who's it Going to Be?

As the goal of equality between men and women now grows closer, we are also losing our awareness of important differences.

In some circles of society, politically correct thinking is obliterating important discussion as well as our awareness of the similarities and differences between men and women.

Michael G Conner, Psy. D Clinical, Medical and Family Psychology

Let's have a look another scenario—

As with any business or company, there are lots of people working there, all have their own responsibilities and each role is considered important as it contributes to the overall success of a company. For most of us the place of employ has become our second home due to the amount of time spent there. We all have our own responsibilities as each role is considered important, but there is one person who has to take final responsibility for the stability and success of the business or company. In other words, the buck has to stop with someone, who's this someone going to be?

Imagine now a different scenario: Here you are at work, and suddenly it's become a place where no one takes responsibility, instructions are ignored or contested, imagine also if decisions handed down by managers were met with a refusal to comply with by staff who do not agree with the instructions issued.

Imagine if no one was held accountable. How would anything be accomplished if employees continually were at loggerheads with their managers and neither one would back down.

The home is no different? Everyone must share the responsibilities, but someone has to be considered the *'head'* of the family. So! Who's the CEO in your world?

I hear you all say, *"But there are female CEOs as well."* This is true and they make great CEOs, BUT! This is your home we are talking about, your man, your life and your future. Do you want your man to feel like a real man or do you want to rob him of his masculinity. You can be the CEO at work, but let your husband be the *'head'* of your household if you want peace in your home life that is.

After all, isn't this the title that has been reserved for men for generations' The man is the *'head'* of the household, the woman is the *'lady of the house'*, you are responsible for the running of the home and it is no easy task, if you come up against a major problem regarding the running of your home, who are you going to approach for assistance, or help with finding a solution—your husband of course!

Your husband is the *'provider'*, his role is to *provide* for and sustain his family *(irrespective of who earns more)* and ensure a safe and comfortable environment to live in. Where is the problem in understanding this? The woman is the nurturer, the caregiver of warmth, love, tenderness, and compassion.

Women are better at multi-tasking while men on the other hand can only do one thing at a time.

The point I am attempting to make is that women are good at doing some things, and the men are good at doing other things, there is no need to compare or feel inferior because woman are by no means inferior by any stretch of the imagination.

Ok, guys are better at doing some things, so what! We on the other hand excel at other things! This is the way nature intended it, just go with it.

Neither he nor she has anything to prove to the each other, what is most important is to make sure that you live in harmony surrounding yourselves in your love for each other.

Stripping your man of his masculinity is depleting him of his worth, his manhood, and this may eventually lead to problems further into the marriage. Can you honestly blame a man for straying, if your partner has been depleted of his manhood because you treat him like a puppet with the strings permanently entwined around your fingers? This may sound harsh, but it's happening.

Your energy and that of your partner could be better spent in showing him/he how important you both are to each other rather than trying to outdo each other.

How much do you want your spouse in your life? I presume that you do, otherwise you would not be with them, right!

Then go ahead and show them!

Guys—you can make life much easier for all by not taking your wives—or partners for granted, show them that even though they may be earning more than you do that you appreciate them and support their career choices and are happy if they are happy.

Never argue with your woman or blurt out in a moment of anger, "So, just because you earn more than I do, think you can treat me like dirt," or something to that effect, you get what I am trying to say here? Show some class, and reassert your self-confidence and your woman will appreciate and respect you for it.

What happens if you both share in the decision-making process? Who has the last say? Or more to the point—what happens if the two who are sharing the decision-making, cannot see eye to eye, and will not agree and neither party will budge—what then?

What *will* happen is that a battle will unfold in the household accompanied by anger with yelling on both sides verbal abuse, name calling, tears, and bitter words exchanged, one will try to demean the other, old arguments could resurface, and any *'hoarded'* complaints will also join the party culminating in mayhem and this could last for days.

The woman may continue to argue her point because she may think to herself, *"Why should he have it his way, I have rights as well, he thinks he knows it all,"* he on the other hand, may think, *"I'm not giving in this time, I'm always the one to give in, she never backs off, she thinks she knows it all,"* and so on and so forth.

What is really happening though?—The two of you are at each other because you cannot come to a mutual decision, and by being this way; you are slowly chipping away at the very framework, the core, of that which is keeping the two of you together in the first place—your love! How can there be any chance for romance to survive within this relationship when both parties and in constant battle.

Compound this scenario by adding twenty or thirty years, till one day you both arrive at—

"We have drifted apart, he seems distant, he's become so serious, he's grumpy, hardly ever smiles, he doesn't make me feel wanted, he never pays me compliments, we never do anything spontaneous anymore, we never go

anywhere together and degrades me around friends, he works back later these days, he has no time for me or the children, we hardly ever talk," etc.

He, on the other hand will state, *"I don't feel close to her anymore, we are forever arguing, any attempt I make at initiating sex is rejected but now I don't even feel like it anymore, can't remember when we last did it, she makes me feel unwelcome in my own home, I think she likes being on her own, she never smiles, we feel uncomfortable in each other's company"* and so it goes.

Relationship expert and sex educator, Dr Yvonne K Fulbright says—

"Given the shopping list of reasons for diminished or inhibited sexual desire, it's practically guaranteed that you will experience it at some point."
11 March 2009. The Daily Telegraph

It is a given then, that boredom will enter our lives at some point and the reasons for this diminished sex life, is not just about the fact that you no longer engage in sexual activity with your spouse as often as you used to. It's not just about the sex it's the whole chain of events that has brought you to this point. However, this will only occur if you allow it to happen.

You really do need to examine your entire life, how you have lived it so far how you have treated your partner, to try and determine how you got to the point where you are bored with each other and why you are not longer attracted to him/her. If you have peppered your lives with continual spats and squabbles day in day out, is it any wonder then, as to why the love and the romance have vanished.

You never want to reach the place that couples reach where one or both partners say, *"We rarely have sex these days"* or *"My wife is just not interested in me,"* or you may confess, *"I am bored, there is no excitement in our marriage and I just do not have the desire to have sex with him like I used to when we first met."* Or one or both of you could say, *"I feel empty, there is nothing there anymore."*

This is what years wasted arguing does! It's like a parasite that eats away at your soul destroying and in doing so chips away at the love you started out with, till one day, there is no more love left, and then, you wonder why you feel so empty unappreciated and unloved.

Worse still, one of you, will probably become involved with someone else, and if it is your husband who does this, you will no doubt blame the other woman, and more than likely accuse *her,* of being a home-wrecker, but she is not at fault.

It is always easier to blame someone else, for seemingly *wrecking* your marriage, but the truth is, your marriage arrived at this point based on the track you placed it on when you first started out, and if that was the fast track to disaster, then it has arrived at its' pre-designated destination. Your marriage will be what you make it and no point in blaming anyone else; you have only yourselves to blame.

If however it is you who looks for love in another man, you will probably end up blaming your husband and say that he just did not pay enough attention to you, or that he did not make you feel like a woman.

Perhaps you are both to blame, perhaps one tried harder than the other, perhaps you rejected him every time he approached you for sex and he got fed up waiting but whatever the reason, do not blame anyone else if your marriage breaks down, blame only yourselves!

How can you reduce the chances of reaching such a devastating point in your lives? Reach out to each other, stay in tune to each other's needs, and fix your problems as you encounter them, work them out together, and reach a compromise by openly discussing your concerns.

If the issue is a major one, as in financial or anything else considered serious which may in turn cause serious ramifications within your lives and you can't agree, then perhaps you should both seek professional advice, if he does not want to seek professional advice, perhaps it may be best to back down, for the sake of your sanity or wait until he has calmed down and approach the matter once again.

If this argument is all about the division of chores and of who does what in the home then for both your sakes, find a middle ground and work it out with minimal fuss. Because honestly, it's just not worth the trouble it causes. What is most important to you, as the lady of the house? What do you consider to be priceless? Is it not important to you, that both you and your husband are happy together, do you really need to argue over every issue that arises and is it worth losing the love, the mystery the romance in the long run?

Don't allow the division of chores to become a major issue—It is precisely for this reason that great importance should be placed on sorting this out to the mutual satisfaction of both parties early on in the relationship.

Set your ground rules if you must, but don't be strict or harsh and always be prepared to show flexibility of these rules towards your spouse.

The sharing of the chores or the *'who does what'* within the home should be constructed amicably, as long as it is non-life threatening, surely you can find a middle ground, talk to each other in a constructive and respectful manner. Allowing this process to degenerate into a slinging match will only contribute to your downfall, later on.

You are supposed to be in love with this person you are arguing with, what are you both going to do when real problems enter your lives?

Once again, compromise, work it out, and if all else fails, let him have the final say. It's worth it in the long run.

Dr Gordon Livingston *best summed it up—*

In fact, what passes for love between adults, more often resembles a kind of unspoken contract for services. Traditionally this took the form of an implicit agreement that the man was responsible for financial security, while the woman provided housekeeping, sex, and childcare. The women's movement resulted in a renegotiation of the contract to include the desire of many women to work outside the home and a reluctance to take sole responsibility for child rearing and household chores.

These laudable steps in the direction of gender equality, has a one side-effect: a heightened sense of resentment and competition in many marriages.

It became an article of faith for feminists that no one relinquishes power willingly; it has to be seized. This attitude is not a prescription for increased closeness. When combined with an increase in the financial independence for women, it is perhaps not coincidental that one in two marriages now ends in divorce.

'Too Soon Old, Too Late Smart' Dr Gordon Livingston

So how do you decide who does what? You can begin by preparing a list of all the chores that need to be done, be it daily, weekly or monthly basis, have a close look at this list before you talk to your husband about it.

Just bear in mind (*as you are already deciding which chores he will do*), the hours he works, where he works and what kind of work he does. Consider the time he arrives home as opposed to your arrival be sensible and practical.

Are there any children that need to be taken into consideration? Who will collect them from school or childcare? Chances are it will be you, the mother, if this is the case do not be resentful towards your husband, if this solution is not possible, then reach a compromise, remember you are both working towards the common good of your household. I have seen many men pushing a stroller in the middle of the city taking their child to childcare no doubt. Obviously in this case, the other parent was not able to take the child to childcare, a perfectly understandable arrangement.

Women do work just as hard as men and trying to fit it all in a day becomes challenging, but some men have jobs that require them to be totally focused because millions upon millions of dollars are at stake, now imagine your husband who has not slept (*because he was up all night taking care of the baby*) and bleary-eyed, off he goes to work. Do you as his wife find this to be an acceptable arrangement?

How effective and capable do you think he will be, of making those important decisions, when all he wants to do is crawl into a corner and have a nap? Don't be unreasonable with your demands on him.

You are the *nurturer,* and unless you are sick, it should be you nursing your child. It's called loving someone above and beyond—loving your child, and loving your man, and he will appreciate you even more.

It's also called *sacrifice* and there will be a lot of sacrifice throughout your marriage as it is all part of being married and caring for someone else. Look at this list honestly and don't try to palm off chores to him because you can't be bothered doing it, be honest and considerate about your decision. Once you have studied it closely, talk to your husband about it, and give him the option of selecting the chores he would like to be responsible for, you may find that he will pick some you have already mentally assigned to him (*he does not need to know that*). If you allow him to choose first, then chances are he will not mind doing them. If you force them upon him, you will be contributing towards the resentment that will inevitably accumulate in time, eventually to be used against you at the appropriate time.

Let's assume something unexpected has arisen and you require him to do that which he normally does not have to do. You have every right to ask him for assistance, but do so in a respectful manner, don't demand—ask! It is a case of give and take, *'give'* back love by *'taking'* each other's needs into consideration.

Whatever you do, think twice before you slap an apron on him the second he steps inside the door and hit him with, *"I just got home too, and anyway, it's your turn to clean."* This is not what he wants to be confronted with, particularly if he has had an extremely bad day at work. Ok, you have had a bad day as well, does this mean that you both now have to put your boxing gloves on?

He is not a child, do not turn him into a kitchen hand (*unless of course he wants to.)* Perhaps I should clarify this further. Today as never before, lots of men enjoy spending time in the kitchen. If your man is one of them, you are very lucky in fact it can be compared to winning the lottery. If your man wants to throw himself into the kitchen every night and cook for his family, good luck to him and to you, but if this is not a part of his persona, and he does not feel comfortable in the kitchen, will this mean that you will all starve—as you are also refusing to go into the kitchen for the simple reason that it is not your turn to cook?

The kitchen, primarily is or was the woman's domain after all, and if you are too tired, ask him in a positive, sweet manner, *"Darling, would you mind cooking something simple this evening as I am so tired,"* etc. I am certain that if he loves and values you, he will oblige (*providing he knows how to cook, if not order in)* but the important thing to remember here is that you do not demand this of him or order him to do it, you are so setting yourself up for a full-on argument, again more of the *'chipping away'* of any romantic inclination, love, sex, long-term happiness, contentment, which places each of you on a very sad path indeed.

By remaining calm, he will be more inclined to remain calm as well, he obviously won't be able to conduct an argument all by himself so if you don't snap back at him, he won't have cause to snap at you, and if he does, just walk away, you do not need to qualify his actions right then and there on the spot. You will only end up arguing and nothing will be achieved. If you love this person, exercise a little patience. What about the women who do not work, but still refuse to cook for their families and still expect their husbands to wash the kids, cook and clean even though the wife has been home all day?

For the rest of you who have to work very long hours, come to some kind of an arrangement with your partner in order to allow maximum use of the time you both have once you both arrive home, particularly if there are children to consider.

*Guys—you have to be considerate towards your partner—*and you too must take care of your responsibilities around the home.

*Ladies—You absolutely must plan and be organised—*when you arrive home you have the time to take care of your family's needs without all the drama. There are ways of getting around everything. Plan, plan, plan, you are a wife/mother and it is your duty to your family to take care of them in the best way you can with a positive attitude.

Since we are so good at multi-tasking, we should be able to go to work, come home and be able to prepare a simple meal for the family and still find time for ourselves as well. It all comes down to organisation. I got through it as have millions of women around the world.

We have read countless times how the women are the '*nurturers, the care givers*' but I wonder how many women are paying attention or even realising how significant this piece of information is and what role it plays within our lives. If women can grasp this concept, then most of the problems that exists within a relationship will simply vanish.

Be compassionate and understanding by reassuring your man that you are there to assist him as he should always be there for you too. You should both rely on each other (*this is a union after all)* but with respect and regard. Try not to be harsh with each other, but forgiving, in other words, cut each other some slack.

The main point to remember is, not to allow household chores to cause tension within your marriage, it's just not worth it, communicate with each other, and make sure that your requests are reasonable and be open to compromise.

Men have always been *the 'providers',* that instinct is buried deep within their DNA since the cave men walked the earth, it's the way they were made, what purpose would it serve to make them feel inferior.

If the female earns more, take care to reassure him that you are in this together, that both your earnings service the one home and most importantly, don't throw it up in his face every time you argue, unless you wish to place your marriage on the endangered or worse still, on the extinct list!

If you do earn more than he does, endeavour to make him feel good about himself by assuring him how much you love, respect and appreciate him.

Never make an issue of who brings in more money; it's just not worth it. Bringing it up is the same as liken it to an open invitation for either one of you to demolish each other's worth. Hurtful words spoken with anger are very hard to forget and all you will be doing is chipping away at your relationship and your love. Show him how much you love and need him in your life, and make him feel appreciated.

Making him feel less of a man is not going to achieve anything?

Is it going to enhance your life?—No! I can tell you right now, most men need to feel that they are the power and strength in the relationship whatever you do, don't take that away from him.

*Guys—you can assist by not taking your wives or partners for granted—*and certainly don't bring up how inferior you feel for not being the major financial contributor every time you argue, let it go! As already mentioned—Never argue with your woman and blurt out in anger, "So, just because you earn more than I do, does not give you the right to treat me like garbage," or something to that effect.

Every time you have an argument, expect that old issues will resurface, yes that's exactly what happens.

Neither sex has anything to prove to the other, what is most important is to make sure that you do all that you can to live in harmony and trust and you will both appreciate each other even more and understand that what you are really doing is SAVING your marriage.

Therefore, the key to a happy future is not in the planning of the perfect wedding day with all the trimmings—they key to a happy life is the planning for both of your future lives together and endeavouring to make your marriage become as strong as a fortress.

Unbelievably, in some cases, there are some men who stay within an unhappy marriage, even though they are the mega major financial contributor to the home, while their wives are home meeting with the gardeners and the cleaners, all of which the husband provides the funds for, she contributes nothing; yet she *'rules the roost'* and these men continue to exist living each day in fear of upsetting their wives.

Example 6—Daniel and Maggie—True Story

Daniel, a major head of a billion-dollar company, who overseeing hundreds of employees, exerts his power and authority in the work place where his word is considered law. Not to mention his earnings per year running in the millions. Now imagine this very same man arriving home arriving home to a wife, who has no regard, respect or anything for that matter for this poor soul. He fears and basically trembles in her presence for fear of doing something that may displease her. Can you imagine telling your spouse that you are thinking of taking some time off work, and to be told by Maggie, his wife, that he is not wanted at home?

Then there is the other story of how he would ring his wife during the day to inform her that you are not feeling well, and to be told, "Well, you're not coming home!" Can you imagine? How pathetic and tragic this situation is, whereby the man having a major position at work, controlling hundreds of people at work, goes home and immediately recoils, tail between the legs, head down and presents himself to his wife, who by the way does not contribute one single dollar to the household, yet this man (who exerts so much power at work), is brought to his knees at home, how can this be, and the question begs to be asked, what happened? Why is he allowing this to continue? He earns the millions of dollars; she contributes nothing, yet she is in charge. How? Better still why?

No matter which decade we live in, a man essentially wants to feel that there is purpose in his life and that he is the power, the strength, he is the provider. You have nothing to gain by stripping away the very essence of his being.

Buried deep down, underneath a mountain of studies and research, lies the remnants of what relationships used to mean and it seems that it was so long ago. It certainly was not as it is today, and while I'm sure it was not perfect then either, at least men and women knew their roles, and knew what was expected of them.

To modernise does not automatically mean the result will be for the better or a guarantee of success, nor does it mean that what's considered to be trendy or fashionable as far as relationships are concerned, is the best way, either.

By over modernising relationships, today's generation has lost its way. No one really knows what their roles are, what should happen, and what should not happen within a relationship. It's all become a mish mash of who does what.

"It's your turn to wash the kids, or cook or clean or do the laundry," she tells her husband, because she has been out working all day as well.

It is here that confusion arises and trouble begins to brew, particularly if the man has no intention, interest, is just not *him*, to be involved in the kitchen or the laundry (*unless of course you were sick and he was just helping out).*

Remember what you read earlier on, the woman essentially is the caregiver, the *'nurturer',* the man is the *'protector'*—the provider, these roles have been mixed up now and the male may be a little confused by having to perform tasks which essentially were the woman's role.

It's time to go back to basics. Don't take it personally, he is not trying to give you a hard time deliberately, it just feels alien to him, as I mentioned earlier, allow him time to adjust, and let him decide which chores he feels comfortable performing.

Ask for help, but ask it in a nice way, don't demand it and turn it into a major argument.

If you both care for each other, you will be accommodating to each other's needs and by being diplomatic you will achieve this without depleting him of his masculinity in the process.

Guys—you need to understand that while we women realise—you are the hunters and the protectors, there will be times when according to individual family situations, that your woman will need help in whatever way she deems necessary, so unless you have an absolutely valid reason for not being able to assist, then, you too can just do it!

The point is to not wait for her to ask you, observe what is happening, and rather than be asked, 'offer' to assist her. Her happiness within the home should be paramount, when your wife is happy, you should be happy as well.

Communicate, without demeaning each other and just do what you need to do to help each other within the home without quarrelling.

Let's try to regain some of that, which was lost by the modernisation of relationships, show regard, respect, flexibility and utmost consideration towards your partner.

There is no reason why a husband and wife cannot remain civil towards each other during the course of their life together; if you are open and honest and respectful of your individuality, not forgetting that the reason you two are together is because you chose each other above everyone else.

Ladies—because you have him now, is no guarantee that he will stay—if he does not want to be with you or if you drive him away with your actions. You cannot make him stay if he has become disenchanted and falls out of love with you.

Guys—of course not forgetting, that this also applies to you—if you cause your spouse to fall out of love with you due to your actions and inconsideration, then you have no one to blame but yourself if she becomes disillusioned with her marriage.

Before you begin reading the following pages, I ask you both to write a short poem, or verse or even just a paragraph on the man/woman you are about to, or just married, or entered into any form of serious relationship.

No matter how long you have been together, write a love poem about him/her. It need not be a masterpiece and it does not have to rhyme. If you really love your partner, you certainly should be able to string several sentences together, in order to demonstrate to yourself, if nothing else, what this person means to you and how you feel about him. Go ahead, you can do it!

I have supplied the title of the poem, now you go ahead and fill in the rest. Take a deep breath and visualise him/her, now look deep into your heart. What would be your worst nightmare of your partner? Pretend for just a minute that something has happened to them and they are gone, can you feel the desperation, the heartache, now imagine in an instant, that you have your partner back again, there he/she is in front of you.

Go ahead and describe exactly how you felt when you believed you had lost them and the relief you felt realising it was in your imagination.

If he/she walked up to you right now, this person that you fell so much in love with, enough to marry them, what would you say to him/her?

Example:

TODAY, TOMORROW, FOREVER

You found me so many years ago and you managed to change the course of my life
Have you any idea how it feels, to think about the same one man for the last 20 years
I don't think a day has gone by where my thoughts have not turned to you
And lingered around you for a while
I think of your smile, and I smile
I think of your lips
And I touch the lips that you kissed
I think of your heart
And mine skips a beat
I think of your crystal blue eyes
And my eyes suddenly see

170

I think of music, and I hear your laughter
I think of your arms
And I am enveloped in warmth unlike anything I have ever known
I guess what I am trying to say is
I love you darling more than anything
Today tomorrow and forever.
F.M.H.

Now it's your turn! (Write something from the heart.))

EVERY TIME I THINK OF YOU

This exercise will determine the extent of your feelings for your partner and if you have trouble verbalising your feelings directly to them, writing this poem will give you the opportunity to change that.

Put this poem or short verse in a safe place, maybe even frame it and place it somewhere you can both see it then each time you pass by it, stop and read it. Allow these words to permeate deep within your sub conscious, where they will resurface as positive feelings, which will become evident in the manner in which you speak to and treat each other.

You will be surprised how positive these loving words can be and how they can affect your mood and his and it can serve as a reminder each day as to the reasons why you married each other. One thing's certain, change is in the air, and with the passage of time change is inevitable. Sometimes the *'change'* can depend on how you have treated your man or how the man has treated his woman.

If both have treated each other well, change can be a positive experience, but if the treatment has been bad, this change will not lead to happiness.

Perhaps reading your poem every now and again will continue to remind you of your love for each other, as time and circumstances distract us from the things that really matter, and what matters is the two of you. Endeavour to stay connected by verbalising your feelings and reaffirming the love and trust you both share for each other.

Years from now, you will be able to ask yourself the question—*"If I had my life over again, would I marry the same man/woman."* Hopefully, at whichever stage of your life you ask yourself this question the answer should always be,

171

"yes!" If you find yourself answering no but are still reasonably happy with him/her, then you should be fine, but if you are not happy, then perhaps you need to talk to your partner about any issues you may have, but do so calmly, don't verbally attack each other, speak to him/her in a constructive manner in the hope that you will be able to sort out any underlying issues you may have and reach a solution acceptable to both of you.

As always, if there is physical or substance abuse, you need to seek professional help as soon as you can because your personal safety should always come first. Here then, is your opportunity for those who are not married yet, to take heed and always remember how your life pans out with your partner is dependent on both of you, not just one or the other, but both! Love each other, respect each other and always, always be considerate, forgiving and flexible, this will strengthen your relationship so that if you do have to go through adverse times *(for whatever reason)* the strength of your relationship is what will see you through your difficult time.

Time also changes our appearance, our likes and dislikes vary with the passage of time, and the things we enjoyed once upon a time now do very little to entertain us now but are replaced with something else which may give us more pleasure.

Our taste in food, hobbies, styles, music and so much more, takes on a different meaning, and along with this, *'change'* some may come to realise the person we married is not the person we want to spend the rest of their lives with but we do anyway.

This revelation may shock some, but it happens more often than we think, it's only that most don't verbalise it directly, but it emerges within our mannerisms towards each other because of this deep feeling of discontent, hence we become neglectful, disinterested, resentful, bored, argumentative, etc.

Could this be that other percentage of couples that are still together, but only just? Is this the other half that hardly ever has sex, and when they do, it is routine, boring and mundane because they are no longer, *'in love',* lost the spark but remain together out of indifference, whereby neither party cares about finding anyone else.

Perhaps they feel they have lost their looks, have let themselves go and just plain do not feel attractive anymore.

We all need to stop and think about how much we are prepared to do for our partners, while there are no guarantees, you can certainly do all that you can now in the way you treat each other, to maximise your success rate, so that 20 years on, you will remain *'in love'* with each other.

This is what is important, not the colour scheme for your wedding or how many bridesmaids you are to have, or whether to have a 2- or 3-tiered wedding cake. If you feel the need to *'worry'* about something, worry about something really important and worth worrying about and that certainly is not colours of ribbons and bows. Together, you will endeavour to make your marriage become so strong, that absolutely no one will be able to penetrate it, except the two of you. (*If anything, that's how to affair proof your relationship.*)

It's well and good to have your man say, *'Happy wife, happy life'*, but do you know the real meaning behind this? Could it be that the main reason men feel the need to keep their wives happy is because, they just want to keep the peace and not because of any romantic inclination. Basically, they do as they are told, to avoid being nagged at by their wives. Well, at least all the men that I have spoken to vouch for this and for their male counterparts as well.

Is this what you, as a woman want for your man; to keep you happy, so that you won't nag him? You do realise that this is damaging your relationship don't you! He will soon begin to tire of having to do things just to keep you happy for the sake of peace at any cost, and you will notice a gradual decline in the quality of time spent together. The day may well come when his pandering to you now, will come back to bite you in the behind big time.

He should do things for you, because he wants to, not because he *'has'* to, just to keep you happy at his and your own expense. Wouldn't you prefer to hear him say, "*Wonderful wife, happy husband, great life!*" I guess what I saying is your "happiness" should not come at the detriment of your partner.

Ladies—how many times have you ever said to your husband—"I'm your wife, not your mother?" Well then, which way is it, I'm confused, it's no wonder men are confused as well.

We keep ramming it down their throats that we are not their mothers, yet we treat them like children. We expect that they have to obtain permission to do whatever it is they wish to do to then be told, *"No you are not going, or you can't do this, that or the other"* because we the women don't want them to go off with their male friends for any form of activity (unless we allow them or we can go with them.)

If we are not their mothers, I suggest we all stop behaving as if we are and start treating them like men who happen to be our husbands. Did the priest not say, *"I now pronounce you husband and wife"* or did he say, *"I now pronounce you 'child and mother'."* Sounds ridiculous, doesn't it?

Guys—*Do not disrespect your woman, care for her, value her*—love her show her how important she is in your life and above all else, make her feel secure and show her that you can be trusted. Do not exclude her from all of your activities, surprise her by retaining spontaneity, and plan something you can both participate in on a regular basis.

Love your woman with the same intensity as you did when you first met, and it will take someone who possesses wisdom to understand the significance of what I mean by this. I hope this is you!

22

How Do You Know
If You Married the Right One?

You don't, you just hope you did! Marrying the right person is like winning the lottery it does happen sometimes to someone, somewhere.

They are the small percentage of happy couples out there that can look at each other 25 years on and profess to still be in love with each other, again proving that the strength of love can endure.

To all the people who believe they married for love, would you marry the same person if you had your life over again? If he/she is truly the right person and you are extremely happy together, then the answer must be obvious.

What if, the answer is *"No"* what then? Does this mean you have just wasted years of your life? Let's assume that you have been married for some length of time, it could be five years or ten years or longer, and your reply is *"No,"* does this mean that you are currently very unhappy in your relationship and have just wasted ten, twenty or thirty years of your life? That's a lot of life to have wasted.

Could it be that you are looking for a way out? Or are you reasonably happy, have no intention of leaving. However, if you had your life over again, would you marry the same person? Which category does your relationship fall in?

If you are reasonably happy, considering all that you both have been through and have managed to come out of it still sane and still caring for each other, then you have done very well. If on the other hand your relationship is in tatters, does this mean that you are doomed to spend the rest of your life, trying to make it work or is one of you going to give up?

The following is directed towards unattached people, this is your chance to learn from other people's mistakes so that you do not find yourself in the same situation years from now.

Hopefully, when you select a partner, you will go through your check list of what you like and dislike in another person, and while there are no guarantees, you would have minimised if nothing else, your chances of picking the wrong person as we have already mentioned it is inevitable that people change. This does not necessarily need be a bad thing, but the trick is to change *together* and for the better, and still be able to retain some of your individuality within your relationship *(which after all is the reason why you both fell in love)* which will continue to keep both of you connected to each other. If the changes that will occur in your lives end up distancing you from one and other, then this relationship will be heading for trouble.

Don't put yourself in this position in the first place for twenty years or however many years, is a huge chunk of your life to have been wasted in this way.

Can you appreciate the importance of making sure that everything associated with planning your future with the man/woman you select must be given top priority?

If I asked a married woman right now, *"Are you still in love with your husband?"* Her reply should be *"Yes."* If she hesitates and then replies, *"I think so."* I'm no psychologist, but that *shows* that she has doubts and one must ask why she hesitated and what has occurred in her life to cause her to have doubts. Her reply of *"I think so,"* more than likely means that she wouldn't. You should know if you love someone or not, you can't just, *'think so'* about anything, you must know, it should be a definite, loud and clear *Yes!*

Look at it this way, if we have several boyfriends and we pick number five, when all along number 1 would have been more suitable, what then?

Can you imagine how devastated your partner would be if you revealed to them years from now that you have nothing in common because you have changed and you have outgrown them, are going to divorce him/her.

If the person you married has changed into the kind of person you no longer like, love or desire, what will you do?

Remembering this is the person whom you fell in love with all those years ago and have spent the major part of your life with, has now changed into someone you no longer wish to be with, or worse still, they have remained the same, but *YOU* have changed because now, you feel that you have nothing in common or have outgrown your partner.

The fact is when two people decide to marry, particularly at a young age, while it is the ideal age to begin a family it's not always a good idea to marry too young as both still experiencing and learning about life therefore it lessens the possibility of still remaining together 30 or 40 years on. This is the down side of marrying too young.

On the other hand, if we began a first-time serious relationship when we are older, the down side to this would not be that it is not very practical for having children (although many do and are successful parents) it is not always the case with some couples for as we age become less patient *(although in some cases, some older people have more patience)* perhaps not as much energy unless one is quite fit and healthy.

Then *of course,* there are couples who are at the prime of their lives and able to have children, particularly the career minded with lots of money to spend and the freedom to do it *(have also cultivated a great social life)* do not want their lives taken over by the responsibilities associated with the raising of a child. They become *'selfish'* in a way, and I am not saying that there is anything wrong with that, it is their prerogative and it is totally their choice, their right.

So, it's either we are old enough to have children but too young for a long-term relationship to last the distance, or a little old for kids, but better placed to maintain a long-term relationship—which is it to be? I am completely aware that it varies from person to person and there is no set right age to marry, but allow common sense to prevail, experience as much as you can with life's complexities do all the things you want to do, see as much as you can of the world and when you feel comfortable with yourself and you feel that your experiences have enriched your life, then you are ready to enrich the life of your *'one and only'* that's when you take the next biggest step—the Everest of your life—Marriage!

The longer you allow yourself to experience all that life has to offer, the greater the opportunity you have of forming a more balanced perspective of life.

Having a mature and sensible outlook on life places you in a better position to successfully merge your life with the one you choose to marry.

Life itself is the greatest teacher, it enables us to experience and learn things about ourselves and others for with experience comes the wisdom, with wisdom comes the ability to recognise the importance of the essential qualities that will be a prerequisite throughout your life.

You need to be confidant enough to seek out the desired traits and qualities you are searching for but also possess the maturity to recognise these qualities in the other person.

We spoke about change, but now we will go that one step further here is one more question regarding 'change'. Are we to fool ourselves into believing that we are capable of changing them back to the way they used to be or can you, for that matter, change back to the way you used to be? Can you continue to live with a person whom you have outgrown?

This is the time when the marriage contract option to review and renew would be appropriate.

So, what are you to do? Must you stay together, even though you no longer want to be there? I am simply pointing out, that these things do happen and you need to assess your own life and decide what is best for you.

No one can tell you what to do or what not to do, you know how you feel and you and only you must make that decision.

Whatever the reason, you both need to weigh up your feelings and decide if there is enough love left to build some kind of future on.

Restarting an *'out of date'* or *'stale'* relationship is not going to be easy but if you are determined and committed and both have the real desire to readjust your relationship to suit each other *(if this is your true desire)* you will get there through sheer perseverance.

It may be that some couples may want to end their marriage when they realise, through fault on both sides, that they have grown apart and have nothing in common anymore because they allowed themselves, without even realising it to drift apart and fall out of love.

Falling out of love is also a part of life. It may be easy to fall in love with someone, but it's just as easy to fall out of love as well.

Every second of every minute of every day is important when it comes to your spouse and yourself, don't waste the minutes of your life that will shape your days, months and years together. Make every day count, every day you need to enhance each other's lives because it is this that keeps you bonded and *in love* with each other.

I can say with 100% certainty that I loved my husband when I married him. We moved to another part of the world where I began to notice that his character began changing and he became intolerable.

Finally, his infidelities began to emerge and because of this and the unbearable circumstances he placed me in, we divorced. I knew what I had to do as my life unravelled before me. I realised that my husband was not the man I married. Yes, I waited for twelve years, in the hope of seeing some kind of improvement, but it did not happen.

Twelve years is a long time to wait, and I would not recommend this to anyone, but I waited because of my determination at not wanting to see my children grow up without their father and their grandparents. I did not want my children to suffer in any way. Believe it or not, I also thought of his parents as well, I actually did not want them to miss out on seeing their grand children grow up.

I did everything I could to make this marriage work, I was the perfect wife to him, and by perfect, I mean, I never asked for anything, I cooked, I cleaned, I basically did everything for him, but where did this get me? Nowhere, do you know why?

The love was not reciprocated, or maybe his love was not strong enough, either that or my ex simply didn't care, it certainly was not the kind of love that one could build a future on.

Was I not someone's daughter as well, did I not have a mother who cried and wept for my unfortunate life, more to the point, did my ex-in-laws not have a daughter that was also about to be married as well?

Did they not stop to think for just one moment, *"We would never wish this kind of life on our daughter, so let's not inflict this upon our daughter-in-law."*

I could have continued to tolerate this situation, and stayed within the marriage and still be with him today, but I would have aged before my time, and my spirit would have died if I had to continue to live in the way that I did.

Should I have sacrificed my life to try and make it work, even for my children's sake? What kind of environment would my son and daughter have grown up in, one of great unhappiness and despair, and who knows probably some kind of depression on my part, which would have been brought on by my unhappy life. Was my life not as precious as the next persons?

Can I believe that one possible way of saving my relationship would have been me going off to a holiday resort with some new sexy underwear for a romantic getaway and this would have been the element missing in my life and all's good on the front!

Love cannot be one sided, it must be returned it must be given and received willingly and freely. It's called unconditional love!

In my heart, I know that the decision I made to leave was the right one both for my children, and for myself as I have no regrets because I valued my life, for I too had a right to happiness just as much as everyone else, and having reached the point of no return, I ended the relationship and took my two children and departed.

Sometimes, when it becomes obvious that there is little hope left, you need to let go and save yourself, but it has to be your own decision.

Marriage, or a committed relationship, *is* wonderful, but it's only wonderful and everlasting, if the combination is the right one and the love is given freely and returned freely, if it is not, it can be a living hell.

Hopefully, you have spent or will spend your life with your partner laying down solid foundations, and with each day that goes by, those foundations will become stronger. Understand that in order to ensure an ongoing loving relationship you need to nurture it right from the very beginning, not mid-way through your marriage not later on or towards the end, but *right in the beginning…and never stop!*

You are going to discover that one of the things you must do is accept that at times you will need to sacrifice something, if it means that your sacrifice *(whatever it may be)* will benefit your partner this of course applies both ways.

Guys—the same will be expected of you at times for the benefit of your partner, as the occasion arises. After all, this is the 'give' and 'take' we speak of.

There will come a time during your life that you will have to do something for them or go somewhere for them or accept something that they want, because it is what he/she wants, and not necessarily what you want, but at that instant you must put aside your own 'wants' and do what your partner desires. This is what sacrifice is all about and it won't be just the one time, this will be an ongoing necessity throughout your lives together.

Once the children have grown up and have their own lives, it will just be the two of you again, ready for the next phase of your lives. You now need to plan for this next stage of your life, which is even more important and can be even better than the beginning of your relationship if you have both thought and planned well for your future.

If you're thinking is *"Oh, I've been there done that, I've done everything for him/her (at least you think you have), I don't need to do anything more he/she knows I care,"* you are sadly mistaken.

Can you relate to the scenario below:—

She/he says, *"You never say I love you anymore!"*

He/she says, *"Well you know I do must I have to keep telling."*

She/he says, *"Yes I know you do, but I still like to hear it from you, never stop telling me that you love me."*

Have I made my point, you can't stop telling your partner you love them just because you think they should know this anyway, you need to express your love to them on a regular basis and never assume they should know it anyway.

If your relationship with your husband has been a happy and fulfilling one, you have nothing to worry about, but if it has been marred constantly over the years with squabbles, and arguments and the million and one things that can occur in a marriage, then I would be concerned.

Men for instance, and particularly the type who have been financially successful in business, have now this new found freedom and have the capacity to do as they please where money is no object.

They are thinking, *"Hmm, I wonder if I can still pull a chick in—do I still have it!"*

(If they start to think along those lines—they will do it!)

When men reach this point later in their lives, it could be at age 50 or 55 or even 60, they could make changes in their life that will automatically affect your life as well and do you know why? Because they are of the mentality, *"I do, because I can!"*

They could be at the local hotel enjoying a drink where suddenly he observes another woman, who has caught his attention by her outgoing personality and smiles at her, or she may smile back at him and he decides to see how far he can go with this woman. It is only human nature as we age *(and we are all getting there),* that we want to know that there is still some life left in us and we want to enjoy it. I guess this is the point that the other woman may well enter the picture *(if your man allows her to that is.)* I hate to say this, but if you have given him just cause in the past with your bad treatment of him, then he might just do it.

If he has made the decision at this stage in his life that he no longer wants to be with you, there is very little you can do.

So there it is ladies, no amount of threats or tantrums will keep the man at home if he has already decided that he wants to leave.

You cannot make a man love you or want to be with you, if he has stopped loving you and no longer wants to be there. Change is inevitable, that being the case, how many people actually stop and think about this in the beginning when they are preparing for marriage?

Think it all through and make sure that you know exactly what you are doing, ask yourself, *"Could this be the one? Is this person I want to be with?"* It is for this reason that the selection process is of the utmost importance, try, try, try, to find someone who is as close to the kind of man/woman you desire, and hopefully you will have fewer dramas along the pathway of discovering whom you really married.

If only there was some foolproof way to find the right person, but unfortunately there is not. The things we like in our youth are not necessarily what we prefer as we mature. Staying with someone who is making you so unhappy is not the right decision, should I have stayed with my husband? Should I have sacrificed my life for my marriage? Just when is enough, considered to be enough?

Don't place yourself in a situation whereby years from now you may well be asking yourself, *"If I could go back and do it all over again, would I make the same decisions and would I have married the same person?"*

The answer to this question should never be *"NO,"* for if it is, it means that you married the wrong person. You may have some feeling for him, but is it real love and will it last the test of time.

Will you still long for him to touch you and make love to you, or will you be sleeping in separate rooms, not for the mystery factor, but for the fact that you cannot stand to be near him, or you hate him touching you because he has become unbearable.

Whatever the reason, it equates to one thing, waste of two lives. Let's remind ourselves that statistics tell us that of all the marriages that take place, 40% of them will fail. What happens to the rest? Does this mean that the remainder will succeed? No! I don't think so, what it means is that of the 60% that are left, more than likely half of them live in unhappiness, be it alcohol or drug abuse or wife/children abuse, and the rest of the marriages survive on indifference. They just plod along within the realms of boredom, the usual nagging, and the usual acceptance of their monotonous reality that has become their life and no doubt they accept this because we are all reminded daily through the media that this is what happens to relationships, it's normal—oh no it isn't, not where I come from!

If it does happen to you, it is because you both have allowed this to happen, so sit back and watch your marriage crumble around you, as the years dissolve away the last memories of your wedding day and along with it all the hopes and dreams that you nurtured, what is left now is a kind of emptiness, a void that can never be filled because there is no love left.

Why should husbands spend their lives keeping *busy making sure their wives are happy at any cost, because if they are not happy, they will be deprived of intimacy or a better word for it—SEX!* Should they not both be trying to please each other, why does it have to be one sided? Is it any wonder then, that this marriage will crumble, it's inevitable!

Thought—"Why on earth did you bother to get married in the first place," or more to the point—"What kind of expectations do you have from your marriage?"

Ladies—do you still think it is a good idea to deny your man intimacy? Would it not be better to talk to him about why you are feeling the way you do and resolving it?

There is a whole lack of knowledge about what makes a healthy marriage. Spouses need to deal early on with money, sex, in-laws, deciding who is going to raise the kids, and who is going to work. Or, if both spouses are going to work, they need to decide how they are going to share the responsibilities of the house.

Elizabeth Kutner, Atlanta, GA. "The Divorce Lawyer's Guide to Staying Married" Wendy Jaffe Esq. Volt Press 2006

23

Magic!
Is It The Two of You!

This poem is for you, to help you to remember those moments or you may even have a romantic letter he wrote to you, find it and frame it, you will need it!?

MAGIC

There's magic in the trees
In the clouds and even the rain
There's magic in the wind—
That softly whispers your name
There's magic in the ocean—
The stars and silver moon
There's magic in everything—
As long as there is you
There's magic in your walk—
Your laughter and your sighs
The stars may as well fade—
When compared to your gorgeous eyes
We are the magic—I know this to be true
This magic is forever—
As long as there is you.

F.M.H.

This is the magic I am referring to—Did you feel this kind of magic on your wedding day and if so, did you take some of the magic with you, into your lives?

Let's go back to the time you met the man/woman of your dreams. Remember how this felt, how excited you became when you knew this person was on their way to see you. Those warm balmy evenings walking on the beach or enjoying a glass of wine, the way you held and kissed your man/woman in the moonlight.

Ladies—Has he ever told you, that you are the most beautiful woman in the world and how much he adores you and just you? Can you remember how wonderful you felt, how your heart pounded whenever he touched you? Do you remember the magic feeling you felt whenever the two of you were together?

Look upon this *magic* I refer to as the low GI or *'slow-release'* key ingredient that will slowly seep into your very beings to act as a constant reminder of the love you share with the love of your life. It's this magic that will keep your love from fading as you go through life together.

You spend so much time planning your wedding, from A to Z, everything must be perfect right down to the minutest detail, yet not much thought goes into planning your life that will expand beyond your wedding day. Your wedding will be all over in one day, your life together is supposed to last a lifetime, don't think that once you are married, your work is done!

As I have already mentioned in chapter eight of this book, getting married is the easy part, staying together on the other hand is difficult this is where you both need to acclimatise to each other, it's the same as climbing Mt. Everest—you need to acclimatise for both.

On the mountain, you must acclimatise to the lack of oxygen due to the increasing extreme height as you slowly ascend. If you don't, you will die.

In marriage you need to acclimatise to each other, in a way you will be ascending to unchartered territory. If you do not ascend slowly and acclimatise to each other as you go through life, you will have no life (*not together anyway.*) to go through because your marriage will not survive.

Therefore, you both need to ease into your new roles.

Allow him to ease into his new role as your husband and again I repeat myself, whatever you do, do not become his mother—he has a mother, he's left his mother, he now wants a wife, an equal partner, which also means that you should not treat him as a child by telling him he can't do this and he can't do that or whatever else he enjoyed doing before he married you.

This includes his Friday night drinks with the boys as well, whether he wishes to partake in this or not is his decision, not yours. Show him, prove to him, that just because you are married, does not mean he has lost his freedom *(he will appreciate and value you even more)*.

Let him be the one to make changes or adjustments to his activities, it has to be his decision. By using this logic, you will be diffusing potential problems, which may appear in the future thus strengthening the foundations of your marriage.

The best thing you can do is to reassure him that you do not expect him to give up the activities he loves and the people he enjoys spending time with. Don't make him feel that he is your prisoner. What's good for the goose, is also good for the gander, you too can expect the same privilege.

If you decide that his business is your business and demand that he stops it would be the first of a series of mistakes that you are bound to make and these mistakes will only serve to weaken the very foundations you should be strengthening. Learn very quickly how to treat a man and how to handle his ego.

Marriage is give and take, but problems arise when there is more take than give. You have selected the right person to spend your life with, finding a perfect balance should not be difficult.

Above all, you need to be patient, you both need to focus on each other, but it should not have to be a nightmare and you certainly should not have to resort to trick tactics in order to achieve this. Whatever you do should be done with love and for the benefit of both.

Don't give him reason to one day say to you, *"Because of you, I have lost all my friends."*

You must be willing to sacrifice something if you wish to keep your man/woman happy, with actions and the freedom of wanting to be with you through love and not force.

I have already mentioned, don't for one minute think that *"Oh, I'm married now, I don't have to try anymore,"* because the real work has just started.

Try to recall the way you used to behave in front of each other when you first met. We all know that when we first meet someone, here are some things we do and some things we don't do in front of them, correct! Well then, just because you are now married to each other, doesn't mean you have to drop your etiquette of what you can and cannot do in front of him/her.

Guys—help me out here, I think you know what I mean—right!

Take it from another woman, she does not want to hear any sounds coming from you other than your words of love from your mouth and I don't care how 'natural' any bodily function may be. There is no faster way to allow familiarity to take hold in your life than to make such mistakes. You both may think it's cute at first, but trust me, 15 years later, it won't be cute.

Ladies—the same applies to you, he does not need to see every aspect of you in the raw, if you know what I mean therefore if you want to keep the mystery alive keep your personal business—personal! Remember the mystery that you had in your relationship when you first locked lips? Never, ever lose it, believe me you will both long for this mystery one day but it will *be too late.*

The message here is if you treat each other as lovers *(even though you are married) it* means that you are nurturing the perfect environment for that elusive *'magic'* to thrive in.

Go ahead, surprise each other by all means, with some real *'together time',* but do it for the right reasons, do it because you want to spend a little time with each other because it *is* romantic and spontaneous and never stop dating, no matter how long you are married, continue to have your date nights once a week or a fortnight or better still let it be spontaneous, it does not have to be at a set time, it can be whenever your man has the inclination to take you out on the town.

This is *"your"* time with him/her right now, don't blow it!

24

Stop Acting Like a Wife
He Wants His 'Lover' Back—YOU!

Your man brushes past you and reaches out to touch you, the woman he fell in love with and married! Remember this man?

The one you couldn't wait to see, can you recall the anticipation you felt whenever you were together? He is the one you thought was the most wonderful man on the face of the earth, can you remember how you felt when he '*touched*' you then?—The elation and the lust of his hands on your body, wasn't it amazing! He must have thought you were someone very special, remember how you felt when he proposed? You were so excited and thought you were the luckiest woman in the world, I know you must have felt this way—because you married him, right—What happened? What's changed?

Can this be the same man that you now accuse of '*groping*' you as he walks past you in the kitchen or wherever inside you home?

If your man touches you as he walks past you, take it as a compliment because he obviously finds you amazingly attractive, it's because he still desires you. Imagine if he never bothered to do this, you would complain he does not make you feel attractive, sexy, and desirable and accuse him of having an affair.

If he ignored you, you would probably complain that you no longer feel like a woman. You may well say that you are bored with your love life or lack of and complain and wonder why you no longer feel sexy, well is it any wonder why?

If you value your relationship and value the man you chose to spend your life with, then rethink your attitude towards him unless he is abusing you in some way, which again should never, ever be tolerated, you really should not be turning your man away.

Be happy that he loves and admires and desires you, the woman he chose to share his life with, give him the opportunity to love and appreciate you, so if you want to feel sexy, let him touch you and give him the opportunity to make you feel loved.

If you care about your marriage and your future, do not demoralise him by making him feel unwanted through rejection. When he reaches out to touch you in his own playful way, it is his attempt to make you feel *desired,* so let him! Don't slap his hand away and tell him that all he is interested is in sex and cares precious little for anything else because eventually, he will find someone else to '*touch*'.

Would you prefer he goes and gropes someone else? Should the *'other woman'* now be considered the, *'home-wrecker'*, honestly just who's the home-wrecker here? I am certain you would not want him *'groping'* another woman. If you don't care whether he does or does not, then once again there is an underlying problem and the best thing you can do is resolve it as quickly as possible, otherwise you may as well give him your blessing to move on because even though it won't be immediate, he will eventually cave in to his desire and you've lost your man.

If you are offended that your man laid his hands on you, there is no doubt that your home is already wrecked long before any other woman comes onto the scene. He is not the stranger on the train or that questionable person at the bar, but your man and in your home, so if he touches *(gropes)* you—guess what! GROPE HIM BACK! Give him a kiss and tell him, *"See you tonight baby."*

There it is—you will have one very happy man right throughout the day, right through to the minute he walks in the door of your home and picks up where you both left off.

How many times must I say this, there has to be give and take in a relationship, why on earth would you turn your husband away (*unless of course you no longer love him*) in which case you have some serious discussions and decisions coming your way. If you love the guy, show him, and stop being such a bore!

You have him, make sure you now know how to keep him by keeping your man interested in you, not someone else and you achieve this by maintaining some form of excitement on his part.

Your man loves you and needs your attention, by neglecting or refusing to give him that which you should *both* desire, is just one more nail in the coffin that will bury your marriage.

Ladies—guys like to touch or hug their women, so let them—all you need to do is to make sure that it's always you he's touching and not someone else— For God's sake, STOP ACTING LIKE A WIFE!

People court their mistress, but not their wife. Couples need to do the same thing for a husband or wife what they would do with a new girlfriend or boyfriend. To keep the marriage alive, people need to keep surprises in the relationship.

Lowell Sucherman, San Francisco, CA. "How To Stay Married," Wendy Jaffe, Esq.

25

Have Your Own Respective
Bedrooms. Wait, *What?*

Absolutely not kidding! Hear me out—I said separate bedrooms, not separate lives, you will still sleep together, but remember early on, I mentioned that you need to take some of the magic from your honeymoon with you into your marriage *(don't leave it behind)* this is where you can put this magic to work for the both of you if only for a while.

Now, I realise space could be an issue, but if you do have a spare room, think seriously think about converting it into a second bedroom for your partner.

Now you each have your own space, you can decorate your room with mystery and romance, he can decorate his in whatever way he desires.

What you are doing early on in your marriage and remember you may not get this opportunity again once the kids arrive you are giving yourselves your own space, within your own home it's like a form of freedom but within the home. Giving him his own space to retreat to, to think in peace, to sleep in peace if necessary to have his "me" time in there if that's what he wants. It also alleviates any well into the future desire on his part to have time apart (for whatever reason), so by giving him his own personal space right from the beginning inside the family home, he won't have cause to ask for it outside the home one day. Does this make sense?

Having your own space is no longer a luxury, it is essential, not just for him, but for you as well, therefore if it is all possible to have separate rooms indefinitely go for it, you won't regret it.

Bearing in mind that once the children come into your lives, you may not be able to keep your separate rooms *(great if you can though.)* So, if you can get started on the right foot now, you would have set a pattern and this will flow through into the rest of your lives and the best part, neither one of you will want 'time out' from each other in the future, because you are getting 'time out' on a regular basis whenever you need to.

If your man wants to sleep alone for whatever reason, let him, if you want to be on your own for a night; so be it, the rest of the time you either sleep in his room or he sleeps in your room and by doing so, you allow a little romance and mystery to seep back into your marriage.

Now let's examine the romantic aspect of such a set-up. Your husband tells you he would like to have a drink with a few of his friends after work on a Friday night and asks what you will be up to while he is out with his friends. What would you say?—You could say that you are also catching up with one of the girls from work for a quick drink, but then you are going home or, you could give him a hard time and demand that he come home or that you should go out together because you are married now, etc.!

Remember, there will be many times that you will go out for drinks together that is a given and you should expect it, but you don't have to expect it every single time. Earlier on, I mentioned that you are together as one, but also individuals who besides enjoying doing things together also enjoy doing things apart, and the 'but we're married now', should not enter the equation. If you want to keep you man, then you need to assure him by your actions to be free to love you and to want to be with you. Let him be the one to make any changes to his pre-marriage activities. When it's his decision to make adjustments to his outings, without you, it becomes more effective, and he can never blame you for it, as it will be his decision.

Let's assume that he is going out with his friends and you with yours or you may choose to go straight home, so you tell him that you are looking forward to just getting home, unwinding with your favourite music wafting through your home, while you prepare a long soak in the bath, then you are going to rub your sexiest lotion all over your body and when the aroma intoxicates you, you will retire into 'your' room and Friday night being satin sheets night, you're having a glass of wine by your bed to accompany you as you drift away to some far-off exotic destination listening to your favourite music.

Remind him, that you may or may not hear him when he comes home, and invite him to try the door of your bedroom, if it is unlocked, he is welcome to enter (asleep or not), if the door is locked, "Sorry darling next time."

How quickly do you think he will down that glass of beer and excuse himself from his friends and be home, he may not even bother to go out at all and even if he did, where do you think his mind will be, there with his mates or you lying on the satin sheets? Tell him that you will be looking forward to his arrival home. He won't be long coming home I guarantee it. How can he resist you; this is just one of many other ways, you can become the '*drug*', he cannot resist and the more he gets this drug, the more he wants it, get it? He will not be able to believe his luck at having found such an innovative, sexy woman who, to top it off happens to be his wife, why would he want to look elsewhere when he has his very own '*goddess*' at home.

I can assure you, his drinks with the boys will slowly become *(while still essential)* just a little less frequent. Remember, just because you are married, does not mean he has to give up all of his previous life before you came onto the scene. It is unrealistic to assume that each party has to throw their persona out simply to become someone else because they are now married. Naturally, you will do lots of different activities with your husband, many times over, but you are still two separate and unique people and yes—you do need to do things apart as well. It's what keeps life interesting. You can actually become '*closer*', by doing some things apart. The honeymoon does not have to end the minute you board the plane and head back home. Bring back some of the magic with you and plant it firmly in your home, water it and nurture it with your love and watch it grow and blossom into the kind of future you want it to be and deserve to have.

Unhappiness in a marriage is more often the result of control by one individual over another causing loss of identity and self-respect. To those about to be married (or married), my advice is to encourage the separate interests of your spouse. Support and nurture your loved one's individuality and creativity.

Joslin Davis, Winston-Salem, NC. "The Divorce Lawyer's Guide to Staying Married." Wendy Jaffe Esq. Volt Press 2006

26

Expressway to a Man's Heart.
It's Still Through his Stomach!

No matter what anyone tells you to the contrary, the way into a man's heart is *still* and always will be very much through his stomach unless of course men don't eat food anymore!

Show me a man who does not like to eat! Show me one man who would not think that he died and went to '*food*' heaven if presented with his favourite dishes. Do you know any man that would not like to come home to the wonderful, comforting aromas of *baking and cooking* emanating from the kitchen?

I realise that time can be of the essence and if you are a working woman and don't have time to do this every night, that's ok, make it a weekend special but you still need to eat each night, so prepare something easy and simple, what's wrong with that?

If I had a dollar for every time, I mentioned this is conversation to other ladies in my presence, the first words that popped out of their mouths were, *"Oh what rubbish, the woman works as well, and women are tired as well, and why should the woman have to worry about what's for dinner when she's been out all day."*

Ok then, you can both sit there at the dinner table and stare each other down, nibbling on some take away food night in night out, oh, and when you have children, they too can sit at the end of the table with you, while they all wait for dad to come home, to either bring some take away, or the other alternative would be for him to throw himself in the kitchen to prepare some kind of dish. How does that sound?

Your man may be a great cook and he may not mind being the one to cook each night for his wife and family, but what happens if he is late coming home or away on a business trip due to work commitments? Are you going to sit there and starve? Of course not!

The point I am making is that as a woman, you need to know how to cook irrespective of whether or not your man loves cooking.

It is inconceivable to imagine that some women do not think it essential that they need to know how to prepare a meal, and we are talking about *'simple'* meals.

Perhaps you can take turns but you cannot believe that it's ok to leave all the cooking to the man, surely not! What are you going to do if your husband refuses to cook, or has no idea how to cook, or has no time to cook because he works long hard hours, what will you do then?

Enjoying the evening meal with your spouse in the early days of marriage, is just one more way of cementing your relationship, it's the together time that you are spending, making it a calm, happy experience, because when the children arrive *(if any)* life will change therefore take advantage of the precious time you have together now. Why would either partner want to jeopardise losing something as wonderful as this relationship when you both strive to make each other happy?

This is just one more way of keeping your husband interested and loving to be at home and one more way of getting your man hooked on you by giving you both the opportunity of turning your house into *'home'* a place you both want to be in. Can you appreciate the importance of this? Let's look at this from a different angle.

You have just married the love of your life *(as has he, you)* but this as we know is the easy part. The real work has just begun because now, you have to set about creating a loving, nurturing atmosphere for the both of you to grow in, to live in, and to love in.

This is how to set roots within your relationship and these roots will be planted inside your house *(with all the little things you do for each other)* and you will water these roots, with your love and nurturing, which is how a house ceases being a house and becomes a home. This is how you make your home impenetrable to unwelcome outside influence. I think we all know what I mean here.

So go ahead and master the art of cooking for your man and with your man, and whatever you do, don't listen to anyone else telling you that you should not have to do this. You do, you both do. Don't think that you have him now and you don't need to impress him anymore because you do, you both have to spend your lives impressing each other if you wish to be with the same person for the rest of your life.

Ladies—Just because he married you, does not make you irreplaceable. If you both contribute towards your marriage in a positive way, how can it not blossom and grow into everything you imagined it would be. This is how you show your man love, by doing things for him—that really count. There are many, many things you can do for him, cooking is just one of them—besides cooking being great fun, it can also become quite addictive when you discover how easy and simple it can be and the rewards are immense.

If you do not want to lose your man to another woman, and once again I stress there are many other factors that will need attention as well, begin by surrounding your man with your love, thus fortifying your home giving both of you a better chance of your marriage surviving. Whatever love you lavish upon him, you will have that love returned back to you tenfold (as long as he really does love you.) Don't just show him you love him—give him a taste of you love as well!

27

Every Action = Reaction = Outcome!

Don't get me wrong, it's not just you that has to do all the work, your husband will have to contribute as well, but his contributions will be different to yours.

You will provide the *'action'* he will react and what follows will be *'consequence'*. This process will be reverse repeated whereby he will initiate an action and you will respond with reaction followed by consequence. If his or your *'action'* is met with favourable *'reaction'* then *'outcome'* should be positive and this is what you need to *'gel'* your relationship.

This positive action and reaction within your *'home'* establishes the two of you as the architects, both laying down (*by your contributions*) the cement that is required, to build and strengthen the foundations of your home and marriage so that you may continue to build your life upon, and depending on the quality of your contributions, they should become *'earthquake proof'* foundations.

If on the other hand the quality of your contributions is of a very low standard, I guess the foundations of your marriage will never strengthen and a continual supply of these negative contributions by either party will act to destabilise the foundation of your marriage till one day there is total collapse.

It is up to you, how easy or difficult your efforts will be, as it all depends on how much you are prepared to sacrifice for your partner after all sacrifice is and always will be a part of marriage. Throughout the passage of time, there will be many more *'little things'* that you will both need to do for each other throughout your relationship and each time you do, there's one more bolt keeping your marriage in place and on sturdy ground.

Ok! Back to cooking—hopefully now that you have a renewed appreciation of the importance of cooking, you should set about polishing your culinary skills, and begin this process as soon as possible.

Find out which are his favourite dishes, invite him to come and help, but only if he wants to, don't force him to, whether or not he enjoys cooking has absolutely nothing to do with it. You can ask, but if he says no let it go it's simply not worth turning it into an argument.

Irrespective of your partners desire to participate in the kitchen, you still need to learn how to cook, and you don't have to be a master chef, just learn to cook easy simple dishes in the beginning and develop your skill in time.

Pay no heed to anyone telling you that you that you don't need to do this, or you don't need to prove anything to him, etc. Tell them in response: *"By doing things for my man does not mean I feel the need to have to 'prove' anything to him, I do this, because he is my husband and I want him to be happy, when he is happy, I am happy, because I adore him. That will put the brakes on them quick smart."* That's all you need to say to them.

There are so many cooking shows on television that it won't be difficult to learn several quick easy dishes that really will not require very much effort at all so you can have a delicious meal ready within half an hour when you know the right kind of food to cook. Salads, grilled meats, fish, quick pastas, fresh crusty bread (*shop bought of course),* a glass of wine and you're done! If you work and not in a position to cook every night that's ok, plan ahead and cook dishes that you can freeze. You can save the baking for the weekend, and yes, why not attempt to make some bread, just for the fun of it, ask your man to help, but don't demand it if he prefers not to.

There is nothing more comforting to the soul, than the aroma of a roast, or bread or a cake baking in the oven, give him these aromas to carry around inside of him every time he is out and about because these are the things (*besides his immense love for you)*, that will keep him from going nowhere but home to you.

By creating this *'aura'* of warmth, comfort, trust and love in your home you are giving him something to look forward to every evening and by doing so you are also rewarding yourself with that same warmth, comfort and love and this is the way to keep your man close to you. Certainly not through any sinister manipulative way, but by showing him your affection, in turn, you allow him the same opportunity of showing you his affection. Just one more little thing you've done for each other, and guess what? It's called love.

Don't become complacent and think that your man will always be there, whether you take care of him or not, for the odds are stacked against you. Hence, I say, get him addicted to you through your actions, and reduce the possibility of him ever wanting to leave later in life. Never underestimate your man, and guys, the same applies to you as well!

Example 7—Joanne and Andrew—True Story

Joanne (*not real name*) was an attractive girl, who never had any problem getting men to notice her, but for some reason she never seemed to be able to have a relationship that would last longer than a few months. She attracted attention whenever she went out for the night and had absolutely no trouble meeting men, which is why I could not understand why she never really had a stable relationship.

Then one day, she met Andrew *(not real name)*. He was a wealthy man, with a large home in and exclusive area. On one occasion, she was at his home visiting and the following scene was played out in the kitchen. There was Andrew, with his pots and pans, busily preparing a meal *(great cook)*, he enjoyed cooking and wanted her to get involved as well, but where was she?

She had positioned herself on top of the kitchen bench cross-legged, holding a glass of champagne and looked oh so sexy *(she thought)*.

"Hey, I would really appreciate it if you could hop down from there and help me," he said to her.

She, taking a sip of her French champagne replied, *"Darling, you know I don't cook, I just like to watch,"* as she kept on swinging her legs in front of him when suddenly he pulled her down from the kitchen bench and demanded that she help.

Being the drama queen that she was, she preceded to smash his very expensive glass, which contained the equally expensive champagne onto the kitchen floor, and an argument ensued. At this point, he demanded that she leave. She of course refused, at which point the authorities were summoned and she was forcibly removed. Needless to say, that was the end of yet another relationship.

The story gets even worse but that is a book in itself for another time. The point I am making is, that this is what happens when you try to force someone to do something they are not comfortable in doing. The situation could have been in reverse. Imagine it being you demanding that your partner put the beer down, get off his backside, and help you in the kitchen. What kind of response do you think you would have received from him?

If it can happen to a woman, it can just as easily happen to a man only in this instance you won't have to throw him out, eventually he will leave of his own accord. No matter how good a cook your man may be, you still need to know how to cook as well more so if he has no idea at all.

The other reason being, don't think that just because you look sexy and attractive, that your man will consider this enough to maintain a relationship, your beauty will take you so far, and then some substance needs to come into play, what are you going to offer him in that department?

Life will throw many, many obstacles at the both of you, some could be big, and some will be small. You may get through the small ones but how well do you think you will fare when a big obstacle comes along. These are the, *'the earthquakes of life'* that I speak of. There will be many more *'little things'* that you will both need to do for each other throughout your relationship and each time you do, there's one more bolt keeping your marriage in place.

Just because he fell in love with you and married you, does not make you irreplaceable, but the things you do together and for each other will make you both irreplaceable to each other. Never, ever take him/her for granted—You are together because you chose to be together not because you are forced to be together. Create a warm nurturing atmosphere at home, fill this atmosphere with the sounds and the aromas that will make both of you look forward to coming home every night. Allow him to feel that this is where he belongs, home with you.

Yet again, one more way of getting your man *'hooked'* on you and one more way of turning your house into a *'home'*. It's the quality of the love that you lavish on your partner that will bind you together for you will both have to go that extra mile for each other, every single day of your lives if your wish is to maintain your marriage. It really is very simple, strong foundations = survival, weak foundations = collapse.

Do you want your marriage to survive or disintegrate? Your choice—if you want it to last, you have to work at it. If you don't care and are not prepared to take care of your man and your home, then you should never have married in the first place, but it doesn't matter because your lack of input will eventually be the catalyst that delivers the final blow marking the end of a marriage you did not care about in the first place.

Experiment—Recipe for Love

The purpose of this experiment is to teach you to master the fine art of *'balance'* the balance I speak of is the art of knowing how much to *'give'* and how much to *'take'*. Sometimes you may need to *'take'* less than you *'give'*, again, this is acceptable, expect that somewhere down the track it will balance itself out.

What is this *'give'* and *'take'* that I speak of? It's the art of communication, the capacity to love unconditionally, the ability to forgive when necessary and the maturity of recognising when the need for compromise has arisen and the understanding that what you do, you do for love that you have for each other that contributes towards the benefit of your marriage.

Below is my own personal recipe and I have named it *'The Sauce of Life'*.

More than likely it will take you a few, maybe even several attempts to get the quantities of the ingredients at just the right amount as I will not be including quantity, you will have to figure that out for yourselves, but when you do, you will understand the enormous amount of effort that will be required into getting the balance of your life at just the right point.

You will be required to apply yourself with the necessary dedication into finding the correct proportions for each ingredient for this sauce but get it right and you will not only have a delicious sauce that you will enjoy for many years to come, you will also have learnt a valuable lesson.

You will have learnt that life needs to be *balanced*, and you need to be *patient*, then you will also understand the amount of focus and determination that will be required throughout your marriage in order to maintain the *'balance'* and the amount of patience that will be required to finding just the right tilt within your relationship that will keep the both of you on the same page as your life unfolds before you.

I will not give you the quantity of each of these ingredients. You need to figure that out for yourself. If you add too much of one ingredient, you will spoil the dish (*this is where you learn the art of balance*).

Think about the person you are preparing this recipe for think about how much you love and adore this person and how much you desire to please him/her. You will be required to supply determination, good intention, love, and passion. These ingredients are a prerequisite.

The purpose of this experiment is to show you that by learning to balance the quantity of the ingredients, this will also go a long way into teaching you patience, perseverance which is considered essential ingredients for life.

Think about the ingredients, each one plays an integral part towards the outcome of the finished product. Taste and smell the spices as they represent the very essence of life. Create your own miracle, and you can, it just depends on how determined you are.

Now open up your heart and let all your love pour into the sauce you are preparing.

Good Luck!

For the Chicken Stock:

Method:

Chicken Stock *(This can be prepared the day before)*.

1. 1 chicken *(1.5 Kg)* must be of good quality, organic preferred.
2. Rinse chicken with cold water and place breast side up in pot.
3. Cover chicken with cold water till water level just covers the chicken breast.
4. Add salt (to taste).
5. Bring chicken to boil.
6. Once boiling commences, cook chicken for about 20 minutes, turn off heat.
7. Allow to cool completely.
8. Remove chicken and strain stock then store in clean glass containers for future use. (If placed in plastic containers, they can be frozen as well.

You can now roast the chicken if you wish, and along with some potatoes and lots of rosemary you will have a delicious roast chicken and potatoes, throw in a salad for good measure and there's a meal for you.

Ingredients for sauce:

Butter
Sea Salt
Oil
Onion
Garlic—the rest comes straight from the heart directly to you. Enjoy!
Sprinkle of chilli
Lemon Thyme
Lemon juice and rind
Cinnamon
Crushed peppercorns
Tomatoes (Vine ripened only)

From your heart provide the two absolutely necessary ingredients to make this sauce delicious.

"Love and passion" and taste as you go to get the flavour right!

Method:

For preparation of the tomatoes

1. Place tomatoes in bowl make a small x cut under the tomato and pour scalding hot water over them and let sit for a few minutes. The skin will start to peel back.
2. Remove the skin and place tomatoes in food processor and liquidise.
3. Set aside.

- **Place a large enough pan on burner.**
    1. Add oil.
    2. Butter.
    3. Add finely chopped onions/garlic/chili/lemon thyme.
    4. Sautee, then pour in chicken stock allow to reduce a little.
    5. Add crushed peppercorns and salt (good quality) and taste.
    6. Lemon Juice (to taste).

7. Sprinkle a little Cinnamon (for this one I will warn you, be careful not to put too much in). Taste it for good measure.
8. Pour in tomato puree. Sample a small amount for taste.
9. Simmer for 10 or 15 minutes on low heat.
10. When the consistency is just right, not too thick, or too runny and all the flavours have come through, turn off heat.
11. Add a little butter and stir. The butter makes the sauce glossy and ties up all the flavours.

And there it is!

This sauce can now be either be frozen and thawed as required. If you intend of using it for dinner one evening, take it out of the freezer and allow to thaw in the fridge, when you arrive home in the evening, simply reheat in large pan, boil some pasta, drain the pasta and pour pasta into sauce, stirring gently, as this allows the pasta to absorb the flavours of the tomato base, sprinkle some fresh basil, then serve with a sprinkle of parmesan cheese or cracked pepper and for good measure, a drizzle of either chilli oil or truffle oil over the top of the pasta, and enjoy!

There it is, a great dish to be enjoyed any night of the week when you arrive home, tired from work and it's even something your husband can put together if he gets home before you do. With proper planning, anything is possible.

You deserve to receive the quality of the love you give to him. It's the little things you do for each other that will fill in the mega portrait of your life. Give your partner the kind of love you want returned and remember, you cannot manufacture it and you must never pretend. Make it part of your nature to always be open with your partner and always show your love for him/her with everything you do.

Communication is paramount followed by honesty and trust being critical, without them you have nothing.

Ladies—If you do not want to lose your man to another woman—play it smart and begin by fortifying your home. Surround your man with your love, love and more love and the only way is by you learning how to look after him. If he truly loves you, as he should, he will appreciate your efforts and you will have him for life, and you will not have to chase your friends, sisters, and cousins away from your home for fear of losing him.

To be married is not the "destination," but the beginning—it's the beginning of your journey with another human being, how happy and successful this journey becomes depends on the both of you and your treatment of each other. When you can appreciate each other, put each other first, learn to compromise and understand the meaning and value of unconditional love, then you are well and truly on a happy and fulfilling pathway in life.

28

Once a Cheater—Forgive Him
Twice a Cheater, Forget Him!

Give him the benefit of the doubt until you know for sure, but chances are, if you think he is, he probably is.

If he has been unfaithful to you for whatever reason, think about why he would have done this and you must talk to him as soon as possible.

When you approach him, as much as I know how difficult it would be to be calm (*I have been there myself*) try and listen to what he tells you, your patience will be required at this point if you expect to resolve any issues. Give him an opportunity to explain. You are not going to like what I am going to say right now, but has it occurred to you, that maybe some of the blame lies with you. Question yourself and ask yourself why he would do this.

Don't start screaming at him, no name calling (*at least not really bad hurtful names*) remember every action has a reaction, you don't want to call him horrible names that he will remember when all this is over, particularly if you are going to forgive him. Let him explain to you the why's and the where's allow him to explain to you what happened and why.

Find out what caused him to be unfaithful, give him the opportunity to explain, if he is remorseful and regrets his actions, and as long as you still love him and he you, don't throw your marriage away, give it a chance.

If he asks you to forgive him, try to find it in your heart to forgive him, as long as you both still love each other. Do not make a decision while you are emotional and distressed, you may end up making the wrong decision.

You might just end up regretting your hasty actions and remember, if you throw your man out of your home you had better hope you know what you are doing, because keep your man away from you for any extended length of time, then should you have a change of heart, he may not come back to you.

If he admits it was just a *'one time'* only, and he loves you and he will never do it again, think carefully before you make any rash decisions but everyone makes mistakes, no one is perfect it will be up to you to decide if he deserves one more last chance.

You may wish to seek assistance from a marriage guidance counsellor but ultimately the decision will be yours and your partner's as to whether or not your marriage is worth saving, just don't be in a big hurry to end it until you both have searched deeply within your hearts and whether there is enough love to rebuild your marriage from scratch.

Think about your life and ask yourself what could have happened to make him want to do this, you may or may not be partially to blame depending on your treatment of each other. It does not mean he does not love you. It may have been just this one time, a moment of weakness who knows, but everyone makes mistakes.

A friend of mine once told me, *"If I ever find out that my husband has been playing around, he is out the door, he's history, no second chances, he's gone."*

Well one day, she did find out that her husband was cheating on her; did she throw her husband out? No, she did not, they worked it out, and I am happy to say they are still together today and still love each other.

In the case of physical or substance abuse, there can be no second chances the first time is also the last time. If you are abused in any way, seek immediate professional and family assistance. Depending on how you have both treated each other thus far, and depending on the amount of damage that has occurred it may be possible to still save your marriage but only if you both want to, remember though it cannot be by force or by threats.

Guys—You need to understand that there's a whole lot of trust—that's gone out the window and it needs to be built up again and unless you are determined to go to any lengths to prove to her that you can be trusted again, you will fail.

Ladies—It won't be a happy time but if he really loves you—he should be prepared to do whatever it takes to build the trust between you once more.

He needs to persevere and you need to believe that he will. If he does it again, you have a problem. If a man cheats once, he may have made a mistake, if he cheats again, he's hooked, and he will never really be able to stop.

I would question just where is the love that you two shared, what happened, how did this happen and who is to blame? It may be his fault, but the chances are you both contributed, if only in the smallest way but it all adds up till one day, those foundations I have talked about throughout this book have been weakened so much that they can resist no more and collapse.

No one can go on forgiving a person who keeps on making the same mistakes no to mention the amount of strength required to keep on forgiving him. Once a cheater, forgive him, twice a cheater, forget him.

You deserve to be happy as well and if he really valued what he had with you, he certainly would not put you through it twice. It is easy to say what we would, or would not do if it were not our partner's we're talking about and are not personally involved, and a totally different ball game when we are involved.

Thought:

- Don't be hasty in throwing him out of the house. By this time, you would have invested a huge part of your life with his. I know it will be hard, but somehow, find it in your heart to forgive him if you still love him. Everyone deserves a second chance and certainly forgiveness.
- Be careful when seeking assistance from relatives or friends who tell you to throw him out. Make sure that they are reliable and sensible, certainly hear then out, but sometimes they could have their own agenda particularly if one or two of your *'friends'* were always jealous of you and your partner, or it could be that they did not approve of your man in the first place because now would be the time that they would be telling you to get rid of him.
- Listen to the advice they give you but listen to your heart before you decide your course of action. While it's ok to take on board the advice they may offer, ultimately, you must decide what is best for you.
- He may realise what a fool he's been and it may hit home all that he stands to lose by his foolishness and stupidity and maybe just maybe, this may even strengthen your relationship and bring you closer together.

29

It Takes Two to Tango
Are You Willing to Learn?

The children have all gone and it's just to the two of you once more. The prospect of being alone with your husband can sometimes be a little scary, particularly if you have not had a happy life together.

The strength of the foundations that your marriage was based on over the years will now be put to the test. If your married life was marred with unresolved arguments right from the beginning, and if you both allowed yourselves to drift apart mentally but stayed together for the sake of the children, then now would be the time you should be concerned, because it is not suddenly going to become a bed of roses just because the kids have gone.

There are a number of different scenarios we can examine:

- There are married couples that even after thirty-five years of marriage, or however long are still both very much in love with each other and wouldn't think of being with anyone one else for all the money in the world.
- There are couples who have had a reasonable marriage, peppered with the usual run of the mill problems, lack of interest regarding sex, boredom, etc. but still stayed together and resigned themselves to the fact that this is what marriage is all about and simply accepted their fate.

Some married couples may have huge problems *(maybe infidelity)* on either side but both decide to stay together for the sake of the children.

There are also women, who, in the last-ditch attempt to keep their marriages intact decided to deliberately have a child in the hope that it will save their marriage or prevent the husband from leaving her. Deciding to have a child when the marriage is unstable to begin with is the worst thing you can do, not only for the child, but for your marriage as well because your marriage is already in trouble, bringing a child into the picture is not going to save your relationship.

All you are doing is clutching at straws hoping that your man will not leave you, but you know what? That is the wrong reason for bringing a child into the world, and the wrong way in trying to keep a man, not to mention the selfishness on your part, because this child deserves to have the best in life, it deserves to have loving parents and it deserves to have a stable and comfortable environment to grow up in. Your child does not deserve to pay the price for the mistakes that either one of you have made.

Imagine if you did manage to keep your man through the birth of your child, imagine also, how life will be for all of you, if you still did not get along with your partner.

Can you see yourselves having spent your lives in a state of constant arguments and bickering, then one fine day, this child now grown, has left your home!

If you have used your child as the glue in keeping your marriage together at all costs, what is going to happen when this glue *(child)* has gone? Assuming that you both actually managed to stay together, in the process though, your husband has harboured resentment towards you throughout your relationship, for trapping him in this marriage, how do you rate your chances of any kind of reasonable life with your partner after your child has gone?

You simply cannot trick, trap, threaten a partner, or use emotional blackmail, nor having a baby to act as a *'marriage retainer',* it will not work, or at least it may work for a while, but D-day is coming, wait for it! If you do have a problem with your relationship, then work to sort this out to the satisfaction of both, before you bring children into your lives, having kids will present its own challenges, heartaches and dramas that goes hand in hand with raising children, and this will require the efforts from both of you, therefore the last thing you want to be do is try to undertake these challenges while you are both fighting your own demons that will be poisoning your marriage and destroying your child…

Just how much can you handle? Do you really need the extra stress that is associated with bringing up children while also trying to *'mend'* your marriage?

Fix your relationship first, and only when you both feel that you can move forward together, then and only then should you consider bringing children into the world.

Ladies—remember all the things I wrote about in previous chapters—from this book as to the reasons why it is imperative that you treat your partner with love and understanding right from the beginning?

The reason being is you both need to land on the same page after you children have left, if you are not, he will be going one way, and you the other.

Guys—the same applies to you as well! If you are not happy with your life—or the direction it is heading, talk to your partner discuss and resolve your issues.

If you love her and do not want to lose her, then fix it quick! If one loves and the other does not, you have serious issues to resolve, therefore do what you have to do now, rather than lead her on only to leave the marriage later. Work it out, or move on and do not waste her life, or yours, both of your lives are precious and are meant to be lived within the confines of love and happiness, not despair and heartache.

30

Are We Meant to Be With the One Person
The Rest of Our Life?

If the person we marry is meant to be *'the one'*, why then do so many people divorce and find *'the one'*, the second or even the third time around.

During our lifetime, most will have had several boyfriends/girlfriends (*give or take a few*) and depending on what fate has in store for us (*if our marriage was not successful*) we will continue to meet others during our later years as well, however let's look at the boyfriends/girlfriends you meet during our youth.

How can we know if we have selected the right one, after all we must have liked something about all of them to have dated them in the first place right? What was the defining reason that made *you* pick one over the other?

Could it be in fact, that perhaps, just maybe, we may have allowed the *'right one'* to get away? (I think here we can refer back to the checklist mentioned in previous chapters, of what it is you seek in a potential partner. What are the traits that you need to look for when you begin dating).

I look to my own experience for example. I married the man I loved, so why am I still not with him? I think it's a case of 'wrong person at the wrong time of my life'.

I was far too young to know what I wanted and what love was. How could I possibly have known what it meant to love someone, when the only love I had known was that of my siblings and my parents, loving a man is a whole different ball game.

So, what happened to all the love I had for my husband all those years ago? The point is, I married for love; you married for love, yet some end up in the divorce courts and others live to see another day—Why?

If you do spend your life with the one man/woman and it lasts forever, consider yourselves fortunate indeed, but which *one man/woman* is the right one? Could it have been the very first, or was it the second one that you were in love with?

Sure, there are people who have only ever loved one man/woman. I personally know a woman who has only ever been with one man and that is the man she married and still is with him *(can't help wondering if she is truly happy because appearances can be deceiving.)* She is destined to wonder if in fact he was the right one, or was someone else meant for her? Can you imagine knowing only one man in your entire life? Then again, perhaps she is truly happy and that would be wonderful! People have been known to marry their childhood sweethearts, and are very happy and contented in their marriage.

Example 8—Peter and Helen—True Story

Twelve months after Peter *(not real name)* married his childhood sweetheart Helen, 12 months later they divorced and do know why? They discovered they had nothing in common! That bit of information would have been handy before they decided to marry.

There are others who marry their childhood love and may be reasonably happy, but spend the later years of their lives wondering what else was out there, what have they missed out on—*what if* there was someone else they were meant to be with and never gave themselves the opportunity to explore what life had to offer them.

You may say, *"Why don't they leave?"* Perhaps they may not want to leave because they are afraid of the uncertainty of the unknown because while they may not be madly in love with their partner, there is a certain comfort level they have reach and they may not want to rock the boat or risk losing what they already have for something that holds no certainty a *fear of the unknown.*

It's like a person who has been released from prison after thirty-five years, some can handle it and some can't as they have become too used to a certain way of life behind bars and have lost touch with the outside world. It's referred to as being *'institutionalised'*. The prison system is all they know, and the only place they can function, it has become home for them, if they were ever released into the world, they would be lost.

Unless they had family or friends that would support them to settle into a new environment their chances of making it on the outside would be limited.

So too for some people who have only ever been with one person and are used to a certain way of life, they feel secure even though they may not be entirely happy.

These are all the different scenarios that you should be made aware of. Which category does your relationship fall in, and do you ever wonder if there was someone else out there that you should have been with?

This is why it is essential to not rush into a commitment just for the sake of committing. Become a well-rounded person with life itself, experience life, taste life, do whatever it is you want to do, meet different people, stabilise and *'ground'* yourself, you will know when you are ready for a commitment and you will be balanced enough to find the one that suits you.

The worst thing you can do is commit to another person, then spend the most important years of your life *(when you should be concentrating on your partner, your home, your family),* yearning or wishing you had made different choices or wondering, *"What would life have been with John or Paul or Peter?"*

Don't rush into marriage only to spend the rest of your life struggling to make it work. If someone has to force you to commit—*YOU ARE NOT READY! Therefore, don't do it* and the other person doing the *'forcing',* you have no right to force anyone to commit to you either. If they want to commit, they will not need prompting by you.

There are so many different scenarios, some things that work for some couples and those same things that don't work for other couples, trying to pinpoint the perfect path one should take is like trying to walk to the stars, but by god, get it right and the view from up there would be spectacular.

The passage of time, has allowed me to experience and appreciate life with all its complexities and possibilities and in doing so am better able to understand myself, who I am and the qualities I am searching for in another human being.

Where oh where was this wisdom, when I needed it?

Marriage is wonderful and sacred; but if you marry the wrong one, it can be hell on earth.

31

How Does it Feel to Have Him in Body
But Someone Else Has His Heart?

For far too long the *'other woman'* has been the nemesis for millions of wives or partners around the world and each time she is portrayed as being an evil, deceiving slut, nasty, desperate, manipulative, home-wrecker, bimbo, besides also being ugly with a vulgar dress sense to boot. Maybe there are some women out there who do possess some of these characteristics, but not *all* women are like this.

The *'other woman'* may or may not know if the man is married, what is important though, is that *he (your man)* knows and remembers that he is married, and I'm sure if he valued his wife, life and home, he would not be playing Russian roulette with his life. I realise there are some very silly foolish guys out there that have it all yet still pursue the other woman, but that goes back to what we have already talked about, they are bored with their life and need some excitement, that's why!

The sad fact is though, that men do risk all for that fleeting or elusive excitement and without thinking too deeply, they find themselves saying, *"Well here's a woman who turns me on so why not."* If a guy believes he can get away with it and if you have given him just cause to do so in the first place, then he won't say *'no'* to the opportunity of having a one-night stand or any other type of relationship with any woman.

Even if he is approached by another woman who may proposition him, that is still no excuse for a man to take her up on her offer, unless of course he wants to. I'm sure the other woman is not holding a gun to his head and forcing herself upon him. He will do this only if he wants to do it, and more often than not (believing he can get away with it, he will).

He will go ahead and do this, only if *HE* wants to because you as his partner have given him just cause to do so. Knowing this now, who are you going to blame now?

Do not for one minute think that this *'woman'* has nothing better to do but to pamper herself from morning to night, then dress herself in expensive clothing, heavy with the makeup, perfume, jewellery and off she goes for a night out just to get *your* man. It does not quite work that way.

No doubt there are some disturbed women out there who may fit the above description, but not all women are like that, there are many, many women, who are normal everyday kind of people who go about their daily lives just like everybody else.

You also need to know that most of the time, it's not the woman who approaches your man, it is more likely that your man approaches her and here's another shock for you, some of the women are decent, kind, loving, generous women who are simply out minding their own business and having a good time with their friends. Who knows what's happening in *their* lives right! They may be distressed about something in their life, they may have lost their man through infidelity they may be unhappy at home or work, they could have any number of worries or problems that they are going through so there they are having a drink at the bar, and your man comes along and starts to chat to them. *Why?*

Don't condemn *her*, for sleeping with your man, blame yourself first, then your man for either being straight out deceitful, or if there was a problem at home, for not taking the time to sort it out (*or maybe he tried, and you would not listen to him)*. The variables are many, but don't blame her, it is not her fault, she's not the one who is married your man is, and what if, she was not aware because he lied to her re-his availability status at any rate, what then?

This is not *'Fatal Attraction'* they are not bunny boilers and it could be that your partner is the one who won't let *'her'* go, not the other way around.

Imagine how you would feel if you found out that, your man is seeing another woman whom he has fallen in love with, and this woman wants to end the relationship and it is *your* man, who talks her out of it. Your man who says, *"No, I don't want it to end,"* how would you feel? My point is, it's time to stop blaming the other woman, and look to yourselves for the answers as to why this happened.

Something else—every single one of us, have the potential *(given the right circumstances)* to be, the *'other woman'*, depending on our frame of mind with what is happening in our own lives at the time.

Stop the blame game!

Example 9—John and Rebecca—True Story!

John *(not real name)* approached Rebecca *(not real name)* in a hotel one night many years ago and their lives changed forever.

They had seen each other many times on previous Friday night drinks, and were introduced by mutual friends. On this particular night, he approached Rebecca and after exchanging a few niceties, asked her out to dinner.

"I don't go out with married men" was Rebecca's response.

John promptly replied, *"Sure I'm married, but I wouldn't mind taking you out to dinner."* Now if he valued his life and wife, why would he put all of this on the line, just to take someone else out to dinner.

What happened to them? Well, they both fell very much in love.

It's interesting to note that this gentleman has throughout his life, beginning in his mid-20s found it difficult to remain faithful to one woman, but since having fallen in love with this lady, he had no interest in any other woman.

This is a most unusual situation, he does not have a problem being unfaithful to his partner, but he simply cannot cheat on the other woman because he has absolutely no interest in anyone else.

What does this say to you, ladies? John, being a friend for thirty odd years, has confided in me also that most of his male friends who are all in their 50s or 60s, all have girlfriends, besides the *wife* at home.

I spoke with him and asked why he was doing this and his reply was, *"I feel more alive, I am happier at work, I have become more aware of people around me, I used to hear the sounds of music but never really listened to the words, she has opened up a whole other world that I thought was not important or even existed I have come to realise that it is important and I thank her for opening my eyes and heart to it. I did not know what I was missing!"*

"Thank you, John, for giving me permission to use your story!"

There are many women, wives, girlfriends, who have caught out them men and still hang on to them, unbeknown to them that their man is *still* seeing the other woman, yet they hang on to him believing that all is well. All is not well ladies.

To the women who cling on to the man, knowing that this man may love someone else, I ask you—

How does it feel to know that though you have him in body?
When someone else has his heart!

Would you want to hang on to a man, if you knew that there was a possibility he may be in love with someone else?

I know I wouldn't!

32

Don't Want 'Her' in Your Life?
Treat Your Man like a King!

Never forget, if a man wants to stray, no amount of checking up on your part, will deter him. For instance, you may call your husband during the day for the express purpose of checking up on him, and at the time of your call, he could actually be in bed with someone else as he takes the call from you. How are you actually going to know where he is at that exact moment therefore what purpose did it serve calling him to check up on his whereabouts?

Your man was with someone else, so now you, his wife, have hung up the receiver, enveloped in a false sense of contentment and secure in the knowledge that all is well. What did your call prove? Absolutely nothing!

It simply reaffirms that a man will find a way to do whatever he wants and as I mentioned earlier, unless you are prepared to handcuff yourself to him, you will never be able to know for sure, what he is up to. He will find a way, if this is what he really wants to do.

Allow me to repeat this…if you want to avoid this happening, you both need to do the right thing by each other right from the start of your marriage, love and trust each other and always be there for each other. Find your own brand of remaining *'in love'* with your partner then put it into practice and never stop.

If you can do this every day of your lives, then he would have to be an absolute fool to do anything, which would result in losing you. You can always say to him jokingly of course, *"Honey if you ever fancy another woman and you feel like sleeping with her, can you tell me before you do, because I might like to try this with another man."*

This comment, would have a bigger impact than you telling him, *"If I ever find out you have slept with anyone else, you are history, it's over, gone!"*

Threats like this will not deter, but give him a verbal taste of his own medicine *(in jest of course)* and watch how he will think twice about his actions.

While men like to think they can have anyone they like, they certainly don't relish the idea of some other man doing the same with their wife.

So you see, the other woman can be someone who has to get up every morning and go to work—9–5 job, then go home and look after her family.

She may be divorced, she may have never married, or she could be an unhappy wife at home. She could also be a wonderful person, talented, happy, warm and caring, passionate, compassionate woman, with whom your man or any man could easily fall in love with, because he will discover in *her*, what has long been searching for and missing in you.

I make no apology for the shock factor, because this is the truth, you need to know that if your man strays it may well be because he found the kind of love and understanding in another woman that he always hoped or thought he found in you.

You need to make sure that you and only you are all of the above mentioned. You must be the warm, loving compassionate woman, who greets her man, looking the best you can be, nothing wrong with a little splash of perfume either.

Pamper yourself and take care of your appearance, but when was the last time you made sure that your man received a little pampering as well? You visit the beauty salon so you can look good, why not give your man a facial, or send him off to a professional and while he's there he can have a manicure as well. Don't be busy just taking care of yourself, think of him as well.

Here is a story, which while it is slightly amusing, it is also sad:

Example 10—Phillip and Rachael—True Story

Phillip *(not real name)* chose his bride then again, some parental influences on both sides would have also played a part because, Rachael *(not real name)*, his betrothed was a virgin as was the requirement that her background and culture demanded.

The day of their wedding came, and off they went on their honeymoon, which simply meant time on their own, not necessarily going anywhere in particular.

On the wedding night, Phillip was in for a surprise; no more of a shock actually for when the time came for Phillip to consummate the marriage the moment of truth had arrived. Rachael was not only a virgin; she had never had any part of her body waxed. She only ever shaved her legs and that's it! Waxing or shaving anywhere else on her body was considered to be non-essential—need I say more?

There was no consummation of any marriage occurring on this night. Poor, Phillip was so put off with what he saw that there was no way he was going to have sex with her. Rachael was in severe and urgent need of earth moving equipment to move in and clear up the thick impenetrable overgrowth which covered her lower region, we are talking *'black mat' here spanning from one thigh to the other and everything in between!*

The next morning, he pleaded with her to book herself into a beauty clinic and have some of it waxed, at least enough for him to see his way around, but she refused. Rachael's argument to him was, *"Why can't you accept me the way" I am* she said, *"This is the way God made me!"*

Try as he may to convince her that there is nothing wrong with a little waxing on the body, she continued to refuse, and nothing was done about it.

It has been at least a year now, and as this couple's religion does not condone divorce, he has remained with her but his heart is broken. Their sex life has dwindled down to zero, she remaining adamant that he accept her the way she and continues to refuse any form of waxing while he has resigned himself to the fact that this is how it's going to be from now on. Phillip is too embarrassed to approach her parents, as this is certainly not something one talks to her parents or anyone about.

He has indicated to a few close male friends, that if something does not change, he will be forced to resort to cheating on her with other women. No doubts if her parents ever found out, guess whom they would blame? Certainly, won't be their daughter, even though she inadvertently, is the cause. It must be hard when one comes from a strict background or culture and having led a very sheltered life, but if she only knew the damage that is being caused to her marriage, I wonder if she would reconsider.

Perhaps with time and patience on Phillips part, he may eventually be able to convince her to do a gradual waxing, however I hold little hope for this as trying to change a person's ways or beliefs is extremely difficult and we have already discussed that you cannot force a person to change to suit yourself.

Good luck Phillip, I hope you will be able to work it out.

Ladies—Try to be more flexible and sensitive to your husband's wishes— as long as they are not unreasonable. You may one day need for him to show you that same flexibility. Don't neglect him, give him the attention he seeks from you (it may be a while in the making) but if he does not receive it from you, he will find someone else to give him the attention he seeks. Treat him like the man he is and give him the love of a woman—his woman—that means YOU!

So go ahead, give him a kiss on the cheek when he arrives home. He may be tired, hard day at work, in a bad mood, has a headache, you be there for him and just plain take care of your man!

Don't start complaining about how tired you are and how you can't be bothered with cooking anything, and "Anyway, it's your turn to cook, or wash or do the laundry," while you sit there and do nothing you will be asking for trouble. You have the opportunity now to take care of your man—try fixing it when it's too late—is too late!

Yes, married women have affairs with married or single men, and single women have affairs with married/single men, but what we should all be aware of is that, they are normal everyday women/men, just like you with the same desires, fears, anxieties all searching for that love of a lifetime.

No man can be 'taken'…unless he wants to be!
No woman can be made to stay…if she wants to leave!

Points to Remember
- Don't treat him like or a child, you are not his mother. You may be his wife but he still wants that *'woman'* he fell in love with.
- Do not begin or end the day with an argument.
- Do not send him to work in a bad mood as a result of any argument/disagreement because you are placing your relationship in very dangerous territory.
- Do not nag him.
- Get this combination right and you will become the d*rug* that he won't be able to live without, let him get addicted to you—not to her!

If you want to be treated like a Queen treat him like a King!
(You'll be glad you did)

Shifting blame elsewhere may give you some temporary satisfaction, but this won't solve your problem, when the problem may be *your* treatment of him.

It may be his fault, it may be your fault, it may be both your fault, whatever it is.

Understand this, if you continue on this destructive path, and continue to be at each other's throats and forever arguing about every single little thing that life throws at you, then perhaps you two should not be together anymore.

Before your life takes this kind of turn, look around you, your lives, your home, is there anything happening right now that you fear may lead him astray.

Is there something that has been an ongoing issue that needs to be resolved, if there is, do it as quickly as possible, do not allow it to stagnate any longer sort it out now.

Give yourselves the opportunity to be happy at whichever stage of your marriage you may be at, and if both of you are truly happy, then why would either one of you do anything to jeopardise this happiness.

If you have reached a point in your relationship and you have not been happy for a long time now, search your heart deep down inside you must know what you want.

Whatever the answer to this is, you need to have an open and frank discussion with your partner without delay and resolve your issues whatever they may be.

Hopefully there will be enough love there to enable to two of you to get through this but this time really listen to your partner, understand what he/she is asking of you and have a clear understanding of what you both expect from each other.

Guys—Irrespective of the fact that you may or may not be from mars—I ask you, "Do you love your wife/partner?" Very simple question really no matter which planet you come from, "Do you love her?" Oh you do! Then you had better get busy bridging that rift between you by communicating with your wife, and try to understand how she feels and where she's at in her life. Recognise her fears, wants and desires and be prepared to accommodate her if need be.

Ladies—If you are going to give your relationship another chance—begin by letting go of the past, and in doing you elevate yourself and your partner to the next level with renewed love. When you re-energise yourself, you re-energise him, this is turn will give you the stamina to move forward with renewed hope for your future together.

Begin by putting back a little of that mystery we talked about, sprinkle some of that magic I suggested you carry forward from your wedding day, do you remember? This is the time in your life that you need it. Reinvent yourselves if you have to, if you have made a commitment to recommit, then you would both want to try anything that will assist in your reconnection only this time it should be on a much deeper level.

Do not pressure him/her, don't nitpick on trivialities, love him/her and remind each other every day, in every way, that he/she is the most gorgeous man/woman alive and how lucky you are to have them. If you both give to each other, more than you take from each other—How can you go wrong?

You chose to marry him/her, above all others, so go ahead and ignite that passion once more and your partner will follow suit.

The above is all good as long as both husband and wife have decided to revisit their love but if either one has concluded that there is no desire to try again particularly if either party has fallen out of love, then fighting for your husband/wife will prove to be futile if not already too late particularly if either party loves someone else.

If your partner no longer has the desire to be with you, more to the point, if they have fallen out of love, you cannot force this person to *'want'* you, or love you again?

(Perhaps you were never meant to spend all of your life with the one person?) It can happen!

Depending on individual circumstances, if too much damage has been done, it might be better to start a new life with someone else and hope that you have learnt from your mistakes first time around and promise yourself that you will never make the same mistakes again.

Once, a long time ago, I thought my life, my dreams and all that I hoped for, were lost forever when my first marriage ended. I was wrong—the best was yet to come!

Some may reach a point where the realisation that your marriage is over becomes reality, as hard as that is *(take it from someone who has been there twice)*, be sad, but don't despair, because there maybe something better waiting for you around the corner. This *'corner'* took me twenty-five years to get around, but it led me to a love that is the love of all loves!

To him I have given every ounce of my love, there is nothing I would not do for him. As I see it, I had to end a twelve-year marriage, walk away with two small children and in doing so, placed myself on a pathway with many detours, some good, some bad, but all paths lead me to where I want to be right now.

The love and the passion you felt for each other when you first met is the 'pilot light' that will enable the two of you to continue on through life together.
Never allow that pilot light to extinguish!

33

Can an "Affair" *Save a Marriage?*

"There was an article published in the Daily Telegraph recently on Mira Kirshenbaum, who is the clinical director of the Chestnut Hill Institute, a psychotherapy and research centre in Boston, Massachusetts, she is also the author of 'When Good People Have Affairs'. Ms Kirshenbaum who has over 30 years' experience as a marriage therapist, says the 'right kind' of affair can be a positive thing, acting to jolt people from their inertia."

Ms Kirshenbaum, reminds us that her book is not aimed at—

"Creeps who think they can cheat with impunity, but at decent people who know they have made a mistake."

"These people are suffering terribly and need to be relieved of their sense of guilt and shame because those emotions are paralysing," she said.

"You could think of it as a radical but necessary medical procedure. If your marriage is in cardiac arrest, an affair can be a defibrillator."

By Laura Clout—Daily Telegraph, 26 August 2012

I see it more as, "If your marriage is in cardiac arrest, an affair will be equivalent to switching off the life support machine, it will flat line, in other words—Dead!"

No doubt there are women out there whose husbands have had affairs.

Ladies to you I ask, how many believe that your marriage was *'saved'* because of the affair? Are you even with their husbands and how many of you are happy now that your once ailing marriage having been *'helped'* by the affair is now on steady ground and you are living in matrimonial bliss?

Perhaps there is a particular kind of situation within a marriage that may be helped by an affair, but try as I may I simply cannot come up with a suitable scenario. Perhaps if a couple is young and inexperienced and one strays for no apparent reason other than the opportunity was there and he took it, not realising it was a mistake but even then, something is amiss, can they be that immature and foolish? If they are they should never have married in the first place.

Maybe they are the ones who would also be suffering from *'guilt'* because there are gentlemen who do go down this path who are not only NOT suffering from guilt, but they happily carry on their *'affair'* with the one woman for many, many years.

Hence, I do not believe that *'affairs'* can save a marriage, the only way to save a marriage is to not allow it any cracks to manifest themselves within your marriage.

For a marriage to be in trouble means that one of you or both of you is doing something detrimental to each other, be it in the way you speak to each other, the way you treat each other in general. It means that one or the other is not satisfied at home for whatever reason and feels the need to look *(for whatever is missing in their relationship)* at home, outside the home. Therefore, what it all boils down to is what I have been saying in the previous chapters.

If you do not want this to happen to your marriage then you both have to do everything you possibly can for each other from the second you say *"I Do"* and for the duration of your life together to never take each other for granted and treat each other with love and respect, be thoughtful, considerate and understanding. You basically have to become a saint in order to get through the rest of your life with the one person. If you do not wish to do all of the above, then you have *'affairs'* to look forward to and you needn't worry about blaming just the *'cheater'* for more often than not, you too would have contributed to your husband's philandering whether in a big or small way.

Rather than ask yourself, *"What am I going to do about this?"* once it's happened.

How about not allowing it to *'happen'* in the first place.

Do not blame *'the other woman'*, blame yourself!

34

Until Death *Do Us Part!*

Marriage Vow 1

I, __take you ___to be my husband/wife I promise to be true to you in good times and in bad, in sickness and in health. I will love you and honour you all the days of my life.

Or the American version, which read as follows:

I, ___take you, ___for my lawful (husband/wife), to have and to hold, from this day forward, for better, for worse, for richer, for poorer, in sickness and in health, until death do us part.

Wow! I l love those vows, they always bring a tear to my eye because they are the perfect words for the perfect love of two perfect people pledging total, perfect commitment. Marriage vows are sacred but is it just me? What chance do these *'perfect vows'* have of surviving in an imperfect world with less than perfect human beings who may be fraught with self-doubt and insecurities? How can religion or society expect imperfect human beings to abide by these perfect vows? (Perhaps this is why so many people write their own vows, but even so, somewhere within these vows too will be some kind of pledge to love each other forever, etc. and more often, it never lasts.)

Let's take a closer look at the traditional vows and see what relevance they have in our lives today.

Marriage Vow 2

"I. ...take you...to be my husband/wife."

No problem here! Certainly the names of the two who are about to be joined in holy matrimony, needs mentioning.

Marriage Vow 3

"I promise to be true to you in good times and in bad, in sickness and in health."
(American Version)
"To have and to hold, from this day forward for better, for worse, for richer or poorer, in sickness and in health."

This is all well and good, assuming that during the course of the marriage he will be good to her *(bride)* so that this love will continue and yes, she will certainly be there for him in sickness and in health in good times or bad. On the other hand, if he became sick and the marriage was *not* a happy because of abuse or violence, or if the bride lacked any conscience, I can't see the bride sticking around in sickness or in health, in good times or bad, and if she did it would be out of guilt or fear and not because she really wants to be there. Sad—but true!

Marriage Vow 4

"I will love you and honour you all the days of my life."
(American Version)
"Until death do us part."

As long as she has not been mentally or physically abused and as long as there is no drug or alcohol abuse and she has never been attacked or beaten or disrespected, yes, she will love him all the days of her life!

If both spouses are happy with each other and treat each other with respect and understanding for the rest of their lives and if any disagreements do arise *(and they will),* that they handle it and never let the sun go down on them without resolution and forgiveness, in order to continue loving each other every single day of their lives.

'*Forever*' in love—does not mean '*forever*' in misery.

Now let's look at the vows in their entirety from both the Bride's and the Grooms perspective.

Marriage Vows

"I. ...take you...for my lawful (husband/wife), to have and to hold, from this day forward, for better, for worse, for richer, for poorer, in sickness and in health, until death do us part."

Yes, you are my lawful husband, so I guess this means that I as your wife will be treated with respect and you as my husband will not do any unlawful things to me like, mistreat me in any way shape or form, as mentioned above.

If we become poorer in wealth as long as you have been good to me and we love each other, we will work through his financial disaster, just as long as you my husband have treated me well and always with love, so I as your wife, will be by your side to support you in any way that I can, till our lives are whole again because if you, as my husband have not treated me with love and respect throughout our marriage and you have beaten and abused me, I will not be around to suffer any more should another disaster befall us... If there are children, then the kids go with me as well.

***From the Groom's perspective*—Yes, you are my lawful wife but—**if you take from me my freedom and expect that we will forever live happily basking in each other's glow and believe that I will accept this, I can tell you now, I will not.

Furthermore, if you as my wife neglect me during the course of our marriage, and nag and torment me, disrespect my family and friends and expect that I will accept this, I will not, and if you as my wife will use our intimacy as a bargaining weapon against me and pretend to be asleep when I come to bed and continue to say no to me, then don't expect that I shall remain faithful to you.

If this continues throughout our life, then I, as your husband will be forced to seek solace elsewhere.

I on the other hand am still trying to get my head around the vow *'For better or for worse',* can someone please explain to me exactly what does this mean? *Worse* as in how? Worse, as in an unhappy marriage due to constant arguments leading to infidelity, *'worse'* as in drug or alcohol abuse, *'worse'* as in being married to a wife basher and putting up with it, and what does, *'Until death do us part'* mean, *'death'* as in when the alcoholic and drug induced husband murders his wife in a drunken rage while his terrified children cower under a bed?

There are couples that will stay together for the rest of their lives and death will indeed part them This will happen either when one party dies of old age *(unless there is terminal illness)* perhaps they have been together during the good and bad days but always in love with each other and basically, they have grown old together but these couples are far and few in between and the reason they continue to stay together till one dies, is because they've never stopped loving each other.

Death will be the force that parts them because they have no desire to be with anyone else, and even though they may have fought during their lives, they never stopped loving each other, therefore the vow, 'until death do us part', applies to such couples, not to the abused and violence fuelled relationships. These special couples had enough love in their lives during the good times to get them through the bad time, that's the difference!

As I mentioned earlier the only time *'death'* would part couples living in violence is when one party has killed the other in a drunken rage. It happens!

"For Richer, For Poorer."

Hands up, who dreams of getting married and not mind becoming poorer for it? No one wants the standard of their living to drop we all expect to better our lives, don't we? Don't you? I fully understand that adverse things happen, the global financial crisis sent millions of people bankrupt and many lifestyles changed but we pick ourselves up and try again, no one would just sit there in poverty without working harder to recoup financial losses, we would try again and get back to that same place because let's face it, we cannot live without money, we all need it, everything we do costs money. The old saying of money not buying happiness really makes me laugh.

The people who say this are either the ones who have it and wasted it, or have money but greed got the better of them, hence their belief that money does not make one happy, or they have so much money that they can do anything and with anyone they like, now this would be ok if they are single but it won't stoke the flames of harmony in the home when one party seeks sexual attention from outside the house. I know of certain wealthy people, to the rest of the world they seem to be happy, but behind closed doors, I have been privy to what goes on. The husband is having affairs and do you know why? Because he can! *(This is the response I was given by his wife.)* There is very little joy in that household!

Take this to the other extreme; there are people who will never have money, so they say, "Money does not buy happiness," in order to make themselves feel better.

They convince themselves that they don't need it (*because they do not possess the capacity to earn lots of money*) I have yet to see people who after they married not having enough money to buy food, clothing, pay their rent, buy clothes for their children or pay their everyday bills, maybe a holiday every now and again, with wolves at their door, and here they are the happy couple just lounging around their home rejoicing at how great life is without money. I appreciate a good vow, but only if it is realistic and it actually means something.

In conclusion—

- For better, for worse.
- For richer, for poorer.
- In sickness and in health.

These vows are all applicable and have relevance within a relationship that seeks to build strong foundations and build upon those foundations with their love, their understanding, their commitment to each other, their capacity to forgive, their ability to grow together and not apart and the desire to communicate and compromise throughout their lives together.

If couples live within an unhealthy, unforgiving relationship where the trust is gone, abusive behaviour prevails, arguments, neglect and lack of affection become the '*norm*', it is unfair to expect that they must now endure this life because they are compelled to stand by their vows, that were unrealistic to begin with would be an absolute and total waste of life.

It would probably have been more appropriate if at the end of those vows there was a notation stating that if the couple do not get along with each other and if the husband becomes violent and abusive and beats his wife or if the wife neglects and disrespects her husband, then neither husband or wife will be bound by said vows. This I would understand, but to bluntly state that a marriage is considered as *forever*' when clearly, it's not, seems to me to be ridiculous and the number of divorces that occur each year is testament to this.

How many couples do you know that have included conditions in their marriage contracts to accommodate any exit vows?

Vows should be more realistic and perhaps if there was an *'exit'* vow or two maybe then, couples would take greater care of spouses.

Perhaps once upon a time these vows were appropriate or acceptable, but sadly, not in today's day and age. We all recite these vows at the altar, but forget them very quickly because some husbands abuse their wives and are unfaithful, some women fall out of love with their partners because of the abuse or for any other reason rendering these vows as no longer relevant.

'Until death do us part' is as unlikely as me, boarding the red eye on the next shuttle to the moon.

The chances of a marriage lasting for the next forty, or fifty years under the strain of not seeing eye to eye, raising children, financial problems, affairs, squabbles, jealous fits, controlling spouse and physical abuse, is unrealistic and it becomes even more unlikely when the couple about to be married are either too young, ill informed, an have no idea what they want from life.

How many times have we said of women in abusive marriages, *"Why does she stay with him, why doesn't she leave him?"* Has anyone ever said, *"Well she married him for better or for worse, so she has to grin and bear it"* and exactly at what point does the vow "Until death do us part" kick in?

Is that when her drunk and abusive husband goes one step further and chokes her to death after another drinking binge? Perhaps the vows need to clarify what kind of 'death' they make reference to!

When a marriage has failed, either both parties try to work it out and succeed *(perhaps)* or they attempt to work it out and fail, and end up going their separate ways.

Why are vows so hypocritical? Couples are supposed to stay together until death parts them, but we know that when the situation at home gets so violent and abusive, that the person being abused should leave or else it *will* be death that parts them. There is no point to vows that are not realistic. Then again, if they were, no one would want to get married.

Life is too short, and we are but on this earth for a very brief moment in the grand scheme of things, and that time needs to be spent with purpose, with meaning, with love, if a wife is being abused by her husband, should she stay with him? Absolutely not!

Please understand that I in no way disrespect marriage vows, but in today's day and age some of them seem to be extreme. Therefore, the promise of, *'Until death do us part'* is ludicrous. Perhaps marriage should come with a 5-year option to review and renew.

Don't laugh, think about it, it gives both parties a chance to sit down and discuss how they feel about each other and their life together five or ten years into their marriage. If any changes need to be made, that may be the time to do so; while both learning about each other.

Change is inevitable, but the change I am referring to is the change that comes about with the passage of time, it will be up to you both to ensure that these changes will be for the better and you can achieve this *(as I have already mentioned)* by growing together and not apart. It's expected when two people with their own ideas and mannerisms commence a life together under the same roof, conflict can arise very quickly, it's how you both handle this conflict that makes all the difference and the first step is in keeping the lines of communication open and flowing and to being flexible with your attitude.

Either one of you can instigate a heart-to-heart discussion, allowing you both the opportunity to sort out any underlying issues. If there were problems, this would be the ideal time to bring them out in the open and sorted out mutually.

Reaffirm your feelings and your love on a regular basis, I won't lie to you, it will be an ongoing requirement for the entire duration of your relationship, you can never stop trying, stop caring or believe that you are secure and you need not try anymore. You are only as secure as the last conversation you had with your husband/wife, was it happy or was it an argument over something trivial, or major, it does not matter, fix the problem!

*Ladies—how did you send off your man this morning? Was he happy—*or did you argue over something and parted on angry terms? The opportunity to diffuse any ill feelings is always there for either one of you to say "I'm sorry," or "I love you," and if your deepest desire is to continue your journey through life with your chosen one, then I suggest you take advantage of every opportunity of ensuring that you are both travelling on the same path and minimising the chance of one of you straying in another direction.

If your love has not survived the first five years, ask yourselves why? You both have the opportunity to discuss your feelings and both decide where you go to from that point.

If all couples knew that five years after they marry, they will be having discussions regarding the first five years of their marriage, it may encourage

both to be a little more patient, more understanding, love more and argue
less.
Should there be a more radical change of the marriage vows, should they be
more realistic?

Helen Goltz, believes so, and because of her belief she has written a discussion paper on the current marriage licence laws in Australia.

This discussion paper in based on the future of marriage licences in Australia and also the abolition of such licences in place of a fixed term marriage contract of 5 and 10 years with an option after this period of time and if both parties agree and upon a successful 10-year marriage term that the couple can elect to have an 'eternity' contract.

Helen Goltz goes into greater detail of explaining exactly why this is essential and how the fixed term marriage contract will be integrated within our lives, the details can be found on the internet under ***"Fixed Term Marriage Contracts,"*** *if you wish to read it, in its entirety and it's definitely a "must read."*

Helen Goltz, BA Grad. Dip QUT, Dip Counselling AIPC

It makes perfect sense and little did I know when this idea dawned on me years ago that someone somewhere was actually doing something about it and started the ball rolling by doing this study and writing this discussion paper.

Under the present conditions within a marriage, if neither party makes the conscious effort to set time aside and discuss any and all issues that both are not happy about, nothing will ever get resolved.

This in turn becomes compounded by bitterness, resentment, and the continuation of bickering becoming the constant source for the escalation of hostility and negativity within this relationship. How can a marriage thrive within such toxicity?

When too much water has passed under the bridge, it becomes much more difficult for reconciliation to occur. When all communication has broken down, and neither party wishes to discuss or work through their problems, at some point, one or the other will seek to leave the marriage.

Ultimately, once again, the decision is yours, make it your priority to address issues, better still, don't let situations escalate to the point where the damage is done, be considerate in your treatment of each other and hopefully your lives will be a true reflection of your love and commitment to each other.

You only get the one chance with the man/woman you selected, don't blow it!

35

Anything You Can Do
I Can Do Better!

We have discussed any times throughout this book, that in order for a relationship to flourish and bloom, close attention needs to be paid, firstly to the way you interact with each other in private, how you interact with family and friends, and even more importantly, your interaction towards each other within a social circle.

How often have you gone out with your man/woman to a social gathering, and found yourself standing alone even for just a few minutes. When you glance across the room, you notice that your other half is busy chatting and laughing with other men/women.

Ladies—**have you ever noticed other woman checking your man *out from across a room*,** and this being the case, does he enjoy the attention he receives from the opposite sex or is he completely oblivious? How does this make you feel at that very moment?

Guys—the absolute same can be said for you too how would you feel—if you noticed other men were admiring your woman? How would that make you feel?

Ladies—Have you wondered why women are attracted to him? He may or may not be good-looking, but women still get attracted to him. Why? Could it be his personality, is he an open, confident person, does he interact with others quite easily because if he does, people are naturally drawn to people who smile, laugh openly and seem approachable and genuine. This kind of man does not feel the need to pretend to be someone he is not and most people are drawn to people who exude confidence.

Ladies—What would your reaction be? Would you get angry—glare at him and give the other women dirty looks or perhaps drape yourself all over him as if to show them that he is yours? Perhaps, you walk up to him and begin an argument. Or maybe, you approach the other woman and tell her to keep away? Do you find that he becomes agitated as he tries to convince you that you are imagining things? Do you retreat into 'sulking' mode for the rest of the evening only to escalate it to sarcasm status resulting in an all-out war once you have arrived home?

STOP, both of you!

First of all, it is not your husband's fault if he is being 'checked out' by the opposite sex. Instead of being angry, you should feel flattered that other women admire him, getting angry about it and turning it into a massive argument won't solve anything and it will do nothing for your love life either. Don't give him a reason to question how he could have married such a jealous woman. You may get away with it a few times, or several times but if you continue this on a regular basis and spoil each outing you have together, he will be out there on his own eventually. He married you because he loves you; don't give him reason to question his feelings for you.

Do you know the extent of damage you are doing to your relationship when you both resort to constant arguing? This devastating effect will eventually drain the very life out of you and the same can be said of him. You surely can't expect that your relationship is going to survive, let alone grow under these conditions?

What you are doing is inadvertently storing all this negativity and resentment within yourselves only to emerge the next time you both find something to argue about. All you're doing is contributing towards to the downfall of your marriage. It's called the *'chipping away'* process of your love for each other, and you encourage this chipping away process by continuing to bicker, till one day there's nothing left. Whether it's the man who feels threatened by his woman's popularity or the other way around, getting upset and causing grief for each other is not the solution. Jealousy is an ugly trait for both men and women and no good will ever come of it. Be happy that your partner is popular, be proud that he/she is with you and don't you think it kind of makes for exciting times, when you both get home.

When we are admired, we feel good, when we feel good, we are in positive mode and when we are in positive mode, people around us will also feel good. The opposite happens when we don't feel good. If you put your partner in negative mode, who is going to suffer? On the other hand, if you put your other half in positive mode, who is going to benefit?

Both of you!

Be accepting of the fact that other men/women will always be a part of life, and you won't solve this by banning the human race from your lives.

You may as well accept that they will always be there and use this to your advantage. How boring would life be if no other person existed on the face of the earth, but for the two of you.

Instead of turning yourselves into bitter, jealous partners *(which will only serve to turn yourselves off each other)* wouldn't it be better to appreciate and enjoy your man/woman, by trusting them.

Ladies—Perhaps you were once a happy and confident woman—but somewhere along the way you became lost in a world of insecurity, arguments, loss of trust, etc. Don't allow these emotions take a hold of your life. Disperse them by allowing your natural self to come through once more and people will see you as the confident and magnetic person you are.

Accept the fact that these other women will always be out there, proceed to use this to your advantage. If your man can attract attention, then guess what?— So can you! Hey, it's called keeping each other on your toes and that can be a good thing. There is no room for complacency in any relationship, let alone a marriage that is supposed to last forever.

How do you do this; first you have to change the way you think about yourself.

- Love the person you are, and have a love and caring for all people around you.
- Be genuine, if you are a caring person, magnify it by showing it, if you feel beautiful on the inside, believe me it will show on the outside.
- Possess the passion and the marvel of life itself; this is where your magnetism is recharged.
- Have kind loving thoughts for all that life represents, this will reflect on your face, if you are a passionate person, show some of that passion within your mannerisms or your laughter and even your disappointments.
- Your man can look at you conversing with other men and think to himself, "You can look and chat to her, but you can't touch her cause she's with me." This can be a positive thing and it is just one more contributing factor towards having an active and mutually satisfying sex life.

Never threaten your partner by trying to make each other jealous through your conversations with other people, there is nothing wrong with being a little flirty, but one thing you should never do is to deliberately lead another man/woman on by allowing them to believe that there is something more to your friendly and approachable manner.

Your flirtatious side could be reflected in the way you laugh or in the manner in which you speak, or the way you tell a story, it can be in *mannerism* rather than direct suggestion or action. Glance in the direction of your partner, smile at him/her and blow them a kiss, this is your way of telling them, *"I love you darling, no matter who I'm talking to, I only have eyes for you!"* Because I'm not forgetting who I'm going home with tonight!

Check yourself out in the mirror, what are you wearing? Do your clothes look a little tired outdated are they rather plain and uninteresting? Look at your garments and ask yourself, *"Would I have worn this if I were going out on a date,"* if the answer is *no'* then that's the very garment you should not wear.

Select something classy but sexy, and if you don't have anything quite like that, go out and buy some new clothes. It does not have to cost the earth either.

Look at your hair, if you need help with this, visit a good hairdresser. They will be able to suggest a suitable more appealing hairstyle for you but you must also be comfortable with the new style as well, and make sure you will be able to manage it yourself. Check out your makeup, when was the last time you bought a new lipstick or nail varnish?

Time to book yourself in for a makeover! Any of the department stores will be more than happy to create a look that will reflect the new and exciting you. Your clothes, hair, makeup, nails, all important but let's not forget about the lingerie, you go for it, and just do it!

Do it because you deserve it, but also do it, because you may never get the chance again.

When you look fabulous, you will feel fabulous and when you feel fabulous you will be a much happier person and you will show your other half that you care about *you*, about *him* and about your *life* together.

I think most men like it when their woman attracts attention, except for the jealous men that is! He may be your husband, but treat him like he is your lover, make him wish he could race you home right now.

You have now become that attractive, sexy woman by his side when next you go out together. What chance then, does any other woman have with your man?

Absolutely none! Remember how it felt when you first met? Now hang onto that thought. Tell him how your heart skips a beat whenever he is near you, tell him how much you adore him, and tell him how gorgeous you think he is.

Recall what it was he loved about you, when he first met you, and keep that quality within you, never lose it, if you have, get it back quick smart—find it! You need it!

If your man on the other hand, is the quiet introvert type, and is not too keen on you being an extrovert (*I question why you married him in that case*) and he does not appreciate the attention you attract then you will either have to tone your mannerisms down to keep him happy, or assure him that you love him and only him. If he accepts this, great, if not; as I said, you should have thought of this before you married him, this being the case, you may one day have to make a choice–then this is why it was so important to find that right personality to suit your own, right in the beginning—when you were dating.

Can you appreciate the importance of why it is so imperative to find the right person and why you should never *'make do'* with anyone; both sexes will be able to enjoy their lives together when they are compatible by being in tune and in harmony with each other.

Be true to yourself, by finding the one who will be true to you.
This is the match that is truly made in heaven.

36

Re-Igniting Your Love
Don't Allow that Pilot Light Extinguish!

Sometimes marriages reach a point whereby monotony and boredom sets in and there is no passion, no excitement in anything you do and life becomes mundane. If I were to tell a friend, *"Guess what, I met this fabulous guy, he is so wonderful and I am madly in love with him"* the response will be, *"Yeah, yeah, but that doesn't last forever the love changes when you get married, it settles down and from there it's downhill all the way."* Have you now reached this point?

If your love life is suffering it is probably the culmination of lots of little things you have not done throughout your life, and because you did not bother and nor did he, you arrived where you are today. You may decide or have been advised that going away on a romantic holiday will put that spark back into your lives so of you go to that far-off exotic destination. However, your lagging sex life did not get to this point without some help from both.

Ask yourselves in what way did you contribute, or perhaps it was just one party. Whatever the case you allowed it to continue and you did not resolve as problems came up. Do you really believe that a holiday will dissolve any resentment that may have accumulated between the two of you? Will a holiday take away the hurt of him having been rejected for so long, or you having been hurt by something he said and never apologised for! Do either of you actually want to go away together?

The bad news is that if you now need to go off somewhere attempting to re-energise your love life, chances are it is probably a little late.

There is certainly no harm in trying, but what happens when you have to return to the normality that put your love life there in the first place. Question is what will you do, to make sure this never happens again? Are you both willing to make changes to ensure that old wounds are never opened again? Real love, passion and just plain caring for someone unconditionally, is priceless. You cannot pretend nor can you substitute, it should be natural and effortless, it should come from within.

Therefore, if you are still in love with each other, then this should come about naturally, however you will need to maintain this indefinitely.

You will not find this magic on a vacation somewhere, each of you have this magic inside you, remember how you felt when you first met, try and bring that out to the fore. This feeling should be reciprocated and when both feel the same, why you could be sitting on a park bench with your man/woman and you will feel just as elated as any far-off resort, you should not need to go away to reignite passion for each other—just look into your heart, this is where passion lives, find it and bring it out and let it wash over you again.

The best thing to do is to not allow yourselves to lose it in the first place keep those fires burning all the time. If you do not want to lose your man to the other woman, who more than likely is not that much interested in your husband in the first place, because she is not the one perusing him, he is probably perusing her, and why? Because he is bored at home. If you don't want to lose him, keep him happy and content all the time, be there for him, love him, show him how much he means to you, pamper him and spoil him with your unique quality of love.

Show me a man, who would rather be out with his mates when he knows he has a wonderful loving, caring woman waiting for him at home. No tricks are necessary to keep your man, just love! Love!

And more love!

37

Spoil Each Other
You May Not Get Another Chance!

Ladies—**If you fear of losing him then chances are, you probably will**—Don't let your fears materialise, think positively about your life with him, think yourself lucky to have found someone who has given his love and life to you. Don't spoil it now with negativity. Don't even think about keeping him through trickery and mind games or threats. You will only keep him through love and trust. Love is the most powerful emotion we will ever feel and to be able to share this with another human being is a blessing. You have his love now, so don't lose it.

Spoiling your man has nothing to do with equality. Once in a while, whenever you feel like it, make it a point of pampering him, yes! Wait on him hand and foot if you have to, and show him just how much he means to you.

Be the person he met and married and don't turn yourself into the missus, be the exciting woman he fell in love with, no room for complacency just because you are married, you have to be a step ahead all the time. Marrying him was the easy part, *keeping him will be the real challenge.*

Guys—Just because you managed to get the woman of your dreams—does not mean now that you can let it all hang out and not concern yourselves with keeping your woman interested and happy. How happy and content she will be depends on how you are going to treat her from this point forward.

38

Staying Together
For the Sake of the Children

This is always going to be very difficult and a lot of thought needs to go into any situation where children are involved.

I chose to remain with my husband for the sake of my children but it was all in vain. I had to endure many years of pain and anguish instead my husband was more concerned with his social life rather than the state of his life with his wife and children. He would be preparing himself to meet with his female companion, when I would ask, *"Where are you going?"*

His reply would be, *"Out."* When I asked again, he replied, *"Out with my girlfriend."* I was then instructed by my mother-in-law *(whom I lived with during those years),* that I was not to approach him, that I was to let him do whatever he wanted to do, and if he chose to go out with other women, then I was to say nothing, and that I should consider myself fortunate in that he was still coming home to me each night.

The only reason my husband came anywhere near me was because he once told me, he felt *'sorry'* for me because I had not one, so out of pity for me, he would approach me and for no other reason. I came to regard myself as a piece of furniture. I was like Cinderella, just there for cleaning and scrubbing the floors. I don't think he actually wanted me to be happy. I can't help believing that every time I tried to come out of my shell and attempt to be even remotely happy, he would come along and wipe that smile off my face. I would sit by the window, watching life go by followed by countless hours in my bedroom crying.

My freedom was taken away from me as I was not allowed to leave home on my own, and if I did want to go out, I had better have had a good reason. If I needed money, I was told to get some from my father-in-law, then of course he had no money to spare so I received zero.

If my husband loved me, it was a very strange love, if my in-laws loved me then I would not wish that kind of love upon anyone. My life was extremely unhappy, I felt as if I were in prison, always on my own as my husband was away on business trips and my in-laws were visiting their now married daughter who lived in her own home.

Many, many evenings would be spent on my own, while they all went out to enjoy themselves. Was my life not worth anything? What was my reason for living?

Ending a marriage is never going to be easy, but when there is nothing left between two people and each party dreads going home to face the other, then there is really nothing much left to fight for. This may sound harsh, particularly if there are children involved, but if a marriage is doomed, then it is not a matter of *if,* but *when* it will end.

Both parties deserve to be happy and to live life to the fullest, if every avenue of reconciliation has been exhausted and failed, what else remains? Staying together for the children, is compared to a *'stay of execution'* it's a time bomb which *will* explode.

Would the children be happier growing up in an unhappy home with two bickering parents? Better to have two happy parents who are apart, than two parents under the same roof and living in misery. Don't let your lives get to the point whereby you don't even converse with each other anymore. If you have reached this point, your marriage is in trouble.

This after all was the person you selected from all the others and you were sure this was right, and it probably was right at the time, but that was the easy part, the hard part is to finding the right balance between your intimate life, your family life, your social life and your work life if your marriage is to succeed. Are you determined to make a genuine effort to make your relationship a happy one?

Thinking back to your wedding day and where you are right now, how important do you think the colours of your bridesmaid dresses or the icing on the cake or the ribbons in your bouquet are now? I think you get the picture.

I thought long and hard about why I felt I needed to stay with my husband. The first reason was, I loved him and I could not imagine my life without him. My next consideration was that I had two small children under the age of 4, and I wanted my children to grow up the way I did, with both parents, and both sets of grandparents. I had no desire to deny my children the right to grow up with their father in their life. I also did not want to put my parents through the humiliation of having a divorced daughter. In effect, I put everyone else ahead of my own life, my own needs. What was my purpose in life, did I not have a right to happiness as well.

They were the darkest years of my life. Perhaps I should never have married him in the first place, but I was blinded by love and the romantic notion of marriage. I bear no animosity or ill feeling whatsoever towards my ex-husband or his family and I wish only the best for them all. I am very happy that he and our children have a great relationship. We can't change the past; we can only move forward with forgiveness in our hearts.

Example 11—Anthony and Louise—True Story!

Anthony *(not real name)* was a twenty something just married young man. Five or six years into his marriage, he began cheating on his partner. After some time, Louise *(not real name)* his wife caught him out, now they remained together for the sake of his daughters—but today *(20 years later)* this same man is still out there doing what he did when he was in his twenties.

Not too long after he was caught out, he found out that his wife too had an affair as well during the same time he did. Who's to blame? Who cheated first? Who's at fault? Why did they both feel the need to do this to each other and yet remain together and one partner is still doing what he did all those years ago?

Sometimes men or women digress from their lives, just for the sake of trying something different and whether or not they continue to love each other is not the point. Neither one wants the nightmare that is associated with divorce, so they continue to remain together while living separate lives under the same roof.

Life is far too short, and we all deserve to be happy, but by the same token, life can be too long, if it has to be lived it in unhappiness.

39

'Use-By Date of a Marriage'

Have you ever heard the saying, *"Oh he is past his use-by date"* or *vice versa, or "their marriage has reached its use-by date."*

Let's think about this for a moment. We meet the one we want to marry, we then marry him/her, and then we go about living our life. What is the governing factor that determines the *use-by date of a relationship?*

Then it occurred to me! The use-by date of a marriage is automatically predetermined by our interaction and treatment of each other. How you treat your husband, and how your husband treats you. Chances are that if you both treat each other with love and understanding throughout your lives together, if you truly love your partner and show them just how much they mean to you, by doing all of this, you are giving yourselves a very *'long use-by date',* which is great, and if all goes well, *'death'* will indeed be the factor that parts you both…

If on the other hand, you are not treating each other well, you are depriving your husband of love and compassion, constantly arguing, he may not be treating you right, therefore constantly bickering or you both end up losing this *'magic'* that you had when you first started out together you will discover as the years go by, so too does the love, then it stands to reason that you are setting yourself up for a *'short use-by date'.*

Again I emphasise, treat your partners with love, right from the beginning, and while there are no guarantees in life *(except change)* you are at least spending your life with some quality attached to it while lessening the possibility of a failed marriage years down the track.

For each one of us, the reasons are different as are the causes and the circumstances, but we are also aware that sometimes, a couple can appear to be happy, but the man still finds it necessary to have someone else on the side, and

I will never understand why a man would want to jeopardise his family and home this way, but they do.

The reasons for my husband doing what he did for instance would be very, very different to the reasons of someone else's husband. Sometimes, it's no one's fault, you may have during the course of your life drifted apart. Had you realised at the time, you may have been able to take the necessary action to save your relationship. You may have been able to avoid this had you handled each other differently, but sometimes the relationship has run its course and what is lost cannot be recaptured.

It's at this time that the relationship has reached its *'use-by date'*. What you decide to do from this point is entirely up to you and your partner as only the two of you know what has transpired between you and what is in your hearts.

Seek professional help if required, as it may assist you in deciding what will be the next phase of your life that you will face either together or apart.

40

Loaded Questions
Does My Bum Look Big in This?

Most women have done this, and still continue to ask their husbands loaded questions. There are many, but I think the most popular one is:

"Do I look fat in this?" or *"Does my bum look big in this?"*

What man in their right mind is going to answer this honestly? Do you really think he is going to take his life in his own hands, by telling you the truth?

The only thing you will achieve in asking him such questions and by no fault of his own is to force him to lie to you so as not to upset you. Your husband will *'white lie'* his way out of a sticky situation in order to spare your feelings and his life. If he lies once, he can do it twice and get quite used to it.

Don't ask him loaded questions, because in doing so, you encourage him to lie to you and this is putting him and you on a dangerous path. If you get him into the habit of lying and he continues to spare your feelings and get away with it, what else will he find to lie to you about next time?

You are teaching him bad habits that could backfire on you one day.

Keep him honest, by not asking him a question that you already know the answer to.

If you feel need to ask someone whether or not you look fat in something, then in all probability you do look fat in it. You already know the answer, you just want someone else to tell you that you what you need to hear to make yourself feel better.

So—if you think you look fat, then you must be, but that's ok if you have put on a little weight, it's not the end of the world—watch what you eat, get into some light exercise, walking is good, maybe a little swimming and you will be back in shape in no time. Just take good care of yourself. If you have gained weight after a pregnancy, you should make it your priority to regain your normal size as soon as you can.

It may be an old wives' tale, but I was told that by breastfeeding your baby, it actually helps the mother regain her shape much faster. In any case, as long as there are no hormonal issues, light exercise and a sensible diet will see you back to normal quickly.

Guys—you can help each other out by making it a joint effort to walk together regularly.

Ladies—keep yourself in top condition throughout your life—If you notice weight creeping on find out what works best for you and always aim at maintaining your weight throughout your life. It is not just for your partner that you would be doing this for, but for your own well-being as well. It can be done and it is worth it.

For instance, in my younger day I used to be a XSSW, that is interpreted as extra small, small woman. I think that equates to day's measurements to an 8. Present day, after now two adult children and 3 grandchildren, I am still a size 8 and I have always told my family that I will be buried in my stilettos.

When you care about the quality of food you put into your system and eat well and exercise, you feel good, when you feel good, it will reflect on your face and you will look good. Your man will appreciate it, but most importantly, do it for yourself because you deserve the best!

41

The Three Loves of Your Life

There are three different zones to a relationship and all three are crucial. There is the mutual intimacy *(you and your partner),* family time *(you, your partner and children)* and then there is *'me time'*—time set aside for you and only you. *(This applies to both of you.)*

Intimate Love—Between you and your partner and how you treat each other during the daytime hours determines how successful your night time hours *(sex life)* will be.

Family love—Your wife, you and future children you may have. When the children *do* come along life will change yet again, but it does not have to be scary. Remember in the early days how you both used to say to each other, ***"Darling I am busy, but I always have time for you because I love you!"***

What makes you think that you don't need to say this anymore? Actually now, more than ever before you definitely have to say this to each other because it's all the little things that you continue to do for him/her and your family that will contribute towards *'affair-proofing your relationship',* so you see it is possible, just not in the way you imagined.

***'Me Time'* Love—Guys and Ladies**: Understand that even while married, you both need to retain your individuality and give yourself *'me time'.*

Can you see how unrealistic it is to expect to get through your life together by always being in each other's pockets without getting on each other's nerves eventually?

That's a lot of life to get through, how you get through it and how pleasurable you make it, will depend on well you also take care of yourself. For this, you need to set time aside where it will be *'me time'* this is the time you can recharge your batteries, this is the time you can recharge that spark in your life which is the pilot light I have spoken of in previous chapters.

Don't allow that pilot light extinguish, it's just as important as the air we breathe. Oxygen gives life to our body, that pilot light enables our body to feel the passion of loving someone and a reason to live.

Set time aside to take care of you, do the little things that make you happy. Spoil yourself, pamper yourself, and re-energise yourself! Remember, each of you needs to retain your individuality that is of the utmost importance, it's who you are, it's the reason you chose each other in marriage.

Learn to 'love' **yourself—in order to love each other better!**

42

What a Man Wants
And What He Doesn't!

Ladies—"Any omission of the points mentioned below should be considered as 'fuel' for the mid-life crisis event which is inevitable!"

- Unconditional love.
- Don't take his freedom away.
- He wants you to be forgiving.
- He wants his *"me time."*
- He does not want to be nitpicked or nagged constantly.
- He does not want to be treated like *a 'house boy'.*
- You are not his warden, don't treat him like a prisoner.
- Don't interrogate him.
- He past arguments to be left in the past.
- Don't deliberately withhold sex as punishment or to prove a point.
- He does not want to be told what he can or cannot do.
- He does not want to be told where he can or cannot go.
- Don't force him to do something he is not happy with.
- He wants affection—from you!
- He does not want to live in each other's pockets.
- Never reject him.
- Never lie to him and be fair.
- Open communication with him.
- Do one special thing for him every now and again.
- Never degrade him.
- He wants love and care from you and not be afraid to show it.
- He wants you to be his lover, his friend and his partner in life.

- He wants a woman who will stand by him and support him in every way.
- He wants you as his *'equal'* in life.
- He wants a little romance in the relationship.
- He wants spontaneity and surprise.
- He wants to be treated like a *'man'*.
- He does not want you to attempt to change him.
- He wants to be told you adore him.
- He wants you to be patient with him.
- He wants compliments (*whatever they may be.)*
- He likes to receive loving notes for him to read.
- He wants you to give him time with his friends *(the boys.)*
- He doesn't mind being kept on his toes, but in a good way.
- Compromise and flexibility.
- He wants you to have a sense of humour.
- He wants to chill out with a little frivolity together, sometimes.
- Sacrifice.
- Respect.
- Treat him like a king.

43

What a Woman Wants
And Expects!

"Otherwise, don't even think about getting married, guys!"

All of the above plus:

- Unconditional love.
- Forgiveness.
- To never ever raise your hand against her.
- To never treat her like a servant.
- To allow her to enjoy some *'me'* time.
- Don't yell at her *(for any reason)* but if you do, apologise quickly!
- Compromise.
- Patience.
- Consideration.
- Understanding.
- Never lie to her.
- Sacrifice.
- Don't be jealous or controlling of her.
- Treat her with love and respect.
- Compliment her, but genuine compliments, not forced (*she will see right through it).*
- Never, ever call her demeaning names, she will never forget them, and nor will you!
- Tell her you worship and adore her.
- *"Handle with care"* be sensitive and be there for her when she needs you.
- Take care of her needs and requirements.

- Open communication.
- Retain spontaneity and surprise your relationship.
- Sense of humour.
- Don't argue with her over trivial matters (*not worth it.*)
- Treat her, and love her, like you just met her!
- Take her out on a date nights.
- Leave a love note for her every now and again.
- Never forget her birthday.
- Give her time with her friends if she desires it.
- If you love her, never cheat.
- Tell her she is the most beautiful woman in the world—she will make you feel glad that you did.
- Buy her flowers, for no other reason other than your love for her!
- Romance her.
- Respect.
- In other words, treat your woman like a queen.

Finally—One last thing that women want.

Flush the toilet, after use and put that toilet seat down! Just leave it the way you found it, please, please, please!

It's so simple. We like to leave the bathroom neat and tidy (*or at least most women do*) and by leaving the seat up you oblige us to run around tidying up after you which in turn prompts us to complain resulting in you, accusing us of *'nagging' you.* So, to avoid all of this unnecessary bickering, I urge you all, simply lower that toilet seat, then we won't have to run around after you, therefore rendering any form of complaint obsolete, and in turn you won't have to call us *'nags'.* Is that fair enough?

By the way, unhygienic habits in the bathroom do little to ensure the *romantic'* element survives in your relationship.

You do, after all, want women to be romantic, don't you? Then just do this for your woman and by doing so you are giving her the consideration, the love, the patience, and the respect that she deserves. Remember, judgment day is coming but not in the way you think. When he reaches the mid-life crisis point in his life, everything that has transpired between the two of you over the years will play back like a movie in his head. He will re-access his entire life, past and present and if this life spent with you was not a happy one due to the many reasons we have discussed in this book, this is the time that he will decide what he is going to do about it.

During the course of your married life, did you afford him the freedom to pursue his hobbies or interests, or did you prevent him from doing so? This too will be taken into consideration.

Did you ever prevent him from fulfilling his goals? You did—How do you rate your chances of keeping him now?

What about all the times you said no to him leaving him feeling angry, frustrated and rejected? Did you succeed in stripping him of his masculinity throughout the years? As a result of all of the above, have you both lived your lives within a stagnate marriage where boredom and indifference were considered a normal state of being? Are you getting the picture? You do know that your marriage is in big trouble at this point, don't you. I don't want to rub it in but remember the *'payment day'* I mentioned earlier in the book—well this is it!

The good news is that all of this can be prevented and you need not fear your husband reaching this point in your life as long as you have loved your man the best way you know how and allowed him the freedom and time to himself to be who he is and every man is different, but one thing never changes, they want their freedom, they don't want to be hen pecked, they want to be loved and respected.

Love is made a lot of little things we do for the other person, when the little things you do start to diminish, so too does the love.

44

Food for Thought

What if—

The one we are with is not the one who can truly make us happy.

What if—

There is another love out there that is meant for us and is the right love that can make us happy beyond our wildest dreams.

What if—

We marry, have our children, spend 30 odd years with the same person then discover that there is someone else out there that we are meant to be with all along.

What if—

We are not necessarily meant to be with the one person all our life?

What if—

We are meant to be with one person during one stage of our life, and someone else at another stage of our life?

Who's to say—

We must stay with one person forever, and what is "forever" anyway? Is it *"forever"* for as long as it lasts, or *"forever"* till the day we die?

What if—

They change later on if life to become someone that we do not wish to be with? After all, *"change"* is a certainty!

What if—

The decisions we made in our 20s were only made by a heart and mind of someone who could not possibly know then, what time and maturity will undoubtedly teach us about ourselves in the future.

The things we liked in our 20s are not always the same things we will like in our 40s or 50s. Our taste in music, clothes, ideas all change, as we get older, so who is to say that our taste in men and women will not also change?

What if—

We never give ourselves the second chance at happiness due to society's expectations of what is considered right and wrong within a relationship and the quest to honour vows at any costs.

What if—

We finally meet the love of our lives much later in life and realise that this is the person we are meant to be with.

Why—

Are we expected to make decisions and enter into commitments so early in our life at a time when we are so inexperienced and lacking in maturity where we are only beginning to learn about ourselves, let alone take on another life, then proceed to tear that person down in order to relieve our own insecurities?

Conclusion

It has been said many times that the universe, is the last frontier left for man to conquer.

Yet the greatest frontier, and the biggest challenge, that awaits the greater majority of us, resides within us all. What is this frontier and what is the challenge that awaits us?

It's the fusion of two lives that will create this frontier where these two people will now reside in as they face the greatest challenge of all, and that will be, having to learn to live harmoniously with another human being. It will be this process of *'discovering'* who we really married, what marriage really means and how to get through it that presents the greatest challenge of all. To have mastered the art of loving only one man/woman and remaining *'in love'* many, many years from now will be a great accomplishment.

To master the art of selfless loving is no easy task, and certainly not for the faint hearted, which is why so many marriages burn out and disintegrate within this frontier their union created. Most of us will continue to search for that one in a million *'forever'* love that will provide the perfect universal conditions within our own galaxy where there are only two stars residing, your loved one and you!

In a world where so much has been said about the pitfalls of marriage, the end of romance, the self-doubt, the loss of the *'wife'* replaced by the arrival of a *'warden'* thus marking the end of freedom and the beginning of a prison sentence in a home that has become the jail, people still marry believing that theirs is the marriage that will defy all the odds as theirs is going to be the one that will last forever, forgetting that in order to achieve this they need to maintain their relationship from the minute they take their vows, and for the rest of their lives if this is their wish.

All too soon though, the man will complain, *"Where is the woman I fell in love with?"* While women will confess, *"He does not even notice me anymore, and he never tells me, I love you, and I don't feel appreciated."* While the rest of the ladies will avoid sexual contact at all costs and spend their lives thinking up ways of avoidance.

Men will yearn for the *'lover'* in their wives, and women will either wish they were loved more *like* a lover, and the rest will hide altogether.

What women do not realise is that if you want to be romanced you need to incite that feeling in your man with your actions and the way you treat him.

The men on the other hand must understand that if you want your wife to act as if she is still your *lover*, you need to make her feel very special. The problem arises when neither party knows how to carry forward the way they used to be, before they married.

When 40% of marriages continue to fail it means that couples are doing too many things wrong.

Perhaps what is needed is a redefinition or an outlining of what marriage is really about and what conditions need to come into play in order for the marriage to survive let alone shine brightly in this galaxy that we have created but one thing is definite, something needs to change.

I hope that the contents of this book will shine on as a beacon, down a pathway that has been left in uncertainty for too long, as we all forged ahead with the latest *'how to'*, being the flavour of the month. Let's not lose sight of what women are supposed to represent and re-define the role that our men should be playing within our lives.

I will leave that to each individual to look into their heart of hearts and through honesty and the sobering thought of the reality of married life, to think about and implement the changes you feel will be acceptable to both of you for the purpose of further enhancing your lives and place you on a happier successful path that will enable you to conquer the great unknown and the final frontier that is—*MARRIAGE!*

About Love and Romantic Love

By: Michael Grayson Conner, Psy. D

Love is mostly tender and quiet.
Love is a light that allows people to see things that are not seen by others.

Romantic love is a deep emotional, sexual and spiritual recognition and regard for the value of another person and relationship.

Romantic love can generate many powerful feelings. It can provide a profound ecstasy, and a deep suffering when frustrated. To some people, romantic love is irrational. Romantic love can seem like an emotional storm.

This paper is really a collection of experiences, thoughts, readings, and the result of my discussions with people falling in and out of love. I began writing on this topic in 1989. I was first inspired to write *"About Romantic Love"* when I first read a book by Nathanial Brandon on the topic of romantic love. I revise or add something to this collection of thoughts several times a year. I am most inspired to write when I meet someone in love or someone feeling crushed when their love was lost.

I have had countless experiences talking to people who believe romantic is followed by disillusionment. These people come to believe that romantic love is a false hope. They began their relationship with romantic feelings. They had dreams for their future. They felt that life was finally rewarding and worthwhile. But eventually the relationship began to fall apart. It was a painful experience. They remember when they were in love. They feel tortured by their inability to see how or why their love was lost.

Despite these experiences, people are still drawn to something they seldom reach. It is a profound longing. A desire that is difficult to extinguish. Romantic love is not something that must crumble when faced with practical realities. Romantic love is not something just for youth. Before going further, I should talk about the institution of marriage. One kind of marriage is the *utilitarian marriage*. In this type of marriage there is an absence of mutual involvement or passion.

This type of marriage is usually held together by social, financial, or family considerations. In a utilitarian marriage, the relationship is made tolerable by long separations, community activities and usually infidelity.

The other kind of a marriage is the *intrinsic marriage*. In this type of marriage there is passionate emotional and sexual involvement. The experience of life is shared. The relationship is considered more fulfilling and interesting than any social activity. In this relationship, there is a tendency to avoid activities resulting in separations.

Marriage itself does not create or sustain romantic love. To love someone, and for that love to endure, requires the ability to see that person with clarity. For example, we have all seen how some people will idealise or glamorise their partners. They exaggerate their good qualities, and they ignore and avoid considering significant differences and potential problems. Why do they do this? Many reasons, but mostly because they need to see the person in this idealised way. People can fall in love with the idea of a person who doesn't really exist and then hope the relationship will endure.

Most people never learn how to sustain a loving relationship. The reason is simple. Nobody showed them. The mere fact that a man and woman feel love toward each other does not guarantee they will be able to create a joyful and rewarding life. Love does not automatically teach a person communication skills. Love does not teach a person how to resolve a conflict. Love does not teach people how to weave their love into the rest of their life.

For most people who fall in love, a time will come when they sense the beginning of problems. They know that romantic love can produce great joy and happiness. But with time, they begin to feel more alone. They experience self-doubt and they feel the consequence of their unmet needs. They begin to see the other person more like they truly are and not what they needed them to be. They usually begin to find faults in others and they may become jealous, angry, bitter, sarcastic, or cynical.

Many will separate or remain together in misery. They will often have children and try to raise a family in an effort to revive the relationship or to feel better. Many will have an affair. When they separate or divorce, some will get involved in another relationship too quickly. They try to find some way to ease the pain. They idealise this new person in their life and the cycle starts over. They say to themselves, "I'll never be hurt like that again."

The exact origin of the desire to love is difficult to comprehend, but can be appreciated in many ways.

When a man and woman encounter each other in midst of love they seek intimate contact. In a general sense, love is a response to something we intimately value. Romantic love is the experience of joy in the presence of a loved one, joy in being close to a loved one, and joy in our interaction with a loved one.

Someone we love enters the room. Our eyes and heart light up. We look at this person. We feel a growing feeling of joy within us. We reach *out and touch their hand. We feel happy and fulfilled.*

I believe we all have a profound need to find things in the world we care about and feel inspired by.

Life is worthwhile—at any age—when we find something worth pursuing.

Psychologists have long recognised that both children and adults need something in their environment that is a source of "pleasure." Maybe pleasure is a not the best word, but we do have a need to explore those things which are interesting and exciting. We search for that which will charm us and bring us in touch with the awe and wonder we experienced when we were children. We know that children are curious and adventurous. But the most important need of children and adults seems to be the expression of their true nature—Being who we truly are is important. I first learnt about who we are, from my friend and mentor Sterling Ellsworth. He called it our Real Self, our identity, and our true nature.

Our Real Self and the nature of people is quite clear when we observe children. Any parent can readily see that children are inherently lovable and capable. And for children to grow into healthy adjusted adults, they need to be treated as lovable and capable beings. They also need to express their lovable and capable nature.

From the moment of birth, we begin looking for lights that will brighten our journey, provide us with purpose and meaning, and make our struggle worthwhile.

It is here that we can begin to understand another important expression of romantic love.

Romantic love is a powerful way to express our capacity to love and to be loved. It is a way to focus our energy, our curiosity, and our desire for adventure. Romantic love is a source of pleasure and inspiration and is worth pursuing. Romantic love is a blessing of life. Romantic love confirms our lovable and capable nature.

At the very core of romantic love, I have observed and discovered a number of important dynamics at work.

Visibility (the Desire to Be Seen)

To live successfully is to put ourselves into the world, to give expression to our thoughts, our values, and our goals. Whenever we express our personality, we make known our values, our intelligence our sense of life, our rhythm and temperament. Each of us expresses ourselves in our behaviour—-how we act and what we say. Whatever we express in our behaviour can be reflected back by the response and the behaviour expressed by others. We see how others respond if we are paying attention. The way they act how they look at us, the way they speak to us, and especially the ways in which they don't respond.

When we encounter a person who thinks as we do, and notices what we do, and values what we do, we experience a strong feeling of contact with that person.

In loving you, I see in you a part of me that is also you... I also see in you something that is really me. And there is you, a person of many qualities—a person who is a mystery—a person I am drawn to.

All life, by its very nature—entails a possibility of defeat. Because of this, we find pleasure and reassurance in the expression of life. Sharing our life and participating in life is reassuring that life is possible. Romantic love is an intense sharing and reassurance that life is possible.

So we find pleasure in the experience of life that endures. We take comfort in the experience of this. This comfort is a greater gift than any explicit words or advice: The sight of a lovable person, the awareness of a capable child. There is something in each of us that finds pleasure in watching the healthy assertiveness in a child make his way into the world. Finding ourselves romantically in love is always associated with a hope that it will endure.

Visibility and Self-Discovery

The agony of not being recognised or seen by others is a source of many problems and insecurities. When we are seen by others, there is always some element of self-discovery available to us. The first time we feel loved, there is an enormous pleasure and excitement in finding someone who sees and values us. A sustained experience of visibility in any relationship that goes to any significant depth will generate self-discovery and expanded awareness.

Visibility and Understanding

The desire to be seen and understood is inseparable. When we are told we are loved, there is something in us that feels joy. And there is something in us that wants to know what others see. The desire for visibility is related to our desire to be understood. For any individual, blind love may help numb or settle anxiety, but it will not answer our hunger to be seen and understood. People who feel misunderstood will often go to great lengths to be seen.

Being visible does not always lead to love. But love devoid of visibility is an illusion.

Visibility and Validation

People often confuse the desire to be validated with a desire to be seen. Visibility and validation are not the same.

We have all known people with low self-esteem. In every case there is an excessive preoccupation with gaining approval and avoiding disapproval. There is an excessive desire for validation and support. People naturally confuse the need to feel good about themselves (self-esteem) with a need to be seen (visibility). The desire to be validated is not healthy when it becomes more important than honesty, integrity, or any expression of our lovable and capable nature.

The desire to be validated is not a sign of low self-esteem. But people with good self-esteem do not run around acting super normal, hiding their faults, showing off, or trying to impress people just to be validated. The more they take pride in who they are and the more they act in a way that makes them proud, the more eager they are to be seen for who we are. Self-esteem means confidence in our capable nature, and it means confidence in a lovable identity.

We are not mistakes. Mistakes are how we learn. We are all inherently lovable and capable. We may not be treated that way. We may even come to believe we are not lovable and capable because of the way people treat us. All love endures between people who recognise their lovable and capable nature and that nature in the others.

When we feel lovable and capable, we want others to see us as we truly are—not who we pretend to be. We look to see if they can see and communicate to us their discovery of who we really are. We want people to see and value the identity we were born with and what we have grown to become. We want people to see us and treat us as lovable and capable.

In romantic love, two people see each other in a unique way… And they experience each other in a deeper and more complete way than any other relationship.

Visibility and Sexuality

We are more than human. We are beings of a specific gender. Contained in every human is the awareness of being male or female. It is an integral and intimate part of our self-concept and our identity. We are not merely human beings. We also experience ourselves as male and female. Our sexual identity is rooted in the reality of our biological nature. Our sexuality is not simply our physical maleness or femaleness. Our sexual identity is the experience of our maleness and our femaleness.

The polarity of male and female generates a dynamic tension. These differences can be complementary and provide a window into aspects of ourselves that were never known.

Our sexual identity is central to who we are. We not only want to be seen by others as a certain kind of human being. We want to be seen as a man or woman. Despite the many differences between men and women, we can complement each other in many basic, mysterious, and wonderful ways.

As far as I can tell, masculinity is the expression of man's belief that the creation of a woman was nature's most brilliant idea. And femininity is the expression of women's belief that the creation of man is nature's most brilliant idea.

We all carry some male and female aspects within us. In men, the male principle is usually predominant in women, the female principle is usually predominant. A man knows what it feels like to be a man in a way that no woman can fully understand. The same principle applies for women. The difference in perspective available to men and women when encountering each other represents, at least potentially, a deeper range of knowing our self and another person. In other words, a wider range of possibilities exists between men and women than between members of the same sex. The deepest level of self-understanding for a man requires interaction with the opposite sex.

In relating to people who are different, especially the opposite sex, we can potentially experience the fullest range of who we are, who we aren't and aspects of ourselves we deny or never realised. The polarity between man and woman generates and accentuates self-discovery and self-understanding.

We have all heard how some people can meet someone for the first time and then experience a sudden shock of recognition. There is an odd sense of familiarity, a mysterious sense of having encountered the person before-as if the person was already known.

These people experience a sense of fascination over this mysterious familiarity and strangeness. Something is known about this person in a powerful way.

In romantic love, we perceive the other as a real or potential source of happiness. Desire is born, desire leads to actions which result in pleasure and joy. If we are frightened or angered by our differences, love withers.

Fascination, attraction, or passion may be born "at first sight." But love requires curiosity, patience, acceptance and seeing people for who they truly are. This usually takes time.

Our Sense of Life and Romantic Love

A soul mate is a person who shares our sense of life. When we encounter another person, we encounter the presence of that person's sense of life. Sometimes we can quickly sense something about the other person's sense of life, how he or she feels about himself or herself, the joyfulness in their approach to life, or the defensiveness and fearfulness they endure. We can sense in people their level of enthusiasm, optimism, excitement, or even their dread with life.

Our sense of life reflects many conscious and unconscious values. It reflects our broadest and deepest attitudes, and is grounded in our conclusions about the world, about life and about ourselves. When we are not allowed to express our lovable and capable nature, and when we are treated as unlovable and incapable beings, we develop a sense of life in which the world is not open to our thoughts, is unconcerned about our feelings, and unaffected by our actions.

Our sense of life can also reflect a strong and healthy self-esteem, a clear sense of value in our life, and a conviction that our world is open to our lovable and capable nature. Or it can reflect the torture of self-doubt, embittered resentment, tragic defiance, complaining resignation, aggressive impotence, a perverse sense of martyrdom, a view of the world that is sordid and senseless, or the anxiety that we may live in a world where we are unlovable and incapable.

There are potential problems whenever a couple has a different sense of life. It is essential that people in love fully recognise, appreciate, and accept differences in their sense of life. Even when they don't, things can still go well initially—especially when people put their "best foot" forward. Eventually the difference in your sense of life will surface with unexpected results. People eventually stop pretending or begin to notice with time how you really are.

Our sense of life and our approach to life develops with the first expression of our Real Self. It matters how our parents respond and it matter how other people treat us. It matters if parents treat us as unlovable or incapable. It matters if our parents treat each other as lovable and capable. When people treat us like we are unlovable and incapable, and when they treat each other that way, life can become a grudging responsibility where people may become no more than objects or a means to an end and new relationships are formed on the basis of social economics.

We may begin to value ourselves, not for who we are, but for how we look, what we can do and what we have, or own. We may develop a sense of life where we shrink our awareness, blame others, give up their responsibilities, or we may come to believe that life is no longer an adventure in which every moment offers the opportunity to learn. When two people who respond to life in radically opposing ways meet, a potential barrier to romantic love may be formed.

Complementary Differences and Similarities

The second principle involves the "similarities and differences" between people. The most basic similarity is that a man and a woman are both are human. The most basic difference is that people are male or female.

In romantic love, a man and woman must experience their differences, at least to some degree, as mutually enriching, and as capable of drawing out untapped awareness and potential in each other. Their intimacy is an adventure resulting in expanded consciousness and the profound sense of being alive.

The key is whether the couple experiences their differences as complementary or antagonistic. This will depend on the willingness and ability of both people to appreciate and find value in the other person. Romantic love offers us the possibility self-discovery through deep contact with another.

If you are in love, you might ask yourself, what part of myself does my lover bring me into fresh contact with? How do I experience myself in this relationship? When I am with my lover, what feels most alive within me?

Rhythm and Energy

Most people possess an inherent biological rhythm that is easy to feel but difficult to describe when you don't know what to look for. This rhythm and energy are deeply connected to whether or not romantic love actually ignites or endures.

Rhythm and energy can be observed in our speech patterns, emotional responses, and body language. Closely related is the observation that some people are naturally more or less energetic than others—physically, emotionally or intellectually. Some people move, feel, think faster or slower depending on the circumstance and their environment. Some people are impulsive or impatient. They may even experience a different sense and relationship to time.

Sometimes two people meet and are on the verge of falling in love. They may have a lot in common and they may be physically attracted on the basis of their appearances. Yet they can feel strangely out-of-sync with each other. They may even feel irritated and have difficulty accounting for these feelings. The person who is naturally fast and eagerly explores life may feel chronically impatient with a person who savours life at a slower pace. The person with a less fevered pace may feel chronically pressured. The person who interprets these differences as personal or intentional by the other will feel frustrated and even angry in the relationship.

Failure to understand the importance of our rhythm and energy, and the effect on relationships, will lead to quarrels and disagreements. These differences can become antagonistic even though they have the potential to become complimentary. When couples don't recognise or appreciate their differences, many will become extreme or try to change the other person in order to create a balance. When this fails, couples begin to look for faults in each other. As the relationship begins to fail, they may begin to explain their problems in terms of the alleged faults. They remain unaware of a deeper reason for their discomfort and acceptance of differences.

When a man and woman meet and feel "in sync," there can be an exhilarating experience of harmony and that their relationship is right. Being "in sync" is an experience of knowing the other in a very special sense. Both may resonate to a marvellous kind of rhythm.

Once you are aware of these phenomena, and notice it in your relationships, you can better understand why people are attracted and irritated by each another. Rhythm and energy are the means to explore difference and similarities and to gain a deeper harmony and compatibility.

The Private Universe of Romantic Love

Another essential principle to understanding romantic love is the concept of "a private universe." Two people in love can create a private universe out of their sense of individuality, their similar sense of life, their differences and similarities, their rhythm and energy, and the capacity to make meaningful contact with each other. This universe can be shared with silent understandings, unspoken words, humorous signals, and focused glances. Conversations and physical contact become wondrous, exciting, and safe.

Romantic love is based on shared sight and is shaped by happiness. Immature love is based on shared blindness, and is merely a fortress against pain.

Romantic love is a sanctuary and a source of nourishment and energy. Sometimes romantic love is the only point of certainty, and the only thing that is solid and real in the midst of chaos and ambiguity.

Understanding the Difference Between Men And Women

By Michael G. Conner, Psy. D. Clinical and Medical Psychologist

[This paper is collection of research conclusions and observations that I have witnessed over the past 5 year that I have attempted to put into a written form that might be helpful, but more importantly stimulate discussions. The real purpose is to increase the awareness between men and women, and to help them set aside issues that are not personal but are merely manifestations of nature. To my way of thinking, it is important to honour and rejoice in both our nature and our individuality.]

For centuries, the differences between men and women were socially defined and distorted through a lens of sexism in which men assumed superiority over women and maintained it through domination. As the goal of equality between men and women now grows closer, we are also losing our awareness of important differences. In some circles of society, politically correct thinking is obliterating important discussion as well as our awareness of the similarities and differences between men and women.

The vision of equality between the sexes has narrowed the possibilities for discovery of what truly exists within a man and within a woman. The world is less interesting when everything is same.

It is my position that men and women are equal but different. When I say equal, I mean that men and women have a right to equal opportunity and protection under the law. The fact that people in this country are assured these rights does not negate my observation that men and women are at least as different psychologically as they are physically.

None of us would argue the fact that men and women are physically different. The physical differences are rather obvious and most of these can be seen and easily measured. Weight, shape, size and anatomy are not political opinions but rather tangible and easily measured. The physical differences between men and women provide functional advantages and have survival value.

Men usually have greater upper body strength, build muscle easily, have thicker skin, bruise less easily, and have a lower threshold of awareness of injuries to their extremities. Men are essentially built for physical confrontation and the use of force. Their joints are well suited for throwing objects. A man's skull is almost always thicker and stronger than a women's. The stereotype that men are more "thick-headed" than women is not farfetched.

A man's "thick headedness" and other anatomical differences have been associated with a uniquely male attraction to high-speed activities and reckless behaviour that usually involve collisions with other males or automobiles. Men invented the game "chicken," not women.

Men and a number of other male species of animal seem to charge and crash into each other a great deal in their spare time.

Women on the other hand have four times as many brain cells (neurons) connecting the right and left side of their brain. This latter finding provides physical evidence that supports the observation that men rely easily and more heavily on their left brain to solve one problem one step at a time. Women have more efficient access to both sides of their brain and therefore greater use of their right brain. Women can focus on more than one problem at one time and frequently prefer to solve problems through multiple activities at a time.

Nearly every parent has observed how young girls find the conversations of young boys "boring." Young boys express confusion and would rather play sports than participate actively in a conversation between 5 girls who are discussing as many as three subjects at once!

The psychological differences between man and women are less obvious. They can be difficult to describe. Yet these differences can profoundly influence how we form and maintain relationships that can range from work and friendships to marriage and parenting.

Recognising, understanding, discussing as well as acting skilfully in light of the differences between men and women can be difficult. Our failure to recognise and appreciate these differences can become a lifelong source of disappointment, frustration, tension, and eventually our downfall in a relationship. Not only can these differences destroy a promising relationship, but most people will grudgingly accept or learn to live with the consequences. Eventually they find some compromise or way to cope. Few people ever work past these difficulties.

People tend to accept what they don't understand when they feel powerless to change it.

Relationships between men and women are not impossible or necessarily difficult. Problems simply arise when we expect or assume the opposite sex should think, feel or act the way we do. It's not that men and women live in completely different realities. Rather, our lack of knowledge and mutual experience gives rise to our difficulties.

Despite great strides in this country toward equality, modern society hasn't made relationships between men and women any easier. Today's society has taught us and has imposed on us the expectation that men and women should live together continuously, in communion and in harmony. These expectations are not only unrealistic but ultimately, they leave people feeling unloved, inadequate, cynical, apathetic, or ashamed.

The challenge facing men and women is to become aware of their identities, to accept their differences, and to live their lives fully and as skilfully as possible. To do this we must first understand in what ways we are different. We must avoid trying to change others to suit our needs. The following illustrates some important differences between men and women. These differences are not absolute. They describe how men and women are in most situations most of the time.

Problems

Men and women approach problems with similar goals but with different considerations. While men and women can solve problems equally well, their approach and their process are often quite different. For most women, sharing and discussing a problem presents an opportunity to explore, deepen or strengthen the relationship with the person they are talking with. Women are usually more concerned about how problems are solved than merely solving the problem itself. For women, solving a problem can profoundly impact whether they feel closer and less alone or whether they feel distant and less connected.

The process of solving a problem can strengthen or weaken a relationship. Most men are less concerned and do not feel the same as women when solving a problem.

Men approach problems in a very different manner than women. For most men, solving a problem presents an opportunity to demonstrate their competence, their strength of resolve, and their commitment to a relationship.

How the problem is solved is not nearly as important as solving it effectively and in the best possible manner. Men have a tendency to dominate and to assume authority in a problem-solving process. They set aside their feelings, provided the dominance hierarchy was agreed upon in advance and respected. They are often distracted and do not attend well to the quality of the relationship while solving problems.

Some of the more important differences can be illustrated by observing groups of young teenage boys and groups of young teenage girls when they attempt to find their way out of a maze. A group of boys generally establish a hierarchy or chain of command with a leader who emerges on his own or through demonstrations of ability and power. Boys explore the maze using scouts while remaining in distant proximity to each other.

Groups of girls tend to explore the maze together as a group without establishing a clear or dominant leader. Relationships tend to be co-equal. Girls tend to elicit discussion and employ "collective intelligence" to the task of discovering a way out. Girls tend to work their way through the maze as a group. Boys tend to search and explore using structured links and a chain of command.

Thinking

While men and women can reach similar conclusions and make similar decisions, the process they use can be quite different and in some cases can lead to entirely different outcomes. In general, men and women consider and process information differently.

Women tend to be intuitive global thinkers. They consider multiple sources of information within a process that can be described as simultaneous, global in perspective and will view elements in the task in terms of their interconnectedness. Women come to understand and consider problems all at once. They take a broad or "collective" perspective and they view elements in a task as interconnected and interdependent. Women are prone to become overwhelmed with complexities that "exist," or may exist, and may have difficulty separating their personal experience from problems.

Men tend to focus on one problem at a time or a limited number of problems at a time. They have an enhanced ability to separate themselves from problems and minimise the complexity that may exist. Men come to understand and consider problems one piece at a time. They take a linear or sequential perspective, and view elements in a task as less interconnected and more

276

independent. Men are prone to minimise and fail to appreciate subtleties that can be crucial to successful solutions. A male may work through a problem repeatedly, talking about the same thing over and over, rather than trying to address the problem all at once.

While there are differences in the ways that men and women think, it must be emphasised that they can and do solve problems in a similar manner. There are no absolutes, only tendencies.

Memory

Women have an enhanced ability to recall memories that have strong emotional components. They can also recall events or experiences that have similar emotions in common. Women are very adept at recalling information, events, or experiences in which there is a common emotional theme. Men tend to recall events using strategies that rely on reconstructing the experience in terms of elements, tasks or activities that took place.

Profound experiences that are associated with competition or physical activities are more easily recalled. There appears to be a structural and chemical basis for observed memory differences. For instance, the hippocampus, the area in the brain primarily responsible for memory, reacts differently to testosterone in men and it reacts differently to changing levels of oestrogen and progesterone in women. Women tend to remember or be reminded of different "emotional memories" and content to some extent as part of their menstrual cycle.

Sensitivity

There is evidence to suggest that a great deal of the sensitivity that exists within men and women has a physiological basis. It has been observed that is many cases; women have an enhanced physical alarm response to danger or threat. Their autonomic and sympathetic systems have a lower threshold of arousal and greater reactivity than men. In both men and women, higher levels of testosterone directly affect the aggressive response and behaviour centres of the brain. Increasing oestrogen and progesterone in men has a "feminising" effect. Sexually aggressive males become less focused on sexual aggressive behaviour and content when they are given female hormones.

On the other hand, changing oestrogen and progesterone levels in women during menstrual cycles can produce a "flood" of memories as well as strong emotions. Increasing or high levels of testosterone can produce an emotional insensitivity, empathic block, and increased indifference to the distress others.

At the heart of sensitivity is our capacity to form, appreciate, and maintain relationships that are rewarding. Even here there are important differences. For men, what demonstrates a solid relationship is quite different from that of most women. Men feel closer and validated through shared activities. Such activities include sports, competition, outdoor activities, or sexual activities that are decidedly active and physical. While both men and women can appreciate and engage in these activities, they often have preferential differences.

Women, on the other hand, feel closer and validated through communication, dialogue, and intimate sharing of experience, emotional content and personal perspectives. Many men tend to find such sharing and involvement uncomfortable, if not, overwhelming.

The Task of Relationship Facing Men and Women

The task that faces men and women is to learn to accept their differences, avoid taking their differences as personal attempts to frustrate each other, and to compromise whenever possible. The idea that one gender can think and feel like the other if they truly loved each is rather absurd. Sure, a man or women could act in consideration of the other's needs, but this would not necessarily be rewarding and honest. Holding the benefit of another above our own is rewarding. But from time to time, and more often for most of us, it is important to be our self and to be accepted, and not to be the source of distress and disappointment in the lives of people we love.

The Role of Counselling and Therapy

Counselling and therapy can help a couple understand and appreciate each other, and even benefit from their differences. Understanding these differences intellectually is not enough. A counsellor or therapist can help point out these differences, as they surface, and guide a couple to a greater level of relationship. Understanding that differences are not intentional and that misunderstandings are merely the result of expectations that are not realistic can make a huge difference in a relationship. The differences that can be sensed between a man and women can deepen their relationship. More importantly, when men seek to understand and appreciate that which is feminine, they come to a deeper understanding of their self. And when women seek to understand that which is masculine in men, they come to appreciate and understand more about their own masculinity.

Understanding the Difference between Men and Women.
Copyright 1999–2010 Michael G. Conner, Psy. D.

Endnotes and References

About the Author pp. 2

(1910) *'A Woman Can Love Only One Man'*, *Men, Women & Wedlock,* Quote 111 pp.40, A & C Black Publishers.

Foreword pp. 15–18

Cardwell, Samuel (2008) 'Many studies have been conducted on couples', *AAP* 29 August.

(1910) 'There is at least one woman', *Men, Women & Wedlock,* Quote 1, pp.15. A & C Black Publishers.

Introduction pp. 19–22 (2009) 'The year 1975 is very important in the history of Australia', *Divorce Law and Separation Advice,* © *Divorce Guide*. All Rights Reserved, www.divorceguide.com

Conner, Michael G. (1999–2010) *This paper is a collection of research conclusions.*

The task that faces many men and women is to learn to accept their differences. Holding the benefit of the other above our own is rewarding.

Understanding the Difference Between Men and Women (Collection of research conclusions and observations.) ©

Chapter 1 pp. 23–27

'If Only I Knew Then… *I know now'.*

(1910) 'Love means the association of two people', *Men, Women & Wedlock'* Quote 113, pp. 40, A & C Black Publishers.

Chapter 2 pp. 28–32
'You Have the Rest of Your Life... *To be a wife'.*
Ebbutt, Blanche (1913) *How to Avoid Discord,* pp.13. *Don't nag your husband, Don'ts for Wives.*

Chapter 3 pp. 33–39
'When Women Were Women...*and guys were men'.*
(1910) 'Many people are busy in the present' *Men, Women & Wedlock,* Quote 2. pp.15. A & C Black Publishers.
Conner, Michael G. *The vision of equality between the sexes has narrowed the possibilities.*
Understanding the Difference between Men and Women (Collection of research conclusions and observations.) © 1999–2010.
Thomas, Skye (extract) *The male is the hunter and protector.*
Thomas, Skye (extract) *What can we do about it?*
'Tomorrow's Edge' © 11 August 2004.

Chapter 4 pp. 40–52
'If He Doesn't Seem Right...*let him go...next'.*
(1910) 'When a fellow tells a girl he will love her always*', Men, Women & Wedlock,* Quote 225, pp.65. A & C Black Publishers.

Chapter 6 pp. 59–62
'Wedding Bells...*or warning bells!'*
(1910) 'There is at least one good point about being married', *Men, Women & Wedlock*, Quote 8 pp.6, A & C Black Publishers.
Jaffe Esq. Wendy (2006) 'All of the people in your potential spouse's life', *The Divorce Lawyer's Guide to Staying Married*, Volt Press.
Jaffe Esq. Wendy (2006) 'There are three important rules to remember', *The Divorce Lawyer's Guide to Staying Married,* Volt Press.
McMillan, Dina, Social Psychologist *'When women become overly interested in the wedding day'.*
Angela Saurine (2009) 'Inside the World of Brides Who Can't Let Go', *The Daily Telegraph*, 4 April 2009.

Chapter 7 pp. 63–69

'Bachelor Party…*what's* he really celebrating?'

Norman, Greg (2009) *It's an amazing thing when a burden is taken off your back,* 60 Minutes.

Chapter 8 pp. 70–76

Equivalent to Marriage?—*Mt. Everest!*… *You need to acclimatise to both.*

Ebbutt, Blanche (1913) 'Art is a hard mistress', Preface, *Don'ts for Wives*, A & C Black Ltd.

Ebbutt, Blanche (1913) *Don't forget to be your wife's best friend, Personal Relations,* pp. 24 *Don't for Husbands'* A & C Black Ltd.

Chapter 9 pp. 77–82

'Don't Tell Him You Love Him…*tell him you adore him!'*

Ebbutt, Blanche (1913) Don't quarrel with your husband, pp. 12 How to Avoid Discord, Don'ts for Wives, A & C Black Ltd.

Ebbutt, Blanche (1913) Don't think that it is no longer necessary to show your love to your wife, pp.13–14, Personal Relations, Don'ts for Husbands, A & C Black Ltd.

Chapter 10 pp. 83–95

'What's Love Got to Do with It…*absolutely everything'.*

Arndt, Bettina (2009) *'Fifty Thrusts and Don't Jiggle My Book'*, Andrew from Queanbeyan, The Sex Diaries, Melbourne University Publishing.

Conner, Michael G. (2001) *'Utilitarian Marriage is one that shows and absence of mutual passion or involvement'.* 'About Love and Romantic Love', Copyright 2001.

Sternberg Robert J. (1986). *The Triangular Theory of Love: Intimacy, Passion, Commitment.*

Wikipedia, Sternberg, Robert J. (1986). 'A triangular theory of love'. *Psychological Review* **93** (2): 119–135. doi:10.1037/0033-295X.93.2.119. http://content2.apa.org/journals/rev/93/2/119. Retrieved 2007-06-27.

Chapter 11 pp. 96–100

'The More You Do-You Will...the more you don't-you won't!'

Arndt, Bettina (2009) 'Once the canoe is in the water', 'Just Do It;' *The Sex Diaries,* Chapter 5, pp. 81, Melbourne University Press Publishing.

Davis Weiner, Michele (2009) 'Just do it' ('Sex Starved Marriage') Chapter 5, pp.75, *The Sex Diaries*, Bettina Arndt, Melbourne University Press Publishing.

Gare, Shelly (2009) *'In deep schtuck',* The Advertise 27 March 2009, *'Arndt has unashamedly gone in to bat for the men',* The Advertiser, 27 March 2009.

Bettina Arndt (1910) *The Sex Diaries'* Melbourne University Press Publishing 2009.

'Many a man has fallen in love with a peach only to discover that fate has landed him a lemon' *Men, Women & Wedlock,* pp.18 Quote 16, A & C Black Ltd.

Chapter 12 pp. 101–105

'Oh Baby, Baby...*What Are You Going to Do When Bubs Arrives?'*

Ebbutt, Blanche (1913) *'*Don't let your wife devote herself so exclusively to the children', pp. 69–70 *Children, Don'ts for Husbands'*, A & C Black Ltd.

Chapter 13 pp. 106–116

'Till Divorce...*do us part'.*

De Buys, Mabry (2006) 'Marriage is a very serious business', *The Divorce Lawyer's Guide*, Wendy Jaffe Esq. Volt Press.

Chapter 15 pp. 118–129

'Controlling Your Man, Through Paranoia and Manipulation...*dream on!'*

Browne R.N. Ph.D., Marie H, Marlene M. Browne Esq, *In other words, the closer the proximity your mate has to stimulus,* Part 2 Chapter 3 pp.45. 'The Ready Replacement Pool', 'Marital Hazards and Husband Traps' 'Beware Your New Best Friend', 'You Can't Have Him, He's Mine', ADAMS Media Avon, Massachusetts.

Browne R.N. Ph.D., Marie H, Marlene M. Browne Esq, 'Many marriages are broken by interlopers within the couples inner circle of acquaintances', Part 2 Chapter 3 pp.*44* 'The Ready Replacement Pool' 'Marital Hazards and Husband Traps, 'You Can't Have Him, He's Mine'. ADAMS Media Avon, Massachusetts.

Browne R.N. Ph.D., Marie H, Marlene M. Browne Esq, 'Your husband should not be keeping his feelings secret'. 'Where Temptation Waits', Part 2, Chapter 5 pp.79, 'You Can't Have Him, He's Mine' ADAMS Media Avon, Massachusetts.

Browne R.N. Ph.D., Marie H, Marlene M. Browne Esq, *'Mate Retention Tactics'* Part 2 Chapter 5, pp.82–83, *'Infidelity Punishment, Emotional Manipulation, Commitment Manipulation, Derogation of Competitors, Resource Display and Sexual Inducements, Verbal Possession, Physical Possession, Signal and Possessive Ornamentation.* 'You Can't Have Him, He's Mine', ADAMS Media Avon, Massachusetts.

Browne R.N. Ph.D., Marie H, Marlene M. Browne Esq, '*Part-Time Lovers'* Part 2 *Marital Hazards and Husband Traps*, Chapter 3. *The Ready Replacement Pool*, pp.56–57, 'You Can't Have Him, He's Mine' ADAMS Media Avon, Massachusetts.

Fisher Dr, Helen *'Recent studies have shown that when it comes to protecting your mate',* Part 2, Chapter 3, pp.46 *'The Ready Replacement Pool' 'Marital Hazards and Husband Traps',* 'You Can't Have Him, He's Mine'. Browne R.N. Ph.D., Marie H, Marlene M. Browne Esq, ADAMS Media Avon, Massachusetts.

Gottman, John M, 'Good Marital Habits' Part 1, *Assessing Love on the Home Front*, Chapter 1 *Your Husband's Happiness Factor* pp.17.

Browne R.N. Ph.D., Marie H, Marlene M. Browne Esq, *You Can't Have Him, He's Mine'* ADAMS Media Avon, Massachusetts.

Gottman, John M, Reinhold Niebuhr's Serenity Prayer 'Good Marital Habits' Part 1, 'Assessing Love on the Home Front', Chapter 1, 'Your Husband's Happiness Factor'. pp.18.

Marie H. Browne, Marlene M Browne, *You Can't Have Him, He's Mine,* ADAMS Media Avon, Massachusetts.

Livingston, Gordon, 'While it takes two people to start a relationship', 'Any relationship is under the control of the person who cares the least'. pp. 27 *Too Soon Old, Too Late Smart*, Hodder Australia 2005.

Chapter 16 pp. 130–133
'Life is Too Short…and forever is a long time!'
Example 4: 'Mike for many years was not happy at home with his wife'
Livingston, Gordon, 'What gives love its power is that it is shared', pp.93.
'Unrequited love is painful but not romantic' *'Too Soon Old, Too Late Smart',* Hodder Australia 2005.

Chapter 17 pp. 134–143

'Must all Lessons be Learnt...*through our mistakes?'*

Livingston, Gordon, *'To single out an important life task'*, Chapter 1 pp.2, *'If the map does not agree with the ground'*, 'Too Soon Old, Too Late Smart' Hodder Australia 2005.

(1910) 'A safe bet was the one you were going to make, and didn't'. *Men Women & Wedlock,* pp.58 quote 191, A & C Black Publishers.

Chapter 18 pp. 144–148

'Meet the Jealous Mother-in-law...*who is jealous of you*!'

Wolf, Marshall (2006) 'Marriage is hard work' *The Divorce Lawyer's Guide to Staying Married,* Wendy Jaffe Esq. Volt Press.

Chapter 19 pp. 149–152

'Future In-Laws...*do your parents like him and vice versa'.*

Pierson, Pamela, 'All of the people in your potential spouse's life, their family, their friends', *How to Stay Married*, Wendy Jaffe Esq. Divorce.com.

Chapter 20pp. 153–157

'Domination and Control... *Run! Run! Run!'*

Ebbutt, Blanche (1913) *'Don't think you can live your lives apart under the same roof and still be happy'*, Personal Relations, pp.19, *'Don'ts for Husbands'*, A & C Black Publishers.

Chapter 21 pp. 158–174

'Who's the CEO in Your World...*you, me—who's it going to be?'*

Conner, Psy. D. Michael G, *'As the goal of equality between men and women now grows closer'*, Understanding the Difference between Men and Women, Copyright 1999–2010.

Fulbright, Dr K. Yvonne (2009) *'Given the shopping list of reasons for diminished or inhibited sexual desire'*, How to Fix a Low Sex Drive When the Other Doesn't Want Sex, 11 March 2009, The Daily Telegraph.

Livingston Dr Gordon (2005) 'In fact what passes for love between adults more often resembles a kind of unspoken contract of services', Chapter 21 pp. 163, 'We are all prone to the myth of the perfect stranger', *Too Soon Old, Too Late Smart,* Hodder Australia 2005.

Chapter 22 pp. 178–183
'How Do You Know…if you married the right one?'
Kutner, Elizabeth (2006) 'There is a whole lack of knowledge about what makes a healthy marriage'. Wendy Jaffe, Esq. *The Divorce Lawyer's Guide to Staying Married,* Volt Press.

Chapter 24 pp. 188–190
'Stop Acting Like a Wife…he wants his lover back—YOU!'*
Sucherman, Lowell (2006) 'People court their mistress, but not their wife', 'How to Stay Married', Wendy Jaffe, Esq. *The Divorce Lawyer's Guide to Staying Married,* Volt Press.

Chapter 25 pp. 191–193
'Have Your Own Respective Bedrooms…huh!'*
Davis, Joslin, Winston-Salem, NC (2006) 'Unhappiness in a marriage is most often the result of control', Wendy Jaffe, Esq. *The Divorce Lawyer's Guide to Staying Married* Volt Press.

Chapter 27 pp. 197–205
Every Action …equals …Reaction…equals…outcome!*
Example 7: '*Joanne was an attractive girl who never had any problem getting a man'.*

Chapter 30 pp. 212–214
'Are We Meant to be with One Person…for the rest of our life?'*
Example 8: '*Twelve months after Peter married his childhood sweetheart'.*

Chapter 31 pp. 215–218
'How Does It Feel to Have Him in Body…but someone else has his heart!'*
Example 9: '*John approached Rebecca in a hotel one Friday night'* pp. 217

Chapter 32 pp. 219–225
Don't Want her in Your Life…treat *your man like a king!*
Example 10: '*Phillip chose his bride, then again'.*

Chapter 33 pp. 226–227
'Can an "Affair" Save a Marriage?'—Mira Kirshenbaum (2012) 'When Good People Have Affairs' Lara Clout—Daily Telegraph. 26 August 2012.

Chapter 34 pp. 228–236
'Until Death...*do us part'.*
Goltz Helen, B.A. (2009) UQ, Grad. Dip. QUT, Dip. Counselling AIPC, 'Fixed Term Marriage Contracts, A discussion paper on the future of marriage in Australia', April 13

Chapter 38 pp. 245–247
'Staying Together for the Children'.
Example 11: '*Anthony was a twenty something just married young man.* pp. 247'

Papers Included at Back of Book
'About Love and Romantic Love'. *pp. 263*
Michael Grayson Conner, Psy. D. Copyright 2001–2010.
'Understanding the Difference Between Men and Women'. pp. 273
Michael Grayson Conner, Psy. D Copyright 1999–2010.

www.ingramcontent.com/pod-product-compliance
Lightning Source LLC
Chambersburg PA
CBHW060450290526
45791CB00001B/50